NON-CIRCULATING

THE MERTON ANNUAL

6

THE MERTON ANNUAL

Studies in Culture, Spirituality, & Social Concerns

THE MERTON ANNUAL publishes articles about Thomas Merton and about related matters of major concern to his life and work. Its purpose is to enhance Merton's reputation as a writer and monk, to continue to develop his message for our times, and to provide a regular outlet for substantial Merton-related scholarship. *THE MERTON ANNUAL* includes as regular features reviews, review-essays, a bibliographic survey, interviews, and first appearances of unpublished, or obscurely published, Merton materials, photographs, and art. Essays about related literary and spiritual matters will also be considered. Manuscripts and books for review may be sent to any of the editors.

EDITORS

Michael Downey
Theology Department
Bellarmine College
2001 Newburg Road
Louisville, KY 40205-0671

George A. Kilcourse
Theology Department
Bellarmine College
2001 Newburg Road
Louisville, KY 40205-0671

Victor A. Kramer
English Department
Georgia State University
University Plaza
Atlanta, GA 30303-3083

Volume editorship rotates on a yearly basis.

ADVISORY BOARD

THE MERTON ANNUAL

Studies in Culture, Spirituality, & Social Concerns

Volume 6   1993

Edited by

George A. Kilcourse

A Liturgical Press Book

THE LITURGICAL PRESS
Collegeville, Minnesota

Cover design by Ann Blattner.

Artwork: ''Jerusalem'' by Thomas Merton.

ISBN 0-8146-2250-X

1   2   3   4   5   6   7   8   9

The Merton Annual

| Volume 6 | 1993 |

REVIEWS

Foreword

*Victor A. Kramer**

It is with a great deal of thankfulness that I compose these words about this new series for *The Merton Annual*, a project first conceived in the mid-1980s, and which began to develop in 1986. At that time the editors of volumes 1–5 (1988–1992) planned the project which has now evolved into the present publication. During the initial five years of this annual publication of scholarly writing concerning Merton, we have chosen numerous essays, review-essays, interviews, and reviews which examine the continuing critical inquiry about Thomas Merton, someone who ''elected silence,'' but whose voice keeps speaking to an enormous range of persons throughout the world.

Merton has proven to be a catalyst. *The Merton Annual* editors realized that his life, writing, and influence were continuing to have enormous value for serious readers and scholars. What has, in addition, become increasingly clear during the past decade, however, is that it is not just a matter of Merton's work being admired, used, analyzed, or documented. His voice also helps others to make specific applications in the present moment concerning matters of significance which Merton, only indirectly, might have earlier anticipated. As the new series begins, two new editors join in this enterprise. George Kilcourse, with expertise in theology, ecumenism, and Merton studies, as well as Michael Downey, with expertise in Christian spirituality and sacramental theology, bring new strengths to the editorial work of *The Merton Annual*. These editors have assisted in redefining and broadening the mission of the *Annual* which will seek to make more connections between Merton's vision and the contemporary world of scholarship. It is fitting, then, that this first volume

* Victor A. Kramer is the founding editor of *The Merton Annual*.

of our new series (1993) coincides with the twenty-fifth anniversary celebration of Merton's death in 1968 and should reflect in its varied contents many different ways for spirituality to be extended beyond just his life, or monasticism, and Catholicism.

There are many similarities between Volume 6 and the preceding five volumes of *The Merton Annual,* but this volume is different in that it so clearly looks beyond just honoring Merton. We will continue to include unpublished, or obscurely published Merton material, interviews about him, bibliographical materials, and appropriate reviews. What the new editors hope to emphasize, however, is that while we will not cease to be interested in the living traditions which fed Merton, we are now graced with an expanding vision precisely because so many have absorbed Merton's work. Therefore there are so many more ways to demonstrate that these springs feed many lives, and that all of this is moving beyond any narrowly defined focus, while it also becomes more catholic.

Introduction

Spirituality After
"A Prayer Lip Stumbles"

George Kilcourse

Turning and turning in the widening gyre
The falcon cannot hear the falconer;
Things fall apart; the centre cannot hold;
Mere anarchy is loosed upon the world,
The blood-dimmed tide is loosed, and everywhere
The ceremony of innocence is drowned;
The best lack all conviction, while the worst
Are full of passionate intensity.

"The Second Coming" (1920)
William Butler Yeats

Few lines of twentieth-century poetry capture so succinctly the collapse of the modern epoch and the vacuum that followed. Yeats has imaged the loss of communication between falcon and falconer to signal a universal failure throughout Western culture. The resulting anarchy has allowed those "full of passionate intensity" to audition their idolatries, in which everything becomes expendable. Christopher Lasch has described the debate over the proposed "turn" to "postmodernity" as "a debate conducted, for the most part, by those who know only how to shout."[1] Our *The Merton Annual* 6 ventures to decrease the decibels and to reestablish some constructive communication between our falcon and falconer: spirituality and the insights from what academe and the popular culture now call "postmodernity."

1. Review of Albert Borgmann, *Crossing the Postmodern Divide* (Chicago: University of Chicago Press, 1991) in *Commonweal* 119:20 (November 20, 1992) 22–23.

A felicitous constellation of events converged to make the reconstitution of *The Merton Annual* series responsive to such new directions in "Culture, Spirituality, and Social Concerns" (as our new subtitle heralds), as well as to mark the twenty-fifth anniversary of Thomas Merton's death. 1968 itself stands as a watershed year of transitions and symbolic change: the assassinations of Martin Luther King, Jr. and Robert F. Kennedy; the "Prague Spring" presaging the momentous upheavals in Eastern Europe and the former Soviet Union; the Viet Nam war and antiwar protests across the United States; the Medellin Conference of Latin American bishops proclaiming a "preferential option for the poor"; the promulgation of the papal encyclical on artificial contraception, *Humanae vitae*; and the fourth general assembly of the World Council of Churches in Uppsala, Sweden.

Each of these dramatic happenings in some way exposed the myth of Western cultural superiority. More than coincidence found Thomas Merton crossing the false and constraining boundaries of modernity with his own 1968 venture to Asia, and in the writings of his final three years at the hermitage. His assessment then of our social and political crises urged us to recover spiritual foundations for the "hidden wholeness" which related all differences through a deeper unity. A quarter of a century later, Merton's prophetic reflections have earned him the identity of a role-model for engaging spirituality in dialogue with postmodernity.

At first glance it would seem that monasticism has more in common with the pre-modern than the postmodern era. For hermits, doubly so. And yet the 1990 incorporation of The Abbey Center for the Study of Ethics and Culture by the Abbey of Gethsemani acknowledges and reclaims Merton's original vision for the "Mount Olivet Project" (Mount Olivet was the name of his hermitage) as the inspiration for ongoing, broader conversation to focus on "the possibility of the recovery of spiritual and humanistic perspectives in our age."[2] Its distinct concern would be the underlying questions that focussed upon "the apparent collapse of common language, traditions, and values"[3]— the very cultural breakdown diagnosed by theorists of postmodernity.

Thus, the Abbey Center inaugurated its emphasis on "men and

2. The Abbey Center for the Study of Ethics and Culture, Inc., "The Program: The Abbey Center Circle of Friends" (October 22–25, 1992) 1.
    3. Ibid., 3.

women as humans in community, in the image of God"[4] with an October 22–25 conference for sixty diverse participants gathered at the
Abbey of Gethsemani. Three of the essays in this volume were contributed by leaders of that conference. Rosemary Haughton's reflections, aptly entitled "The Fall of Babel," echo Yeats's metaphor of lost
communication. Her trenchant interpretation of the revealing dynamics
of the conference reflects strong undercurrents of postmodern sensibility. Rembert Weakland's personal narrative of "Monastic Values in
an Alien World" speaks poignantly of the paradigm shift in his own
spirituality. And Francis Kline offers impressions of the processes and
personalities that combined to lead the conference in the fascinating
direction where it finally turned. Roger Corless contributes an independent, freelance essay germane to our theme of spirituality and postmodernity with his cogent reexamination of the context for Merton's
interreligious and crosscultural dialogue (spanning some twenty years)
with Daisetz T. Suzuki.

Peacemaking proved the horizon of Thomas Merton's mature
spirituality, and so it weaves in and out of these essays, as well as
through the Abbey Center's charter. That document, too, is ambitious
for a prophetic voice to invite transforming initiatives to counterbalance
the attitudes and actions "which currently inhibit, or even cripple, often
disparate and disconnected attempts to care adequately for our fellow
humans, our environment, and our planet."[5] In the summer of 1991,
I submitted to the Abbey Center a proposal for sponsoring a "Scholars' Retreat" at the Abbey of Gethsemani. The suggested theme of
the retreat was "Spirituality at the Juncture of Modernity and Postmodernity." Envisioned as a smaller gathering of scholars who would
prepare papers to provoke reflection and conversation, this January
9–12, 1993, event was generously sponsored by the Abbey Center and
hosted at the Abbey of Gethsemani.

It proved to be a unique experience for the nine participants, including myself and Michael Downey who planned and coordinated
the retreat. The scholars not only exchanged thoughts on the theme,
but also entered the rhythms and depths of contemplative life with
the monastic community at prayer. Evening exchanges in chapter with
the same monastic community extended this fruitful interchange and

4. Ibid., 1.
5. Ibid., 6.

affected the scholars' conversations. Amid what Merton describes as the "winter rain" of the hermitage, we trod to the Mount Olivet abode and huddled around the fireplace for a lengthy morning session to hear and to discuss Glenn Hinson's insights from Quaker Douglas Steere's interreligious explorations, how Merton resonated with his friend's breakthroughs, and how the two were mutually indebted. It dawned upon us how fitting it would be to accompany Hinson's paper "Rootedness in Tradition and Global Spirituality" with the neglected Steere-Merton correspondence which reveals their tentative planning in 1968 for the very types of gatherings the Abbey Center now hosts.

Four other papers from the scholars' retreat are included in this volume: Roberto S. Goizueta explores the aesthetics of the United States Hispanics' "mestizo community" as a postmodern alternative. Katherine TePas provides a new hermeneutic for reading Aelred of Rievaulx in terms of "mercy" and affords a contemporary narrative of praxis that attempts to enact a way out of our postmodern crisis. Steven Payne reexamines John of the Cross for applications of his apophatic spirituality to the postmodern context. Tina Pippin navigates through the neglected precincts of John's Apocalypse with an informed feminist's postmodern sensibilities.

As always, an interview with one of Merton's longtime friends provides a unique window for *The Merton Annual* readers. Philosopher John H. (Jack) Ford offers a unique perspective on Merton, particularly in light of the role he played in planning for the construction of the hermitage. Ford's remarks about Dan Walsh, Merton's mentor, prove equally engaging.

Finally, this volume offers analyses of Merton studies. Michael Downey's bibliographic essay encompasses major publications, and breaks new ground with his assessment of a necessary new turn in critical appraisals of Merton's contribution and role for ongoing spirituality studies. He signals a challenging ascent to a new plateau for Merton publications, along the lines of Francis Kline's suggestion that we take a critical, "post-Mertonian" perspective (December 10, 1991, Merton Lecture at Bellarmine College). Downey's essay is complemented by individual reviewers' assessments of particular new volumes and tapes by and about Merton; and reviews of books of related interest, all orchestrated by editor Victor A. Kramer.

Without pretending to claim Thomas Merton as a "postmodernist," one can say unequivocally that he chastened modernity for erecting its worldview on the pillars of rationality, individualism, naive optimism, and an unwavering faith in progress. Much of what Merton prescribed as a "monastic therapy" was an antidote for the destructive tendencies of modernity's technological "mass man" who languishes in illusion and a counterfeit, false self. Merton discovered that the "true self" in Christ summoned us to new possibilities. Here, spirituality has found an engaging conversation partner with the postmodern voices. Merton ironically put it in his own antipoetry:

> 43. Voice of a prayer lip stumbles in gross assent. HELLO AGENTS THIS IS RELIGION CALLING FOR HELP. Send Argus to command another. Try that second election. Seize another paramilitary chance. Well-meaning prayer lip again fumbles message. IS GOD IN KENT?[6]

What Yeats had imaged as the collapse of communication has rebounded here in the most personal section, the North canto, of Merton's *The Geography of Lograire.* Here is perhaps an apt metaphor for spirituality at the juncture of modernity and postmodernity. In fact, Merton's own antipoetry moved beyond the particularity of his youthful crises to the broader global crises of exploitation lamented in this unfinished poem of 1968. It signals an openness to the "hidden wholeness" underlying Merton's own life and work. The inclusiveness of this new series of *The Merton Annual* ventures to expand Merton studies in conversations with such new, even postmodern voices. It also signals that this and future volumes of *The Merton Annual* will focus less upon the monk himself as an object of curiosity, and more upon the wider concerns of contemporary culture that Merton himself would have shared and explored.

George Kilcourse
Editor, *The Merton Annual* 6 (1993)

---

6. *The Collected Poems of Thomas Merton* (New York: New Directions, 1977) 514.

Rootedness in Tradition
and Global Spirituality*

E. Glenn Hinson

In a comprehensive survey of religion in today's world Frank Whaling has made much of growing global awareness as evidenced in: (1) a movement toward dialogue and inter-religious understanding; (2) inter-religious meetings to address wider global issues; (3) efforts to interpret different religious traditions as part of a wider whole, the earth; and (4) the emergence of a global spirituality "that uses the insights of the world's religious traditions to uncover the spiritual significance of the total fabric of human life—its rootedness in nature, its relation to other humans, and its openness to transcendence."[1] He has noted that different religious traditions have responded in diverse ways to the challenge of change. (A) Some have chosen not to respond. (B) Others have worked for a creative restoration of tradition. (C) Still others, such as the Roman Catholic Church in the Second Vatican Council, have undertaken to reform and to adjust old things and to appropriate new ones. (D) Others have chosen radical restatement and reinterpretation out of conviction that "Something deeper is needed in order to speak to new conditions of technological sophistication, medical ethics, ecological disaster, nuclear threat and global perspective than a restoration of tradition or reformation supported by a backward appeal to tradition."[2] (E) Still others have decided to abandon their religious tradition to form new religious movements.

In this essay I put in a favorable word for tradition in spirituality in this period of transition from modernity to postmodernity, what-

* This paper was presented at the January 9–12, 1993 "Scholars' Retreat" sponsored by The Abbey Center For The Study Of Ethics And Culture, Inc. at the Abbey of Gethsemani, Trappist, Kentucky.

1. Frank Whaling, "Religion in Today's World: An Introductory Survey," *Religion in Today's World*, ed. Frank Whaling (Edinburgh: T & T Clark, 1987) 41.

2. Ibid., 45.

ever either of those terms may mean. For me to do this may seem a bit incongruous by virtue of the fact that my own Baptist tradition has taken a rather dim view of tradition, by which we usually mean convention or dead custom. I confess that I have had to learn to distinguish tradition as the essence of something from convention as the external form or condition. Viewing this challenge of change from that perspective, I would agree with Whaling that "In spite of the importance of change in today's religion, it is necessary to emphasize that change and continuity go hand in hand."[3] But this is a judgment that I will not claim credit for or venture to advance on my own authority. It is an insight that I have gained, rather, from two persons who hail from rather different religious backgrounds than my own and who have cast their nets farther than I have—Thomas Merton and Douglas Steere. Both Merton and Steere have played significant roles in the development of what Ewert Cousins has labeled "global spirituality."

Professor Cousins, I think, has correctly connected the emergence of global spirituality with a religious "awakening" which has been taking place since the sixties. Like other "awakenings," this one began with a period of disorientation, confusion, and despair associated in the United States with the war in Vietnam, the Cold War, and growing societal problems. This was followed in the seventies and eighties with a period of deepened religious search as westerners floundered around trying to find answers to these problems in the East. In the last decade of the twentieth century we have begun to see emerging the change of consciousness which accompanies awakenings. As regards spirituality, Cousins has pointed out, "we can discern a process involving a spiritual awakening, a recovery of tradition, and a transformation of tradition—leading towards what can be called a global spirituality on the eve of the twenty-first century."[4]

On the Way to a Global Spirituality

Because Thomas Merton's perspectives and contributions have received ample treatment in many places, I will refer only incidentally to them here and concentrate instead on those of Douglas V. Steere,

3. Ibid., 46.
4. Ewert Cousins, "Spirituality in Today's World," *Religion in Today's World*, ed. Frank Whaling, 307.

who had significant contact with Merton during the sixties and composed a foreword to Merton's *The Climate of Monastic Prayer* which was published also under the title *Contemplative Prayer*. Like Merton, Steere has drawn heavily from the contemplative tradition, especially of Benedict of Nursia.[5]

Douglas Steere started down the path toward a global spirituality early in his career. His study of the life and thought of Baron Friedrich von Hügel in writing a doctoral dissertation (Harvard, 1931) may have given him a shove in that direction, for von Hügel himself had a global outlook long before that could have been popular. Teaching at Haverford College from 1928 until his retirement in 1963 doubtless widened his horizons further, for he came under the tutelage of Rufus Jones, a Quaker scholar of exceptionally expansive outlook. The Quaker tradition, with which Douglas and Dorothy Steere formally identified themselves in 1932, is itself unusually well equipped to foster exchanges with persons of other faiths, to put it in words of Abraham J. Heschel, at "the level of fear and trembling, of humility and contrition, where our individual moments of faith are mere waves in the endless ocean of mankind's reaching out for God, where all formulations and articulations appear as understatements, where our souls are swept away by the awareness of the urgency of answering God's commandment, while stripped of pretension and conceit we sense the tragic insufficiency of human faith."[6]

The traumatic experience of the Second World War and the struggle to bring sanity and order into the horribly scarred world after it undoubtedly pushed Douglas Steere, just as it did many others, farther down the path toward a global spirituality. The war touched the lives of people everywhere, but none felt its stroke more powerfully than the Friends, one of the three "peace churches," and Douglas Steere. Steere had undertaken a mission in Europe for the American Friends Service Committee in 1937 where he witnessed close up the buildup of the Third Reich. He returned again to the Scandinavian countries and Germany in 1940 in a risky effort to encourage Friends as the guns and bombs of war already boomed. At the end of the war

5. Cf. E. Glenn Hinson, "Ecumenical Spirituality," *Ecumenical Trends* (July/September 1991) 97–104.
6. Abraham J. Heschel, "No Religion Is an Island," *Union Seminary Quarterly Review* XXI (1961) 122.

he organized a relief effort to war-torn Finland, for which he was knighted in the Order of the White Rose in 1990.

The Second World War gave a new lease on life to ecumenism, broadening it immeasurably, as many discerned the urgency of reaching out not merely toward other Christians but toward the rest of the world's great religions. For Douglas Steere global spirituality involving persons of other faiths took shape swiftly as he shuttled back and forth to Europe and widened his contacts around the globe.

Early in the 1950s he brought Jewish scholars Martin Buber and Abraham J. Heschel and Buddhist interpreter Daisetz Suzuki, who was then teaching at Columbia University in New York City, to Haverford College to lecture, Buber and Suzuki in December 1951. In October 1954 he undertook his first journey to the East to Japan and India. In Japan he delivered the Nitobe Lecture on "The Quaker Message: Unique or Universal?" at the Yearly Meeting in Tokyo, already laying out the main lines for his brilliant paper on a Quaker view of ecumenism under the title *Mutual Irradiation*, the Richard Cary Lecture for 1968. In the significant Nitobe message he challenged Quakers to respond to the open door of religious and cultural interpenetration which stood before them, wherein "the Quaker form of the Christian religion finds itself queried by the deepest levels of Buddhism, of Hinduism, and even in rare cases of Islam."[7] He urged fellow Friends to trust the universality of Christ which would enable them to reach out and engage persons of other faiths in the same way the author of the Fourth Gospel, Justin Martyr, Clement of Alexandria, or Origen once did. They must not insulate Christ "by placing a screen of uniqueness about Him instead of trusting Him to draw to Himself the categories and thought and cultural forms" of different societies and religions. The world does not need a "catacomb mentality" of an overly defensive Christian theology. To take this way is to become vulnerable, as Francis of Assisi did before the Sultan at Damietta, Ramon Lull trying to reach the Muslims of North Africa, or John Woolman going to the Indians to offer peace. All exhibited faith in the universal Christ "that has vanquished fear and defensiveness." The Quaker message fits into the tradition of those who have known the universal Christ and are unafraid of encounter with persons of other faiths or entrusting Christ

7. Douglas V. Steere, "The Quaker Message: Unique or Universal?" *The Friends' Quarterly* 9 (Paril, 1955) 49.

to others in the conviction that He is indeed the universal Man God has sent.

Shortly after giving this lecture, Douglas Steere spent some time with Suzuki, who had returned to Japan for a brief furlough from his teaching at Columbia, to secure names of Buddhists who could enter into the kind of give and take with Christians which would prove fruitful and beneficial to both groups. Suzuki wrote introductory notes for him to some of the leading Buddhists in Kyoto, where he hoped to get a feeling for "something of the vitality of its life in Japan at that time."[8] He was not alone in this quest, however. The abbot of the monastery in Kyoto complained that "So many westerners were becoming interested in Buddhism that instead of the ancient promise that the meditation of the East would reach through the globe and shake the West, the reverse was happening."[9]

From Japan Douglas Steere headed to India, stopping en route in Thailand and Burma to get a whiff of Theravada Buddhism. In India he sought to answer a secret question: "What is the strength of her own spiritual forces in Hinduism and in Gandhi's heritage that would shape the India that is to be?"[10] Out of his visit there came his proposal for a Quaker Ashram in India and a growing conviction that Quakers had a special responsibility for helping the West to understand the world's great religions.[11] The American Friends Service Committee, which had commissioned this visit, approved a Christmas visit to Katagiri in 1956 to explore the idea. Indicative of his advanced ecumenical outlook at this stage, Douglas Steere believed that Gurdial Malik, a Jesuit whom he had met at Barpali, was the right person to head the Ashram. Meantime, on his return from the orient, Douglas Steere electrified readers of the *Christian Century* with an article on "The Quaker Message," in which he called attention to the basic contradiction Buddhists, Hindus, and Muslims found between Christian crusades and the message of Jesus' love and once again reiterated the call for an encounter with the other world religions.[12]

The Second Vatican Council (1962–1965), which he attended as an official Observer-Delegate for three sessions, injected new energy

8. Douglas V. Steere, *Unpublished Autobiography*, 656.
9. Ibid., 657.
10. Ibid., 672.
11. Ibid., 782, and Travel Letters.
12. August 1955; *Unpublished Autobiography*, 734.

into the search for a global spirituality through dialogue between the world's major religious groups. He took special interest in the schema on Christianity and other religions, making a noteworthy intervention to underscore the importance of dialogue (November 17, 1963) and using the friendly auspices of Cardinal Augustin Bea to push for an international ecumenical effort. During the council, moreover, he and Fr. Godfrey Diekmann, O.S.B., organized the Ecumenical Institute of Spirituality, which held its first meeting at St. John's University in Collegeville, Minnesota, in August 1965 on the eve of the final session of Vatican II. Thomas Merton would have participated in that gathering had Father Abbot James Fox given permission.[13]

Douglas Steere's vision of a genuinely global spirituality assumed more tangible shape in the convening of interfaith colloquia in Japan and India in late March and April 1967. Having retired from Haverford College after thirty-five years of teaching in order to become an Observer-Delegate at the last three sessions of the Second Vatican Council, he was elected chairperson of the Friends World Committee for Consultation (FWCC), a body linking the diverse groups of Friends in common efforts around the world, and secured its endorsement and encouragement for the proposed colloquia. In Japan an ecumenical group of Christian and Buddhist scholars gathered at Oiso to discuss two topics of mutual interest—"the inward journey" and "social responsibility for ordering our world"—in a mostly informal and spontaneous way. This Steere-style meeting resulted in a remarkable amount of "self-disclosure," certainly more than one dependent on formal papers. In India a similar colloquy of Christian and Hindu scholars convened at Ootacamund to discuss only the first of these topics, also in an informal manner. Both Japanese and Indian colloquia planned further meetings, but Christian-Buddhists groups proved more adept at carrying through with the plan.

Mutual Irradiation

Douglas Steere's long years of ecumenical exchange ripened in the Richard Cary Lecture entitled "Mutual Irradiation," delivered at

13. Letter of Thomas Merton to Douglas V. Steere enclosed with a letter of Dorothy Steere dated Feb. 23, 1965; Letter of Thomas Merton to Douglas V. Steere dated Sept. 14, 1965.

the German Yearly Meeting in Bad Pyrmont in 1968. I use the word "ripened" because all of the basic ideas and even the phrase "mutual irradiation" had been hanging on the Steere tree for a long time. What I wish to underscore in looking at this concept of interreligious dialogue is not the dialogue per se but the importance of being rooted in one's tradition in the process. Tradition and dialogue go hand in hand; they are inseparable companions.

Douglas Steere discerned in "the ecumenical surge" among Protestants and Orthodox in the World Council of Churches, among Roman Catholics in the Second Vatican Council, and among Christians and representatives of the great world religions "a message of importance for us."[14] He agreed with metahistorian Arnold Toynbee that what would interest historians a millennium hence would not be the "domestic quarrels" between communist and "free enterprise" systems but the mutual interpenetration of Buddhism and Christianity and, he would add, Hinduism and Christianity. Ecumenism means "world embracing," taking down fences and moving them out to embrace and assume responsibility for one another.

Eager as he was to see this mutual interpenetration of the world's great religions, however, he was not calling for the abandonment or loose handling of the Christian tradition. Quite to the contrary, "mutual irradiation" would require a far greater degree of rootedness than the alternatives: (1) destroying or burying the other religion, (2) syncretism, or (3) mere coexistence, for, in this approach, each religion must be "willing to expose itself with great openness to the inward message of the other, as well as to share its own experience, and to trust that whatever is the truth in each experience will irradiate and deepen the experience of the other."[15] To expose oneself and one's religious experience to persons of other faiths would require real security in one's own faith, for what is called for is not a cosmetic approach but a meeting "at the level of fear and trembling" such as the colloquia in Japan and India tried to supply through deep personal sharing.

As a matter of fact, the colloquia between Christians and Buddhists and Christians and Hindus just prior to preparing the Richard Cary Lecture were doubtless fresh in mind as Douglas Steere elabo-

14. *Mutual Irradiation.* [Pendle Hill Pamphlet 175] (Lebanon, Penn.: Pendle Hill Publications, 1971) 5.
15. Ibid., 8.

rated on his concept of "mutual irradiation." As he conceived it, "mutual irradiation" "would try to provide the most congenial setting possible for releasing the deepest witness that the Buddhist or Hindu or Muslim might make to his Christian companion, and that the Christian might in turn share with his non-Christian friend." It is an "existential" process "that goes beyond mere description and has to be experienced in order to be penetrated."[16] The concern to go beyond observation was what prompted Douglas Steere to avoid formal papers, to spend much time in personal exchanges, and to make "the inward journey" the center of discussion. Personal interaction of that sort is possible only for persons well grounded in their own tradition, as one of the Hindu participants at Ootacamund astutely observed. The great Hindu religious thinker Ramanuja had insisted that he "get the best out of" his own tradition before he mingled too swiftly with other religious traditions," that he "must have a center" from which he could determine "a circumference." "Only as I knew my own religion in its depths would I be able to understand the religion of others."[17]

"Mutual irradiation" would demand deeper rootedness than the alternatives, however, not only because of its experiential exactions but also because of its interpenetrating concern for the other. Truly global ecumenism of this kind "feels concern for the outcome of its fellow religionist's situation and can rejoice and find itself enriched when it produces an unmistakable saint, or a groundswell of holiness, and can feel as equally involved in its misfortunes and say, not 'There but for the grace of God go I' but rather, 'There go I.'"[18] Rejoicing in the pains and the failures of the other and regretting the joys and the victories of the other point to an inadequate grasp of the deep things of God in Christianity itself such as the import of *agape*-love.

Douglas Steere ties "mutual irradiation" directly to the Quaker tradition. Conscious that many Friends have entertained serious doubts about the ecumenical movement, he assures them that this globally spiritual approach would not violate the deepest perceptions of their own heritage. He cites luminaries such as William Penn and John Wool-

16. Ibid.
17. Prof. M. Yamunacharya, cited by Douglas V. Steere in "Inter-faith Colloquia in Japan and India," circulated by Friends World Committee for Consultation, 15.
18. *Mutual Irradiation*, 9f.

man as witnesses of the spiritual principle uniting all humankind, common efforts of Friends with others in peacemaking, and participation of Quakers in the Life and Work movement to mobilize Protestant energies to address great social issues. Where they have balked is at efforts to formulate creedal statements or to find a formula for church government on which all could agree. Quakers have belonged, rather, to a "third stream," i.e., one neither Catholic nor Protestant, "but part of the Christian mystical stream that has nurtured them all" and which "might one day draw all back into its current, immersing them in a new dimension of concern for their fellows that would renew the life of both West and East."[19] Quakers have always had "a slumbering revolutionary element" which looks askance at institutional Christianity and has thence suffered from a bit of "denominational egotism" connected with its mystical inclinations. The events of the period since John XXIII (1958–1963), however, force a thorough re-examination of the negative side, for he accentuated the universality of the love of God so starkly stated in John 3:16. The Pope called us "to witness to the operative presence, here and now, of this fathomless love and concern that is at the heart of things: a presence which is already actively at work in the unconscious life of every part of the creation." He articulated a vision which gives real hope to the world. "By more contemplation, more piercing communication and sharing, more costly undertakings of social concern, we might help to emerge above the world's consciousness."[20]

"Mutual irradiation," Douglas Steere goes on to argue, fits the Quaker tradition in another important respect. It is a "functional ecumenism that begins with all of us encouraging each other to practice our own religious tradition to the hilt and to share our experiences with each other in every creative way we can devise."[21] The goal is not monolithic mergers or wholesale syncretism or stealing one another's members but joining with others "in all kinds of common explorations and common tasks":[22]

> A truly functional ecumenism wants to witness to the world
> how much God cares, and if this means stopping a war; or trying

19. Ibid., 12.
20. Ibid., 15.
21. Ibid., 15f.
22. Ibid., 16.

to learn how to share more equitably the world's material resources; or meeting an emergency human need, or joining the poor; or sending brotherly teachers and companions to live and share with those in another area, or teaching one another how to meditate, or how to pray, or how to kindle our corporate adoration, or how to grow in the life of devotion, or how to use the lives of past saints and heroes to re-kindle our commitment; or how great art, painting, sculpture and music can expand the soul; or how personal guidance and therapy may release the deeper life in us; or how the world of plants and animals and water and wind can temper our souls; a functional ecumenism will open us in these and in other areas to the witness of our fellows, whether Christian or the adherents of other world religions.[23]

He invokes the Zen Buddhist-Christian Colloquium at Oiso in Japan and the Hindu-Christian Colloquium at Ootacamund in India in 1967 as examples of the way in which such an ecumenism might work. He notes how natural it was for Quakers to turn to Zen Buddhists because of their "marked similarities to Quakers in the Christian community."[24] At the same time the Zen Buddhist insistence on "going to the mountain," that is to say, contemplation, as the first priority "searched" Quakers in their activism even as Quaker social endeavor "searches" Buddhists. Convened in "a season where our own and the world's spiritual need was acute," the Hindu-Christian Colloquy showed how "the intimate process of mutual irradiation" could perform a "miracle."

Douglas Steere's concluding appeal was to the peculiar role Friends could play in this venture. They are "naturally oriented to start at the right end of this ecumenical endeavor—namely to begin from within and to draw the whole ecumenical process in this direction." They have the proper balance of inward and outward.[25] Friends will probably not contribute much to the intellectual side of the task, as, for instance, Teilhard de Chardin did, but they have much to say about the experiential side, for they have felt "inwardly in the presence of the living Christ both the joy and the misery of the world and having felt our arms being opened to the whole creation, while we may not ourselves at this point be able adequately to formulate a view of the

23. Ibid.
24. Ibid., 18.
25. Ibid., 27.

universal Christ, we can be among those who are most open to it."[26] Encounter with the living Christ in other religions may rob Christians of a conventional western picture, but it may also give them "a new sense of how little we yet know him, and of how much we have yet to learn perhaps through these very meetings with our brothers [and sisters] in other Christian faiths and in the world religions."[27] Christians have scarcely explored at all the "intellectual implications of the universal in this haunting figure of Christ. . . ." Quakers may render the service of providing a frank and open climate for sincere seeking.

Rooted in Tradition

Before attempting some application of this insight, I should like to demonstrate that concern for rootedness in tradition is not merely an afterthought to Douglas Steere in the context of ecumenical exchange but belongs to the center of his effort to guide the Society of Friends in this period of transition from modernity to postmodernity. The fact that the Friends have eschewed tradition in much the same way Baptists have and taken a critical stance toward institutions, emphasizing instead immediate experience of the Spirit or the living Christ, has made them more than a little vulnerable to major changes in society, especially as their numbers have dwindled steadily. Fascination with the mystical has lured many toward the facile syncretism of "New Age" and Oriental or quasi-Oriental cults. Consequently Douglas Steere has rendered a critical and salutary service in recalling the Friends to their roots and to an essential corporate task of representing the Quaker message to the world.

In a letter circulated to members of the International Fellowship of Reconciliation (IFOR) in February 1963, when he chaired the group, he made his perspective on rootedness crystal clear. Some had accused the IFOR of "Pharisaism" in confining its membership to Christians. Noting his own extensive efforts to bridge the gulf separating Christians from persons of other faiths, he proceeded to reply:

> But my own slender experience would point to the fact that this can only be sincerely done by those who stand deeply and firmly

26. Ibid., 29.
27. Ibid., 30.

rooted in their own traditions that have plumbed them deeply enough to be driven out in profound respect and affection to come to know the brothers [and sisters] in the other faith.

He favored keeping out of the IFOR the syncretists, the Bahais, and "the nervous universalists." There are real differences between Christianity and other religions. Some kind of federation of Christians, Buddhists, Hindus, and Muslims might form to engage in peace efforts, but the IFOR is Christian and should not be apologetic about that. It must not alter its requirements to be all-inclusive. "What we would seem to need, in the IFOR at least, is not to lower the qualifications, but to raise the performance." Creedalism is not desired, "but the witness and example of Jesus Christ must remain central for us."[28]

In a letter to a Swedish Quaker, Sven Ryberg, dated April 2, 1973, Douglas Steere emphasized the essential locus of Quakers in the Christian tradition on christology. Acknowledging Quakers had often had a problem here throughout their history, he insisted, nonetheless, that they must keep their anchor in that tradition:

> For me the Society of Friends is and must remain in the Christian stream, he said. This means that the Bible and especially the Gospels must be read continuously by Friends and crossed with their own inward experience. . . . To face the accounts given there of Jesus Christ and of his unerring caring and his pointing to the Father and his "love that will not let us go" is to feel indeed that "in Jesus Christ, God came all the way down stairs" to man and invites man to come all the way upstairs into his presence.

This ought not to cut one off from the Hindu and Muslim and Buddhist, for there is also the universal Christ who was before Abraham always at work,

> and this for me must always be held together with the historical appearance of Jesus. For I find that the Trinity makes sense to me only in Meister Eckhart's terms of the Godhead as the unfathomable and mysterious ground of Being which out of sheer love poured himself out in creation as God the Father, shone forth in the Son as the disclosure of that love, and in the Holy Spirit as ever-present caring and availability of that love. These three streams

28. Letter of Douglas V. Steere to Members of the International Fellowship of Reconciliation, Feb. 8, 1963; Quaker Collection, Haverford College.

of the Godhead's love did not operate once and then recede into
the abyss of Being. They are happening now and they have been
happening all through history.

This is how God now slips into the experience of people of other faiths.

In numerous addresses to Quaker gatherings Douglas Steere has
consistently underlined the importance of securing their faith in their
tradition. The "real function" of a convocation of "Quaker theologians," he judged,[29] was to "kindle one another and drive one another back to the root and encourage each one of us to write or preach
or missionize or live out a fresh insight that has come from this root,
. . ." Listing "Five Essentials of Quaker Faith Today," he stressed
the need for "twin tempers of relentlessness and openness" as key
characteristics. True to their tradition, Quaker scholars must never suppose that the disciplines of theology and philosophy create or take
precedence over experience and commitment. "Only where a theologian is continually re-immersing this awkward structure in the living matrix of personal or corporate religious experience can it keep from
becoming a 'notion,' a structure sundered from reality, a formula easily uttered, easily agreed to, easily passed on to others, and a poor
Ersatz for the immersion itself" (4). Those were the very things George
Fox was protesting in the Puritan groups of his day.

The five "essentials"—immediacy, Jesus Christ, "that of God"
in every person, redeeming love operative in the whole order of things,
and the structures of a waiting ministry and manner of conducting business with attention to the Light Within—will not surprise those who
know the essence of the Quaker tradition, for Douglas Steere un-
abashedly explains and defends these here just as he does in many
other writings. Indeed, those who know his role in his local Radnor
Meeting in Philadelphia, at Pendle Hill, or as chairperson of the FWCC
will discern an ardent apologist for the tradition which took its rise
from George Fox. After describing the first essential—"a witness to
the immediate presence, the inwardness, the accessibility, the utter
simplicity of the relation of the living God to the soul of an ordinary
man [or woman]"—he exclaims, "What stupendous news this is, if
we lived in it and could share it with others!" (4, 5).

29. Unpublished Paper entitled "Five Essentials of Quaker Faith Today,"
Quaker Collection, Haverford College, 1. Hereafter pages cited in text.

Douglas Steere's christology, as should have become clear in the statement made above, is better grounded in traditional soil than that of many other Protestants, but he is quick to honor the accent of his own tradition on the living Christ of faith rather than the Jesus of history. Noting the criticism the Friends have experienced at this point for inadequate attention to the historical Jesus and the scriptural presentation of him, lack of clarity as to whether or not he was divine, and absence of creedal statements—he invokes one of the Friends' most honored saints, Isaac Penington:

> This is He, this is He, there is no other; this is He whom I have waited for and sought after from my childhood, who was always near me and had begotten life in my heart, but I knew Him not distinctly or how to receive Him or dwell with Him . . . I have met with my Saviour . . . I have felt the healing drop upon my soul from under His wings,

and asks, ''. . . can there be any serious ground for doubt that he had known both God and the Elder Brother?'' (6). Douglas Steere goes on to observe that Penington needed scriptures to prepare him for this experience and warns Quakers not to skimp the Bible. Nevertheless, the chief concern of the Quaker tradition is *experience* rather than intellectual cognition or assent.

From these two basic convictions have arisen other distinctive Quaker emphases in anthropology, science, and worship and organization. It is well known that George Fox and the Friends held a much higher view of human nature and the natural order than the Calvinism of the Puritans allowed. Quakers could not imagine God consigning persons created in the divine ''image and likeness'' and redeemed by the Elder Brother (Christ), in every one of whom was ''that of God,'' to depravity and doom. Not even the horrors of World War II sufficed to destroy or diminish Quaker confidence ''in both the constancy of God's seige and in this reachable and reached center in people in their own company in the free type of worship and business meeting that they fashioned'' (8). Friends, likewise, viewed nature ''as open-ended, as neither automatically containing nor as utterly alien to a new order of redeeming love . . . [which] exists here and now and is operative in the hearts of men [and women], but in another sense it penetrates and shapes man's nature only when it is embodied'' (9). Quaker awareness of humankind as a link in a great chain of being has made them "strangely at home with scientific investigation." This explains John Woolman's "tenderness for all creation," concern for blacks, and refusal to participate in war. It is also the reason Fox rejected the Fifth Monarchy Men and Quakers have chosen active roles in society, "seeking to answer to the unquenchable longing for this redemptive order in the place and generation in which they have lived" (10). When Douglas Steere comes to structures of a waiting ministry in worship and of the Quaker manner of seeking the counsel of the Spirit in conduct of business, he discloses vividly the strength of this commitment to and reliance on the Quaker tradition. Readers of his classic on Quaker worship, *On Listening to Another*, will easily detect his enthusiasm for silent worship and the serious doubts he has about the Midwestern evangelical style. "For me, this waiting type of worship is still a way of direct access to God. It is a means of respecting and encouraging this access in every person gathered. It is a corporate vehicle for gathering the group into an awareness of the Presence of Christ, of an inward sense of their membership in the redemptive community, and of ministry to one another out of this gathered power" (12).

Postscript

In many respects the Quaker tradition which Douglas Steere has eloquently explained, interpreted, and defended during his long career anticipated the global spirituality of this generation. Throughout their history the Friends have stressed the inner journey and the application of the contemplative way to the pressing issues of the day— violence, racism, collective irresponsibility and irrationality, and all the rest. Like Thomas Merton, Douglas Steere has grasped the wisdom of the tradition he represents and offered it to a world crying out for enlightenment. I believe he would agree with the mature Merton's understanding of his own task as reflected in this journal note:

> For myself, I am more and more convinced that my job is to clarify something of the tradition that lives in me, and in which I live: the tradition of wisdom and spirit that is found not only in Western Christendom but in Orthodoxy, and also, at least analogously, in Asia and Islam. Man's sanity and balance and peace depend,

I think, on his keeping alive a continuous sense of what has been valid in his [or her] past.[30]

Both Steere and Merton recognized the pitfalls of racing wildly after the latest fads in a time of rapid social change. Douglas Steere frequently threw up some caution flags to his fellow Quakers with their propensity for spontaneity, and Thomas Merton found that the true and tested needed to keep in check his own fascination with change itself. In *Conjectures of a Guilty Bystander* he remarked:

> There is no real need for me to specialize, but I intend to keep to the writers of Christian Antiquity and those of the Middle Ages for a while, to defend myself against the levity of what happens at the moment to seem urgent just because it is popular. I can resist the general madness (not that the issues are not serious, but the madness about them is absurd), and I have done this lately by sticking to Migne's Latin Fathers.[31]

Merton's remedy for "levity" may seem a bit extreme, but it has in it an inescapable insight. What will offer some safeguard for us in a time of accelerated change of the magnitude suggested by the transition from modernity to postmodernity that we not lapse into the worst frivolity is tradition, the essence and not the external. It will be particularly important as we widen our perceptions and contacts on a global scale decreed by the present awakening. Being deeply rooted and grounded in our own tradition will give us sufficient assurances that we can allow ourselves to be irradiated by the light in persons of other religions.

All of this is to say, I suppose, that not many of us are ready for this transition from modernity to postmodernity. Indeed, not many are ready to be world citizens and to receive or to give light. The past generation has tried a variety of spiritualities—secular, charismatic, oriental and quasi-oriental, and variations on each of these—in hopes of finding one which could "speak to our condition" in a culture we have created with our technology which poses a threat to our very survival. What we have not tried sufficiently may be the very thing to which both Thomas Merton and Douglas Steere point us, namely, tra-

30. Thomas Merton, *Conjectures of a Guilty Bystander* (Garden City, N.Y.: Doubleday & Co., 1968) 194.
31. Ibid., 248.

dition. Modernity has not held tradition in high esteem, and it may be the most pressing task of postmodernity to lay aside this disdain for the tested and tried and recover again the essence of things. In spirituality we are seeing some promising trends in that direction in the publication of sixty volumes of Classics of Western Spirituality, including Jewish and Muslim as well as Christian, and twenty-five volumes in the history of spirituality. The winds of change may not sweep us away after all.

Notes after First Visit
and Correspondence 1962–1968

Thomas Merton and Douglas V. Steere

[The following single-spaced notes were typed just after Douglas V. Steere first met Thomas Merton.]

Notes on Conference with Thomas Merton, February 1962

UNION THEOLOGICAL SEMINARY
BROADWAY AT 120TH STREET
NEW YORK 27, N.Y.

February 1962

John Heidbrink, who has been serving the Fellowship of Reconciliation as the secretary for the theological seminaries, had a concern for us to visit Thomas Merton when we were in Kentucky lecturing at the Presbyterian Seminary in Louisville. He felt that Thomas Merton's growing interest in peace was such that someone should see him and find out any possible way that we could serve him and also to thank him for the things that he has written in the interest of a radical position on peace for those who seek to follow the Christian way.

We arranged to come a day early to Louisville and to go out to the Trappist Monastery at Gethsemane [sic] on Monday morning, February 5th, when he asked us to come at nine. We travelled out the new Kentucky turnpike to Lebanon Junction and then got into a little back road called 52 which turned out to be under construction. We wallowed through some open mud and up and down steep rises that

23

were banked with coal refuse from open pit mines and finally got onto the proper road and to the monastery on the stroke of nine. The real way to go is to take #61 at the Ky. Turnpike exit and then 62 to Boston, Ky., and at Bardstown—the great whiskey manufacturing center—31E south to 247 and then to go in to Trappist, Kentucky on this little 247 spur.

We notified the clerk at the gift shop that we had an appointment and after some time in the shop buying books, we went to the dimly lit chapel and there Thomas Merton met us. He was a man of perhaps fifty wearing a monk's robe with his well worn overall jacket on his arm. He took us past the Church entrance with its GOD ALONE inscription over the door and into a little reception room in the hall off the gift shop, and there we had an hour and a half of excellent visit.

We began with his reference to John Heidbrink's asking him if we should not have an American branch of UNA SANCTA. He said that he was not for this since Americans tended to over-organize good things and that there might be a real slowing up of this ecumenical fellowship if it got too formidably organized. He suggested that it remain as spontaneous and personal as possible and that it would go much further on this basis. He spoke of his own difficulties with the Catholic authorities over the Methodist and Baptist seminaries bringing out their students for a day in order to get some glimpse of medieval church life and his organizing this for them and then how out of it grew some subsequent seminar-like visits. The authorities promptly stopped it when it reached this point. As long as it is a case of Thomas Merton's friends visiting him there is no possible question of it, but beyond this apprehension grows. I told him something of our European experiences with UNA SANCTA and of the spontaneous and unpredictable elements being the most rewarding of all, and spoke of my being visited recently by this Discalced Carmelite who wanted to have some Protestant counselors attached to their Spiritual Life Institutes and these Houses of Leisure and Learning that are springing up. We also talked of the meeting with George Tavard and Damasus Winzen and the Protestant Theological group at the College of Preachers in Washington last November, and of the work of the Taizé brothers at Packard Manse, of the Institutes at Notre Dame, of the work of Robert Brown at Union Theological Seminary and of the fresh temper of openness that is developing. He warned that the worst of all is to get expectations too high that some great move will come at once, and then to have them dashed. We are still in the forerunner stage and this is going well and should be encouraged without over publicizing it.

I said that many of us were most grateful to him for his writings on peace of late and asked if he would not like to talk some of this side to which he warmly agreed. He said that he had been in some real difficulties with his position on the peace issue because the authorities found this so touchy as far as the church at large was concerned. He feels that the poverty of our Christian position today is revealed by the unwillingness of ordinary men and women to face up to the implications of storing and preparing the delivery-vehicles and of their supine giving over their willingness for the delivery of nuclear bombs to the military. He feels that it shows the erosion of Christian responsibility to have let the present acceptance of this preparation for all-out nuclear war get to the point that it has, without a major demanding of a show-down. I asked him whether he came out at the full Christian pacifist position at this point and if he would go along with Evelyn Underhill's statement issued in a volume of Anglican Essays on the war in about 1940. He did not know the essay and I hope that we can get him a copy of its substance. He said that he had been one who chose non-combatant service in the last war and that he could personally have no part in killing as a Christian, but that he thought the absolute pacifist position at the moment was less the one to demand of all Christians than to go all out for nuclear pacifism and demand a defense of their country by the only means that could defend it, namely by non-violence.

We talked of the Catholic position at the moment and he admitted that it was very clouded on this issue of war, with so reputable a theologian as John Courtney Murray insisting that the old Catholic principle of the "just-war" still held, and that since one could not any longer make the old designation of aggressor stick, that if there were a major injustice committed by the enemy, that he was open to attack. With theologians divided and the bishops unwilling to take positions in advance of their theologians, there was little hope of getting official pronouncements against nuclear war. The Pope's insistence that all loyal Catholics would bear arms in defence of their own countries in 1956 after the Hungarian affair has also helped to damp down those who would plead for a radical peace witness on the part of all Catholics today. I asked him if he could not go to work on this JUST WAR theory which had backing also from a Protestant like Paul Ramsey, and whether this was not the line of attack at the moment. He assured me that he was not the man for that, that it must be a highly reputable theologian and that the best one would be Professor John Fort [sic] of the Catholic University in Washington, D.C. He had taken a strong position during the last war against obliteration-bombing and had a conscience on these matters, but that he was not optimistic about his undertaking it against the solid storm of public opposition to any undermining of this ancient bulwark of the Catholic war position. He spoke of a forth-coming book by Gordon Zahn of Loyola University in Chicago which was getting at the Catholic record in the Nazi period, and coming somewhat obliquely at the war issue. He asked if Maritain would tackle it and I said that he had shifted his ground from the Gandhian position when France was overrun in the second world war, and had never reopened the earlier chapter to my knowledge.

I spoke of my visits with John Bennett of late who hugs the deterrence doctrine in spite of his horror at the Christian consequences of being willing to deliver what may amount to a destruction of the whole created world. John Bennett insists that nothing will alter the present position unless we have a wholesale revulsion on the part of the people to the insanity and the utter absurdity of the present preparations. This task, he feels that pacifist and non-pacifist alike can participate in and should be about by night and by day. Yet the official church regards discussion of these issues as morbid and tabu in a service of "comforting worship."

Thomas Merton said that he saw little hope from the ordinary methods of waking people up to the present danger. It may have to come by a terrible accident, by something almost apocalyptic. Dorothy Steere spoke of the women's demonstrations and of what Schweitzer had told her in 1957 in Gunsbach that the women who were close to the source of life might finally have to be the ones who called a halt on this threat to wipe out all life. He brightened to this as to almost nothing else on this issue and said that this made real sense to him and that it might well come this way. He spoke of the striking book on *Women and the Salvation of the World* by the Orthodox scholar E[v]dokimo[v] which had been translated from the French. (Try SPCK)

I asked him about the form that a fresh outburst of spirituality of which the monasteries were in some sense the historical landmarks and custodians of past outbursts of spiritual passion might take and inquired what he saw as the need for our day. He admitted that the present monastic life was largely absorbed in keeping the liturgical engine going and that they were heavily mechanical and not able to meet the need of today. He said that as a symptom there was a longing to go off as solitaries on the part of a number of the most intense younger men and that occasionally they pulled it off. He spoke of one going to Martinique where facilities for hermit existence were present in connection with one of the houses. He said that those in the world who felt the call to contemplation could always withdraw and "take to the woods." "There is still woods." The day of this kind of thing being heroic is past and should be. Let them go if they feel the necessity and perhaps something will come of it for them, and through them.

Laymen have the chance. The monasteries have been largely taken over by clergy and the fresh initiative of laymen is gone. The laymen can hang on to a spar in the shipwreck. They can help rebuild the substrate of silence and purpose in the whole of society which has largely fallen away. These would be people who "are nothing on purpose."

I asked him about the life in the monastery here at Gethsemane and he said it was energetic—the monks being mostly Americans and liking to get things done. There are about 180 monks here and about 1000 in USA and the same number in France with one small house in Germany near Aachen and one in Austria. There are 11 other houses in USA. The penitential side is largely gone today. It never purified the men anyway and today it is a more positive way of life that is encouraged. They support themselves here on their farm—cheese making is a major occupation. They receive many gifts as well. There are 20 of the monks who give themselves entirely to the farm and the rest give perhaps two hours a day to the farm work. He has about 2 1/2 hours a day free to go to his hermitage where he can pray privately and write, but most of the brothers are so caught up in the machine of the monastery that they can do little but to serve it. They go to rest at 7, rise at 2 and have choir duty until 8 or 9 in the morning. They take a light breakfast at 6 or 7, the main meal at noon and a light refection of bread and coffee and fruit at night.

I asked about direction for the spiritual life here at Gethsemane and he said that he and a young Father John of the Cross were each guiding a group of novices, he (TM) the choir novices and J of C the brother novices (who apparently would not go the way of the priesthood). He feels that they have several father confessors who have some gifts of spiritual guidance in addition to being confessors but that the life here is so severely regulated that there is little room for anything very advanced being done. When the ordinary paths give out and you come to the pathless, then most give up and return to the machine. It was clear that there was no over-romanticising of the existing system as far as being a school of contemplative spirituality was concerned. We talked of the older Zen monasteries that were open once a month for a week and of how many from the wider community came and worshipped with them for that week. He said that they had facilities for this and that Damasus Winzen did this all the time at Mt. Saviour for men visitors taking them in to eat with the regularly professed monks and sharing the services with them.

We talked of Bede Griffiths and his experiment in Peermade in Southern India and he was so eager to hear of it. He deplored that we had gone in so rough shod to these older cultures who often had most precious treasures of spirituality to share with us and we treated them as if all that they had must be ground out before they could become proper Christians. He is deeply sympathetic with what Bede Griffiths is about and asked us to help him get back in touch with him saying that it was so long since he had heard from him although he had written.

We left with some of his articles which he had brought for us and with his begging us to come again and to bring several with us most informally and to stay at the guest house for a day or two for real visits. He also asked for some Quaker literature and I promised him John Woolman's *Journal* and the *Journal* of George Fox. He saw us out to the door of the monastery and sent his blessings with us.

Douglas V. Steere

The Steere letters were written on Haverford College (Haverford, Pennsyl vania) letterhead stationary unless otherwise indicated.

March 7, 1963

Rev. Thomas Merton
Gethsamane Abbey (Trappist)
Gethsamane, Kentucy

Dear Friend:

It was so kind of you to send me the copy of *The Thomas Merton Reader* through your publisher and I read it with great joy and appreciation. It is a fine collection of materials and I was especially glad to be able to read some of the things in there which were quite new to me.

When we saw you a year ago on the little visit we made down from Louisville, we had some talk about spiritual direction and I managed to buy your little book on that subject there at the book store in the Abbey. You also gave me an excellent mimeographed copy of your lectures on this subject and these have been especially helpful to me. I wrote a long introduction to a volume of the spiritual letters and counsels of Baron von Hügel, which will be out both in England and in this country in the autumn, and did it on spiritual direction, drawing the case study very especially from Von Hügel's handling of Evelyn Underhill. I am so glad to see you really making the proper distinction between spiritual direction and psychotherapy which has gotten very confused in our time and which needs to be most sharply marked out. I think this needs even further development than we have given it and I hope you will go further in future writings that you do on this subject on that very issue.

I have been so thankful for the things you have written on peace and it has greatly encouraged us all to see the witness that you have made. I shall be over in Holland this summer at the biennial Council Meeting of the IFOR. We will very especially remember your contribution there. Are there any special books that I could send you which you particularly want or need at this time? Please let me know if there are.

Dorothy Steere joins me in sending our warmest greetings to you. If we find any way to get to your part of the world again in June when we come up from North Carolina to Michigan, we will do our best to let you know in advance and try to get to see you. With warmest personal greetings and with the deepest esteem.

Sincerely your friend,

Douglas V. Steere

We will represent Quakers at the Vatican Council in Rome in the autumn.

April 23, 1963

Thomas Merton
Abbey of Gethsamani
Trappist, Kentucky

Dear Friend:

Thank you so much for your wonderful letter of April 9th. I am looking forward so much to reading the things you have sent me which have come. It is fine that you are going to have this peace retreat soon and I see it as a wonderful thing for those who can come and be with you.

I have just been up to Harvard for this Roman Catholic-Protestant Colloquium and found a most generous temper there on both sides. I was hardly prepared for the rate at which this friendliness has come. Father Weigel in his banquet speech together with the president of Harvard University, said that things were coming in such a rate that he thought within a short time it might well be that the Jesuits might even join the Roman Catholic Church!

I am delighted that you are working on Fénelon. I just reviewed a French book on his relations with the Bible and in the course of it reread a somewhat superficial book, but one that brought back the life freshly to me by Catharine Little. It made me want to go back and read the letters and get closer to him again. People have very different tastes about him and some of the remarks of people like Evelyn Underhill have not been particularly complimentary. I have always found him a person of real insight and of a great deal of courage. When one thinks of the humiliations he must have suffered for his desire to do justice to what he had found in Madam[e] Guyon and of the vicious way in which he was treated by Bousset, and of the way in which the prince that he had shaped for the kingship should die at the very point where Fenelon might have come into major influence—it shows what a wonderful character he was to have assimilated all of these terrible blows and yet to have gone on deepening in his faith. There can be little doubt that he remained an aristocrat and accepted the high station which he occupied almost as his due, but few have used it to better advantage and perhaps this is the test God will make of his life.

I will write you again after I have read these things and meanwhile, know how much we cherish your friendship.

Sincerely your friend,

Douglas V. Steere

June 13, 1963

Dr. [sic] Thomas Merton
Abbey of Gethsamani
Trappist, Kentucky

Dear Thomas Merton:

It was wonderful to hear from you on the 16th of May and to have your two papers on Fenelon. I read them with the greatest of interest and liked particularly your introduction to the letters which I trust will be published before too long. The fine way in which you showed how Fenelon was belittled and has been ever since by the French establishment is exactly right and I thought you put it extremely well. I sat down and read a little volume of Fenelon following on reading your fine introduction and felt again the profound spiritual wisdom of this great spirit. How seldom those in power even dare to acknowledge the authority of a spirit like this. I think you know something of what this experience is from the inside.

The Pope's passing is a great blow to us all and especially to those of us who were planning to be with him at the Vatican Council this autumn. Dorothy and I expect to be there, but now things may be drastically changed. It will be very interesting to have some forecast from you of what you think will take place although I expect all of us are simply looking into the darkness.

The kind of a question I wish you would write me about sometime if you ever feel free to do it, would be your own thoughts on what kind of a state, or what proposals for a theory of the state, could a Christian revolutionary pacifist set down. I think this is the most rugged question for us to face and one which even Gandhi was unable to do more than to suggest decentralization and a level of life low enough so that it would not tempt your neighbor. Certainly there must be some discipline in order to supply the needed order for an established life in which families can grow up and work out their inner destinies. What could those who believe in a Christian way propose to supply this order both within local communities and in the larger units? A friend of mine named Mulford Sibley, who is going to be on the summer school faculty at Pendle Hill this summer, once wrote his Ph.D. thesis on this subject of the political theories of the pacifist and came up with a rather discouraging report. I really feel that this is the nub of the matter and that we must have something to say on this if we are going to be able to do more than be protesters. This of course goes very deep into the question of the applicability of the question of the Christian ethic generally, but I would be so interested in knowing how you would make this application.

Dorothy Steere and I remember so vividly the happy hours with you and hope that we can repeat them sometime soon. We both send you our warmest personal greetings.

Sincerely your friend,

Douglas V. Steere

Hotel Boston
Via Lombardia 47
Rome, Italy—Sept. 30, 1963

My dear Tom:

I am writing you from Rome where Dorothy and I are planted for the next period as Quaker Observer-Delegate at the Vatican Council. The opening yesterday was the greatest public spectacle that I have ever witnessed and for sheer magnificence could not be matched anywhere in the world. Even the five hours of sitting had its compensation in a way in being present on an occasion where Paul VI showed how deeply he affirmed the best line taken at the First Session of this

Second Council and how determined he was to implement it wherever he could. The new notes were a sharper articulation of his longing for a wider unity and his willingness for the first time almost in history to make a public acknowledgement of error and wrong on the part of the church in occasioning the separations and asking for as well as an offering of forgiveness. His words about the wide diversity and variety that would be acknowledged in the Christian community could an approach to each other be made was again a move beyond the "welcome home" suggestion which would imply that all of the yielding would be on one side. This note is not altogether absent even from this address but it is certainly far less to the fore than in most instances. It is fascinating to see the liberty of the Bishops as well as the Cardinals in pitching into those prepared schemata in the sessions of the Council itself and it helps the Observers to have validated their theoretical realization that there is anything but a monolithic picture behind the scenes. The move away from Council I in 1870 toward a fresh affirmation of the role of the bishops and of the collegium and of the pope and bishops in council together is one that if courageously pursued might make the Orthodox take a fresh look at the situation. The 1870 accent was such an exaggeration of papal authority that was then so largely usurped by the curia and worn by them, that nothing short of a major revolution could restore the situation to one that could even remotely attract the attention of the separated groups for all of their feeling of the sin of division with all of its disastrous consequences. It will be so interesting in the present schemata of the Ecclesia to see how this will be shaped. There are certainly present some powerful voices who feel with one of the Cardinals who alleged that it would take 40 years for the church to put back what John XXIII had undone.

I have just had a letter from Hugh Van Dusen saying that you very kindly agreed to read the Von Hügel *Spiritual Letters and Counsels* book and give them a comment which they might use in launching it. They stand to lose on such a book at best and need any backing that the friends of Von Hügel can give it if they think it is competently done. Hugh would be most grateful if you would write him directly at Harpers and Row 49 East 33rd St. New York 16, NY and let him have a brief comment as swiftly as you can manage it. I can well imagine what is before you on your desk and how far under the pile this may be but both of us would be deeply grateful if you could up-grade it a little.

If there is anything that I can do for you here at the Council, won't you let me know of it. If there is anyone here in Rome who seems to you to be one I should meet who is concerned especially for the life of prayer and spiritual direction, won't you let me know the name and how I may reach him. Dorothy joins me in sending you our warmest personal greetings.

Sincerely your friend,

Douglas V. Steere

Hotel Boston
Via Lombardia 47
Rome, Italy
26 • X • 63

Dear Tom:

Thank you for your good letter and for your great kindness in sending Harpers those helpful words about the Von Hügel book. It is so hard to get a book of this kind off the ground for FVH is not bedtime reading and the American public want something that is written to move and astonish.

I have met Häring and been greatly drawn to him. I saw him the next day after your letter at a magnificent Bach concert given the Council attenders with the Aachen choir and the Rome Opera orchestra and gave him your greetings. The splendour of the Papal establishment was never more regal than at such a concert with Paul VI on his throne and the cardinals in the orchestra seats and all of this ocean of purple everywhere. I do not quite know what this has to do with the Gallilean but it is Babylon at its absolute Sunday best. Häring is a man I want to see as much as I can of and I am delighted that he has some notions of returning to USA for some more lectures. This is the kind of man we so badly need. I am meeting one of your Kentucky men B. Ahearn [sic] at dinner Monday. He is a very lively Biblical scholar who takes an active part in the discussions which the Observors have each Tuesday with the Commission members of Christian Unity and is a friend of my dear friend Damasus Winzen whom he asked me to meet.

The other day I had a letter from John Coburn who is the Dean of the Episcopal Theological Seminary in Cambridge, Mass. and a writer and guide in Protestant circles on the life of prayer. He is trying to get a term off in order to go to England and see what the Anglican scholars have to give him on ascetic theology. I was talking about it in the Coffee bar at St. Peters and asking a Catholic scholar whether they had anything unique to give on this subject in USA apart from your books on the subject. He confessed to the sterility of such studies today as were in the schools. I saw Father Diekmann soon afterwards and mentioned to him the possibility of a little Ecumenical group of a dozen or so from Protestants and Catholics who might look over the field together mentioning the Carmelite Father MacNamara's efforts to spread this kind of thing on a more popular level. We both mentioned you and wondered if a little institution were set up at St. John's Collegeville, Minn. for a week or ten days in the summer of 1965 whether your monastery might be persuaded to release you to join us. He felt that he could set up such a group. I saw him yesterday and he said that the name of LeClerc [sic] had come to him since as another valuable member to have there if he was in USA that summer. I have since heard from John Coburn who would much like to be with us if he does not get this Guggenheim to permit him to study in Europe that summer. My suspicion from his outline is that Guggenheim will think twice before backing so specifically religious a venture but I may have too little faith. I suspect that Britain will have little to give him that he cannot get out of books by reading on this side. My feeling was that if we could look over the field and find what is really being done in the world and then block out some tasks for ourselves that this might be an ecumenical venture of the deepest significance of all.

I am interested that you have the proof of the Görres diaries. I read the Mss. for Harpers when it was being considered and suggested heavy cutting since she had put in so much that was only intelligible in the light of the German ecclesiastical situation although I like its frankness. I know her and have admired her boldness always. They replied to me that the British intermediary agreed with me in principle but dared not brave her wrath to begin to do the kind of cutting that I had advised. I shall be much interested to see how it really does appear. Stransky is also coming to dinner with us on Monday and I will greet him for you. I like him very much and he has been especially helpful to all of us in the Observer group. The intellectual star of this crowd is young Gregory Baum from Toronto and he too has been very helpful to us all.

The Non-Christians Religions venture is apparently being considered by Cardinal Koenig from Vienna who has written a 3 Vol. work on the World Religions. The delicate problem involved is what to do with the Jews. The Sec. for X Unity think that it would be an insult to put them in with the other Non X Religions and intend to bring the Jews into their Commission. This however will almost certainly provoke the Orthodox Jews and rouse their suspicions so that it seems to me quite wrong in its strategy although admirable in its intention.

There is no definite word around about the time the Sec. will be set up but I suspect that there will be observors [sic] here at the next session of the council which may be in post Easter days or next autumn. No announcement has been made. I will let you know if I hear anything soon.

Any other suggestions you may have for me here that would help me explore Rome's hidden devotional resources will be most welcome, Tom. I am seeing that wonderful Benedictine Rector Augustine Mayer at S. Anselmo and am much drawn to him personally.

There is the perpetual power struggle on here and the Curia won a round this week when at a secret session of the 4 Moderators appointed by the Pope to expedite the business of the Council and the Cardinal Council and Presidents over who really had the power to move the meetings along and to frame issues to be discussed in order to get the real points in the schema out before the Fathers the vote was 11 to 9 against giving this authority to the Moderators—a power which they assumed came with their original Papal appointment. In ordinary society they might well resign and ask the Pope to clarify the issue or replace them but here they go on with reduced power and it will be up to Paul VI to decide whether he will intervene or not. The only way around now is for the Bishops who feel the laggard pace of the present arrangements to use delgated speakers after they have threshed things out in their regional meetings and to see that more is done in Commissions and that they meet more often. Dear Pope John wanting not to offend made the almost irremediable mistake of appointing the Cardinal Presidents of the different Congregations as Chairmen of these Commissions and while he repeatedly distinguished between Council and Congregations, he had already delivered over the keys to these insiders who have little interest in speeding up the Commission work and are sure that if the Council recesses and gets out of Rome they can have things much more their own way. But God has his ways and the educative process of this mingling here of these bishops from all over the world is enormous whether anything else is done or not.

Dorothy joins in sending you our best.

Douglas [Steere]

Rome, Italy
19 • IV • 64

Dear Thomas Merton:

We have stopped by at Rome on our way up from Africa and before we leave in the morning, I just wanted to write to you and to tell you first of all how deeply thankful I was to you for that fine statement I discovered on the Harper and Row edition of the *Spiritual Counsel* and *Letters of Baron Friedrich von Hügel* which appears this week in USA and to tell you that in talking with Father Häring, this wonderful Redemptorist who had been helping so enormously in the Council, at lunch today, when I told them that Father Diekmann of Collegeville was hoping very much to get you to come to a spiritual institute that they are setting up at Collegeville in 1965 for ten or a dozen each of Catholic and Protestant scholars of Spiritual Theology, how overjoyed he was to hear it. He has promised me that he would try to arrange to come over for something else and to be there with us. Father Diekmann and I both felt the want of solid work in this area except for such a very few people like yourself and the need for some fresh approaches to it and felt that this might be an ecumenical undertaking that would implement the talk about the bridges that has been going on here. Our hope would be that this could take place at the end of the summer perhaps at the very end of August 1965 for about ten days and that from the Catholic side you and perhaps Barnabas Ahern and Father Häring and Father Diekmann and a Carmelite father who has organized a Carmelite spiritual institute and a French authority on pre-medieval spirituality together with four or five others and from the non Catholic side it has been left up to two or three of us to coopt some seven or eight others. I would be grateful to know candidates in either rank that you would think should surely be there and these can be considered. Father Diekmann felt that with such an Institute in prospect there might be an arrangement made to make it possible for you to come if you would favor us with this piece of your time. I think that it could result in a new impetus to this side of the life of religion in our time and through it we might block out certain pieces of work that different members would agree to undertake. For me personally it would be an unbelievable experience to have such a block of days with you.

I hope that you got a full set of my Letters from Rome. There were five in all. I expect at the next session to get here for the last four weeks at least and perhaps for the whole of the fourth and final (?) one.

I have been seeing some of the people in the Council on this short visit and find that the Commissions have all been most active in the last four months and that most of the schemas have been completely redrafted. Those that have not come up yet were ordered to compress their content into propositions and then have a longer relatio telling what went on to produce these. The schema on the church, ecumenism, lay apostolate have been redrafted and the one on ecumenism has had its fifth chapter completely recast and I am told strengthened. It is the final chapter—the Jews being treated in an appendix. This treatise on Religious Liberty is I am told attached in such a way that it can be detached and separately promulgated if this is the Pope's wish and many feel this would be the best disposition of it. I am assured that the appendix is not a way out for the Jewish document which is almost unchanged except for omitting the reference to the other world-religions in the prefaratory [sic] story statement where they should have been left unmentioned or else a great deal more should have been said about them. The first alternative was taken.

The Pope's speech to the Italian bishops last week made it almost certain that there would be no further pressing for concluding the council with this session as had been implied in early speeches so that now they expect to have a calendar and allot time to the different items and urge councils of bishops from regions to thresh out the substance of their criticisms in regional sessions and then apoint one of their number to speak for both majority and minority opinion in the group. They hope to finish the one on the Church, on Ecumenism, on Lay Apostolate and to air the controversial Commission 17 schema which is apparently quite stout in its present revised form. From the discussion on this, they will revise again for the fourth session so there is no thought of finishing this at the third session. You will be overjoyed, as I am, that Father Häring has been made secretary of this Commission 17 where the issue of peace and war comes up and where there is a chance to get some sentence in that will peg unmistakably that the CO position is an evangelical alternative that a Catholic may take with the blessing of the church or at least without its harsh disapproval as in the case of this priest who received six months in prison and an equal thump from the Holy Office for testifying in a Catholic CO layman's defence that the church did have scripture for such a position and acknowledged it. As far as I know, Häring is as near to being a revolutionary Christian pacifist and as I have ever found in the Roman Catholic Church and in his new post is determined to keep the issue of peace and war before the Commission. This I write to you in confidence and only to let you know that from within the church there is real hope on the things we hold precious. Karl Rahner is also willing to see that the CO has a recognized position in the church although he does not share Father Häring's views.

I am going up to England after a brief visit to Munich and will work away there on a little book on this Rhodesian poet-saint that Dorothy and I have dug out material on in Southern Rhodesia in the past months. She joins me in sending you our affectionate greetings.

Your friend,

Douglas Steere

[P.S.] The Council president MARELLA and secretary HUMBERTCLAUDE have been chosen for a secretariat for the Non-Christian religions.

April 26, 1964

Dear Douglas:

It was very good to get your latest from Rome and to hear the news of your trip to Africa, and especially of meeting Fr. Häring. Yes, he is a marvelous person and I suspect he must have had a hand in *Pacem in Terris*. A brief talk I had with him here was very rewarding. I must write to him and send him a couple of the latest things that have been mimeographed here. I will put them in an envelope for you too.

It is true that Godfrey Dieckmann [sic] wrote and asked me about my coming to Collegeville, and I forget what I answered. It cannot have been very definite because I have not yet taken the bull by the horns and asked permission. I am rather certain that the permission will be refused, and I am not complaining of this really. Thinking the matter over soberly, I believe that it is rather important that I don't get involved in travelling around because if I do the last vestiges of a monastic life will just go out the window. It would be a great joy for me to get out and see places and find out what is going on and especially to meet people and discuss important things. And yet too I think it may be of very great importance for me just to sit still here, and stay in the woods, and try to be quiet [sic] still, and even eventually write less. This has some of the sound of a fond hope, I know, but really I think that the matter of travel and going out for conferences etc represents a sort of Rubicon that ought not to be crossed, unless it were question of going somewhere more remote and more quiet to be more out of sight and take a plunge into at least temporary total solitude. I don't expect you to agree fully, but in any event I think that the Superiors will still look at it somewhat in this light, though in the Order as a whole there is a tendency to fling wide the doors and get more active. I wonder if this really makes sense, though. And I wonder if those who are doing it really have motives they understand, or are just impelled to do it and think their impulsion is a charism?

I know Fr. William [McNamara] OCD. He stopped by here briefly, and his place in the desert is certainly fascinating. If it were a question of going somewhere like that. . . . Well, I won't speculate.

If in the Council we can at least get clearly admitted the right of the Catholic to be a conscientious objector, something will have been gained. And I also hope that in schema 17 there will be something quite definite again about the total irrationality of war as a means of settling international disputes today, a principle which, if once admitted, ought to show the verbalizing about "just war" to be as trivial and as nugatory as it really is. As to the business about the Jews, whatever may be the rights and wrongs of Hochhuth's "Deputy" (I have read it but not seen it, or rather I read enough of it to get the point, and gave up in sheer boredom) this ends up by being exactly the same issue. Failure to come out for the Jews because of political implications and difficulties. The other question: what would have been the real meaning and effect of Pius XII protesting? And the real meaning and effect of this statement? As to the non-Christian religions, I think that is an important venture indeed, though I don't foresee it getting far as yet. For my own part I have been appointed to do surveys of publication in the field of Oriental mysticism etc for the magazine of our Order. That is a start, and I expect it to be interesting.

Tell me more about your Rhodesian poet-saint. I think you mentioned the subject a long time ago but it is no longer clear in my mind. As to Von Hügel, I am glad the Letters are out and hope Harpers won't forget to send me a copy. They probably have and it has been delayed.

Best wishes to both you and Dorothy
Most cordially always in Christ,

[Thomas Merton]

Feb. 20, 1965

Dear Douglas:

I am very glad to hear from you and to receive the booklet on Africa which I will read with much interest, particularly since I have not been able to get much information about South Africa. Many thanks.

Some time ago I had the melancholy experience of having to write Fr Godfrey Diekmann and say I would be unable to come to Collegeville. This decision was not mine, it was made for me without appeal by my Abbot. If the matter had been entirely up to me, there would have been no question of my coming. I know that such an exceptional opportunity would have been a great grace for me, and I would have participated in the meeting with much interest and, I am sure, great benefit. I still regret that I will not be able to come, and if I thought there were some way of getting there I would make the attempt. But I really do not see any way of changing my Abbot's decision, which is final. On the other hand, if he did change his mind there would be no obstacle. The matter is entirely up to him. As I told Fr Godfrey, if he or you want to write to Father Abbot, by all means do so, but I don't think it will do much good. Perhaps Fr Barnabas Ahearn [sic] might be able to suggest to him reasons why it would be important for me to be there. But as for my own efforts, they have no further chance of success, and I think he really does not want me to go at all for any reason. The reason why I mentioned Fr Barnabas is that Fr Abbot knows him well and has great respect for his opinion. But even he would not mangage, I think, to change his mind.

I will write later about the Council. Did you meet my friend Sister Luke there, the woman observer from America? She is a very remarkable person and I think you would like her. She is from a convent a few miles from here.

My very best wishes to both you and Dorothy. When will we see you again down this way? You are always welcome.

Cordially yours in Chist,

[Thomas Merton]

Sept. 14, 1965

Dear Douglas:

It was very good of you to send me the resume of the discussions at Collegeville. I will go through them with interest and will hope to read the talks themselves in Worship. I want to make clear how much I regret that I was not able to be present. That was not my choice, I assure you. I felt bound to do what I could to attend, because I felt that it would be of great benefit to me and to my community in the first place. Also I must say that I firmly disagree with the theology behind the decision that kept me here. This negative and short sighted view of the monastic life actually ends up by stifling the Spirit, I believe. Of course it is quite true that there is some very real danger of activism in the contemplative life, and one must guard against it, but the inability to make any exception whatever seems to me dangerous and in the long run fatal for the contemplative life itself. But there is no possible way of discussing this with the ones concerned. The lines of communication are simply closed.

On the other hand, if you see Fr Häring in Rome, you might seriously ask him this question: while the monastic Orders should naturally maintain their principle of separation from the world and even from active parish work, is it not a real misunderstanding of the present day theology of the Church to *forbid* monastic priests who are qualified and willing, to undertake any form of apostolic work, even as a temporary exception, and even when they are urgently requested to do so by bishops for instance in Latin America. In other words is it really the spirit of the Church to *prevent* at all costs a priest, a member of a contemplative Order, from volunteering for example to do some temporary apostolic work outside his monastery in Latin America? I know that the principle would perhaps lay itself open to some abuse, but it seems to me that simply stifling all initiative in this direction is going to harm the monastic life. But I do admit that the Superiors have a real problem of keeping the contemplative life contemplative. I just do not think that a narrow and negative view is going to get the results they envisage. It has not done so in the past, it is not doing so in the present. And we are losing good vocations because they see that in the monastery the life tends to be to some extent sterile and inert, and any attempt at seeking creative solutions is suppressed before it can even be thought out and discussed thoroughly.

I would have been very happy to have a group of you down here to discuss these and other things. But again, it is a question of the local policy. It is true I have obtained permission to be a hermit and have entered into the new life which, I admit, suits me very well. I am not anxious to get into a lot of activity which would spoil this. But at the same time I do not consider that a rigid, negative, restrictive and suppressive view of the solitary life is the answer. I am afraid that the chief reason why my Superiors have given me this chance is that it enables them to say *"Now* it is obvious that you cannot have any contacts with the outside and that you must lead a purely contemplative life.'' If those are the terms, I accept them, but once again I think that the negative and limited view behind them is unacceptable and out of accord with the theology of the Church. In a word, to say that there must be a class of people, even priests, who *must be prevented* from exercising an apostolate even temporarily, and even when there seems to be a very good reason for it, seems to me to be quite contrary to Christianity, especially today. However, God has His own ways of getting things done. Naturally I will be thinking of you at the Council, and will be keeping this momentous session in my prayers—especially Schema 13. I hope to send you a copy of an open letter I wrote to the US Bishops, when it is printed. It is on Peace.

Thanks again for all your kindness. Do believe that I remain deeply united to you and to all my friends in Christ. The frustrations of the situation here will not hurt me. They are annoying because they are so blame *wrong,* but apart from that I know that there is good in it all for me, and I know the power and value of the Cross—at least I hope I do, somewhat. Certainly the solitary life is very fine. It seems to me that only here in the hermitage have I come to the real fulfilment of my monastic vocation. I also find that a great deal that passes for Gospel truth about the hermit life is simply false: most of the objections have been framed by people who have no conception of what the life is all about.

Again, best regards and blessings to you and Dorothy and to any friends of mine you may encounter in Rome.

With cordial good wishes in Christ,

[Thomas Merton]

Foyer Unitas
30 via S.M. dell' Anima
Rome, Italy
20 • X • 65

Dear Friend:

I so much appreciated your good letter and we have often thought of you in your solitary retirement. I am sure that you will make of it a time of blessing both for yourself and for us all with God's good help. He is always there and always more than willing. But how seldom we let him in. One of the fine things about our time at Collegeville, was Jean LeClercq [sic] on devotional reading. He brought us into the tradition of the ancient Fathers of reading slowly and with another mind and mood from the usual one, with a great openness and suggested that for steady use, this was a kind of prayer that was very acceptable to God. I had run across this kind of reading in the desert where the Coptic fathers in their solitary caves and huts out from places like Wadi Natroun in Egypt read the Fathers that way and make it their daily occupation. I wonder how you are spending your time and whether this has any place in your day. I would be very interested to know what you make of it. For most moderns it would take a course in remedial reading in reverse, for today they teach people to race and scan instead of to pause and savour and receive the blessing which each word may conceal. I ran into a story once of an old rabbi who decided to read a collection of Jewish wisdom and at the end of the first day was still on the first page, and the first week and even the first month ended with his getting no further. His disciples reproached him for his slowness and his only reply was to ask them why he should go on when he found this page so immeasuraby comforting.

I picked up a book "The Thundering Abbot" by Bremond on your founder DeRancé when I was threading my way past the book barrows on my return from taking Dorothy to a retreat over near the Palazzo Colonna yesterday and have read a good piece of it. I wonder what you think of it. It is written with Bremond's inimitable grace and charm but in many ways it is a devastating book. Biography is a fine art but what a dangerous one, for how difficult it is to know oneself and one's motives let alone to know anothers through the veil of centuries. I suppose that the Trappist order has its roots more deeply in St. Bernard than in this fierce reformer who lanced it into being. How do they look on DeRance today?

The Council is in recess this week so we are a little freer than we have been for a long time. The Commissions are working late and early to get the tidying up that is required completed for the sessions next week. I will find out what they are doing on Peace and War at lunch today when Bernard Häring is coming to us. I fear that this Chapter V will not be improved by the work on it yet the speaking of men like Alfrink and Abbot Butler was said to be very fine. I was in England at just the time they made their interventions but I had worked to get them to speak out on the C.O. issue and hoped that Butler would tackle the disastrous sentence in the Schema on regarding the holding nuclear weapons in the present situation as "not illegitimate" and he did not disappoint us. Your fine letter to the American Bishops was most helpful. We do not have many alas in the American camp who are of much use. After long wavering I was told that Cardinal Ritter did not give his intervention which was against the nuclear threat in the aula but chose just to turn it in. It was better than not to have done it at all—but showed his unwillingness to stand up as the foremost American liberal Cardinal and be counted on this issue. Some said he did not want to unleash Hannan again but his word carries far more weight in the Council than Hannan's ever would. In spite of the tameness of the final Chapter V a good deal of education on the issue of peace is going on and this may have its effect in the long pull. The Pope was fine at most points at the UN but as always he took back with the left hand what he gave with the right in this statement about the defensive weapons which must be retained as long as we have the sinful nature of man—this is all the great powers now need to ease their consciences and know that the Church will support them when the showdown comes. This was the same tip-off which this disastrous sentence in the schema made to the great powers.

I have been asked to write a paper on Mysticism and its philosophical implications for a small but rather select symposium that some Foundation is setting up next year. What have you come across that would have bearing on this issue that would be helpful to look at? I have some ideas of my own but would like to see something to try them on. Old E.I. Watkins has always seemed to me to give the best Catholic formulation of the problem in modern times but I probably know your literature too little to know the best place to turn.

You will be glad to hear that Father Godfrey Diekmann is back at the Council and in good health again thanks to a long rest they ordered him to take before letting him come over here. John C. Murray has been in the hospital with a collapsed lung and has only the last days felt he was making any progess. He is frail and has had a huge load on him in these weeks.

Dorothy joins me in sending you our warmest greetings. We see your old friend Sister Mary Luke often. I spoke to Cardinal Suenens the other day and asked him whether it would not be a wonderful thing to have one of the women auditors address the Council before it closed and incidentally mentioned Sister Mary Luke as a good one to do it. He brightened up and said he was seeing the Holy Father next week and would ask him. Nothing may come of it but it would be a fine thing if it happened.

Yours

Douglas [Steere]

Jan. 17, 1966

Dear Douglas:

Thank you very much for the charming piece on Bethlehem. I really enjoy it. What with Angelus Silesius, Pascal, Zoroaster, and the Spirit in all of it. Thanks.

I have owed you two letters for a long time, since the time of the Council. And Collegeville, I believe. I heard more of that from Dom Leclercq who was here in October.

As to the Council, I have had to write a somewhat hasty commentary on the Constitution on the Church and the World, and it is not satisfactory at all. But when I have a copy I will send it along. It is for quick publication (alas) in England, but perhaps when I have had some time to think and amend it may be worth doing more carefully here. Hence I would appreciate comments, if you get time.

As to this little piece which I enclose, I wrote it at the request of Hildegard Goss Mayr for their magazine in Vienna. I have not made any decision about publication in English. I was wondering if Pendle Hill would be interested? It would have to be a pamphlet or a magazine article (or perhaps part of a collection of essays by others). At any rate you can say what you think about that, if you get a moment. I would be glad to hear from you anyway, just to know how you and Dorothy are doing.

The hermit life has been working out very well, in its own way. For one thing I have no longer any question whether it is the thing for me. It is. It seems to me to be the only kind of life in which in a twenty four hour day one can begin to have time to get down to the real business of life. And even here there are other things to be done besides living. But I think that the apparent conflict is by now my fault and not that of just everybody. However things do seem to be pulling together into a real simple unity, meditation, psalms, reading, study, wood chopping, one meal at the monastery, writing and so on. The days are not long enough. Did I ever send you a copy of the translation of an early Carthusian letter on the solitary vocation? Tell me if I did not, and I will.

I understand that things are a little more hopeful about Viet Nam. I certainly do hope there will be some reasonable kind of solution soon.

My very best wishes and regards to you and Dorothy, and all blessings.

Cordially in Christ,

Tom Merton

March 25, 1968

The Reverend Thomas Merton
Gethsamane Abbey
Trappist, Kentucy

Dear Friend:

I have long wanted to write you to share with you a number of things and to make a proposal about a meeting of our little Institute for Contempoary Spirituality that goes on in a very creative way. I think you know that from the very beginning we had so hoped to have you with us and to have you as an integral part of this undertaking of the sharing of the spiritual traditions of the Catholic and non-Catholic groups. That was not possible because you felt unable to leave the monastery in 1965 in the situation where the Abbot was opposed to it. We have not given up the hope that we might have you with us one year. I wonder if, at this long distance ahead, I could ask you frankly whether, if the little group of some twenty-two or -three persons who usually gather the week that begins with Labor Day were to express a wish to come to Gethsemane for their session in 1969, you felt you could come out of your seclusion and be with us, and whether the Abbey would welcome offering this hospitality to this group.* I do not yet know the topic for 1969, but suspect it may be in the field of ecumenical retreats which is coming up before us in a challenging way at this meeting, and probably will deserve a session soon, at least. We have had magnificent people in the group and the spirit of the exchanges has been beyond their best hopes. If you could write me soon and give me some clue to your feeling about this matter, I would be very thankful.

I have read your little book on Zen and greatly appreciated it. I wonder whether you got my letters written during our journey last year—especially the fifth one, which told about the colloquia we had both in Japan and India. This may indicate to you how much concerned I am in this area.

I have just stopped in Arizona on my way back from the West Coast and been up at Sedona, where Father William McNamara has been trying to share the Carmelite tradition with people who are not within the monastic walls. I know how much you would be concerned with what he is trying to do. I shall see him in Connecticut today and carry on some further talks. He is up there with Otis Maxfield, who is much concerned for the contribution of depth psychology to the inward life. There is so much that is creative going on in this area of our concern today.

I have accepted an invitation to give some lectures in Louisville at the beginning of March in 1969 and, if you could receive us, Dorothy and I thought we might drive down from there to pay you a little visit. Perhaps you do not find visits helpful and I will quite understand this. She joins me in sending you our warmest greetings.

Sincerely, your friend,

Douglas V. Steere

* This would of course be financed by us through a gift to the monastery to cover the costs. It would include 2 or 3 women and last 4-5 days.

March 29, 1968

Dear Douglas:

You mention sending five letters last year and not getting a reply. I remember getting two and I think I replied to both or at least to one: but evidently this correspondence was being intercepted. Perhaps because the Abbot was afraid of my getting more of those invitations which, for some reason, he objected to so strongly. However that Abbot has now retired, though this does not mean that I have freedom of movement—but still I have a bit more. To what extent I may be able to attend groups and conferences I don't know, and actually I see I will have to be slow to do so and maintain some pretty strict limits.

As to holding a meeting at Gethsemani, that is certainly possible in principle, but at the time you suggest the diocesan priests are here on retreat and require all the facilities to themselves. This year at another time would not be so good as I have several such meetings (nuns) going and have about filled up the quota of demands I can make on the retreat facilities. But there will always remain a possiblity for this sort of thing. Or I might possibly be able to attend one of your meetings elsewhere.

But this year I think we must still consider it impossible for me. I am sorry.

On the other hand, I shall look forward to seeing you and Dorothy when you are in Louisville in March 1969. Do please remind me when the time comes round and I will see that you have reservations if you wish to stay overnight. There is a separate Ladies' Guest house.

Do let's keep in mind for some future year the possibility of a meeting here.

With my very best wishes always, and cordial regards to you both,

Your friend in Christ,

[Thomas Merton]

April 22, 1968

The Reverend Thomas Merton
Trappist Monastery of Gethsamani
Trappist, Kentucky

Dear Friend:

Thank you for your good letter. It raises one or two problems that I want to be absolutely sure about before passing this word on to Robert Lechner. Do I understand that there might be a good chance of the Monastery welcoming a visit by our group in 1969, but that you will have to wait until the new Abbot is installed before being able to raise the question? Do you think that it is more likely that we could be able to persuade you to come to us at some other Catholic center in that Labor Day week of 1969 than to try to have this meeting at Gethsemane? I think that you see that we are very eager to have you with us in that year and that we would do anything we could to make this possible. There are many places that we can go to on both the Catholic and Protestant side, so that we are not at all pressed for location, but had thought of coming down to Gethsemane in order to be sure to have a session where you could be present. If you could answer these questions for me within the next week or two, I would be very thankful for we must begin to make our plans soon and I did want this matter to be cleared up.

I am mailing you a copy of the 5th letter of these ones that were sent out last year and I think you may find these colloquia interesting to you. The privilege of coming close to these wonderful people was not a small one and I hope that some of this kind of thing may go on beyond this initial attempt. Having the colloquia ecumenical in character made all the difference in the way in which we seem to be able to move with each other,

What a period we are in with Martin Luther King's assassination and the Johnson regime seeming to do everything possible to hinder taking up the wonderful initiative that was proposed to us a fortnight ago. How can we talk about peace in one breath and call up another 25,000 reserves with the other? No one can trust our sincerity any longer after exhibitions of this kind. We must be born from within again and this will certainly be an agonizing struggle. I am not at all sure that your prayers each day may not be nearer to the heart of beginning this renewal than anything that is being done. How can we interpret the power of intercessory prayer in any better way than to practice it with burning intensity? Is not that the place where we must begin?

We shall look forward to seeing you in March, 1969, but let us keep in close touch in the months between. With deep affection,

Sincerely, your friend,

Douglas V. Steere

April 25, 1968

Dear Douglas:

This is an immediate reply, in order to clear up any confusions about possibilities for the Meeting. The chief problem is the *date*. The early part of September is the time reserved for the local diocesan clergy and there is no room for anyone else in the Guest House.

The second slight problem is that though the new Abbot would permit such a meeting, he is trying to cut down on Guest House activities and might conceivably be more favorable toward my simply going somewhere else. But it would be a matter of giving him time, and this year is too soon to bring it up. Also I am not sure of being free this September.

Hence, there may be some hope for the future, but nothing is quite certain yet. In any case I do look forward tentatively to March 1969.

Really the times are exceptionally grave. One feels that there is a sickness in the air which one cannot quite apprehend because it is both too vast and too new: and one still does not "feel" deeply struck and grasped by it. The Plague is very real. And a long struggle will be necessary. I doubt if any of us will see the real issue of it, unless it issues in complete apocalypse.

On top of the general tragedy, I have a small personal one. A dear old aunt of mine, a most sweet gentle person, was lost in a tragic shipwreck in New Zealand with many other people. It was a great shock.

Thanks for your mimeographed letter which I have not yet read. But now I have it, and hope to report on it later.

My very best to you and Dorothy,
in Peace,

[Thomas Merton]

[Undated]

Dear Friend:

This is just a swift note to send with this copy of Edgar Brookes pamphlet that is just off the press. I am leaving for Tennessee in a few minutes but wanted you to have this for it is to me the best statement I know of the way through on South Africa by an old Christian veteran of the most wonderful spirit.

You are still the one whom I so deeply hope will be drawn to join us August 31–Sept. 7 at Collegeville, Minnesota for this gathering on the spiritual life. The Non-catholics met at Pendle Hill a fortnight ago to prepare for this gathering and they were very keen and feeling that perhaps this occasion was one where we should in a very special way see God's purpose for the specific guidance of the spiritual life with which the Christian religion is charged. I know that you will be open for coming if it seems right for you to do so.

Dorothy and I are returning to Rome next autumn for what I suppose will be the closing session and any commissions that you have to lay on us we shall try to carry out. I have been in close touch with Bernard Haring about the CO statement getting in the text and about not letting the forces prevail who would weaken the statement on Nuclear war which the present version contains.

With warmest wishes.

Yours faithfully,

Douglas V. Steere

The Fall of Babel:
Reflections on the
Abbey Center Conference*

Rosemary Haughton

The first conference sponsored by the Abbey Center is an occasion that could be recorded in a number of different ways. I have chosen to reflect on it as part of something that is happening to the Church at this very strange time in human history.

The cause of the Abbey Center is Thomas Merton, who certainly did not envision anything at all like the actuality of the gathering which took place in October 1992. He wanted a place where spirituality and science could encounter one another in a fecund peace, for the sake of a world full of genius but without clarity, apparently bent on suicide by greed and pride. He saw it all perhaps too simply, overestimating the honesty of scientists, the humility of those committed to spiritual pursuits, and the possibility of any of them hearing each other. A common language was necessary, he knew, both as a goal and prerequisite, and therefore very elusive, as in, for instance, so many "peace talks" fated to the frustration of mutual incomprehension and suspicion for lack of common language.

The first conference to be held, after careful and laborious preparation, to initiate the work of the Abbey Center, was at least evidence of two things. One was the intensity of the desire for the kind of encounters that Merton envisioned, even though in the event it became clear that nobody had a clear idea of what was involved. The other

* This essay is a reflection upon the October 22–25, 1993 conference sponsored by The Abbey Center For The Study Of Ethics And Culture, Inc. at the Abbey of Gethsemani, Trappist, Kentucky.

was the strength of the resistance to packaged unity. Nobody knew exactly what they wanted, but equally everybody was prepared to struggle to discover a common direction, yet not at all prepared to accept unity prearranged.

It was a very diverse group, of different disciplines and traditions, different races and ages and political views, and lifestyles. Some, in the common gathering were vocal to the point of prolixity, others spoke when driven by frustration, others were silent. At meals, breaks and at small-group discussions, some who were quiet in the large group found time and acceptance to formulate ideas, begin to build consensus, recognize possibility.

The gathering reflected, in its frustration, its energy, its persistence, its anger, and its openness, a change in the character of thought and relationship in the Churches. The refusal to be manipulated, and the ability to detect and name manipulation, is a new phenomenon in Church affairs, especially in the Roman Catholic Church in which the manipulation of consciences in the name of unity and the will of God had been developed to a fine art. The gathering at Gethsemani discovered in its collective self a willingness to push through frustration and to risk what could seem a waste of high hopes and long journeys rather than settle for something less than authentic search.

Search for what? If the purpose of a gathering is to discover a common language, where do you begin? Evidently you *do not* begin, as had been planned, with texts in a prepared language, however seductively universal.

The group, with surprising (because undiscussed and spontaneous) unanimity recognized the themes proposed as begging too many questions—not a genuine common language but, in fact, the language of a very specific cultural stance. Clearly also, the group did not want to begin with a set of "problems." This is, of course, probably the most common way for a group to be convened; a "problem" is identified (by a pastor, a governor, a president for instance) and a group of people is asked to find solutions. In this case a number of one-day meetings had been held in different academic contexts to surface problems occurring in that milieu. A formidable compilation emerged of very real problems in the experience of those concerned.

But it did not take the Abbey Center gathering long to recognize that something was wrong. Its members were being asked to accept the problems as written, but what if the problems were not problems at all in the sense of "something wrong and needing to be fixed"? What if they were, perhaps, signs of health—a healthy reaction to attack, as a fever is a sign of the body's fight against infection? What if the breakdown of families, for instance, were a painful but healthy revolt against a deep sickness in the structures that impose gender roles?

Recognition of such undermining doubts and questions produced a result similar to the experience of the architects of Babel. Such a beautiful structure, so skillfully put together, so high and holy! Did some apprentice mason ask the terrible, innocent question that confounded the great men, like the child who, untrained in the necessities of social manipulation, exclaimed aloud that the emperor had no clothes? There was suddenly the frightening but also exhilarating realization that people not only did not have common political and social and cultural models, or common ethical definitions, but could actually *say so*, (in spite of being all Church people) and therefore clear the ground for some real building. The collapse of Babel is devastating but it is also liberating because there is no longer the need to pretend that everyone can actually live in this thing. If there is to be a common language, it will not grow because experts devise it and everyone else cuts the stones and carries them. It will grow because people learn to recognize common needs, emotions, aspirations, and so undertake—slowly and laboriously—common tasks that benefit everyone, creating common spaces that leave room for diversity and eccentricities. (The common language, ultimately, cannot be a high-rise block but probably something much more like a cluster of villages and small towns with fields around them and roads connecting them.)

Reflection on such an experience is inevitably very personal. I cannot speak for another's experience, and others present may perceive the event very differently. Perception of the tumultuous three days, with its struggles and anger and laughter and the final achievement of a sense of embarking on a new, long, arduous, scarcely definable yet possible task, is that the entire event hinged on the concept of identity. It seems that the breaking down of the earlier structure of the conference happened essentially because these had been built on an *assumed* identity (in both senses of the word "assumed") in the gathering. The work was to be defined in terms of a specific traditional-liberal-Western-Catholic-male-philosophical mind, and it was to conduct its deliberations in accordance with that identity. It was to establish common language on that basis and reflect on problems occurring in that spiritual context. It was to have as its totem Thomas Merton—a monastic, Catholic, male, spiritual figure, generously embracing other traditions and many causes in his wide liberal sympathies. And all this was to be held together by the monastic setting, which was to symbolize peace, hospitality, continuity, non-consumer values (setting aside cake and cheese), and make it possible to leave outside (as some participants wistfully observed) the frenetic greed and conflicts of a sick society.

It did not work. It did not work because the kind of people who attended the conference knew (some at first not actually knowing that they knew) that clear identity is the first casualty of major social upheaval. All of them had experienced this in one way or another. Some had known it in severe and specific crises of conversion, letting go inherited identity in order to embrace God. For most of us it had been a more confusing and reluctant experience, a disintegration of certainties, a sense of imbalance, an inability any longer to claim nation or Church or family or gender or professional role as solid ground to stand on, with a label saying "American, Catholic, married, teacher. . . ." With loss of faith in such identities goes, often, loss of direction, of purpose, of value. What is this shell I live in? Does it even exist?

I am not saying that everyone at the conference was experiencing, or had experienced, this kind of cultural angst, but that this kind of experience—which is a collective social phenomenon of our time, not merely an accumulation of individual trauma—underlies the general resistance to being identified in this way. The suspicion of manipulative structure, the questioning of premises, sprang from the awareness that common language can only develop among people who either are clear about who they are, or, if this is not possible, are able to accept that fact and establish a working hypothesis from which to begin, open to correction but adequate and honest as far as possible.

This is, in fact, the situation that many of us are in. It is sometimes painful to the point of despair, but it is also extremely hopeful. It is possibly the only really hopeful phenomenon around, because it accepts the destruction of Babel, it knows that we are, at present, living in rubble and confusion, but not in pretense and vain glory. The danger to the world, and also to the Church (which has unfortunately adopted some of the world's worst mental habits) is that we continue to assume that a common language exists—the language of Western culture, a language of dominance, hierarchy, competition and control which claims the right (and duty) to translate all other languages into its own. The hope actually lies in the loss of the identity that makes that assumption possible. Individually it is happening, and culturally it is happening, but when the symptoms of the needed loss of cultural identity appear we cry "problem" and set up a commission to fix it.

There is, indeed, a huge dilemma, for cultural identity of some kind is in fact necessary for survival, so the disintegration of that identity causes terrible, even lethal, symptoms. The drug culture, fundamentalist religion, the increase in casual violence and callousness (especially among the young), the rise of Neo-Nazism, and in many countries atrocious persecution and war are all the results either of the loss of cultural identity, or the struggle to regain identity, or what appears to be identity. For identity gives self-confidence and self-worth, the loss of it means loss of purpose, apathy and cynicism, chronic and even suicidal depression (individual or collective). And even the fear of the loss of identity results in a panic of hatred for whatever seems to threaten it: another ethnic group, a different religion or class.

Yet often the identity that gives confidence and strength is a false identity, based on evil premises: the "master race," the "dominant sex," the "most powerful nation," the "upper class," all mean that identity depends upon the suppression and oppression of some other group or person. Real social and individual health does not and cannot grow from such deeply deceptive systems, yet the destruction of them is, it seems (and for many it really is) the destruction of all that makes life worth living. That is the paradox—the specific paradox of this time of the end of the millennium, but which will no doubt also affect many decades of the next if the earth is not first made uninhabitable by behavior motivated precisely by the need constantly to support the illusions of such false identities.

This is the reason why the confusion and the partial recovery of the Abbey Center conference is so encouraging and why it matters that the pursuit should continue. I doubt if most people present thought of their experience in those precise terms. What is described here is my perception, expressed in terms which are familiar to me because of other work in which I have been engaged and also from reflection on personal experience. But what I perceive essentially is that what such a gathering can do, when there is an adequate level of mutual respect and trust, is to allow the loss of identity to be apparent, and analyzed. Then perhaps the basis of a common language can emerge.

My reason for suggesting this possibility is the location of the Abbey Center and the symbolism of the monastic phenomenon, which is not, fundamentally, that of an island of peace and sanity in a crazy world (though it may often be that, as it has been before), but a place where individual identities are fluid, and the common identity is explicitly expressed in the values of the Gospel. This does not mean that monks are necessarily individually any better than anyone else at letting go of their false identities, but there is a sense in which they actually do so, whether they like it or not. And it does not mean that monasticism has always, or even often, expressed its common identity in values and behaviors like those of Jesus, but that all the same its purpose is explicitly that. For Jesus was a person who had real problems with the identities he had to shed and those that were thrust on him, but he attempted to share with others a language of common identity whose source of security, continuity, and strength was God and other people, experienced as inseparable spiritual/practical reality. So it is conceivable that in a setting which explicitly symbolizes that kind of identity there can be a source of spiritual security of the right kind, sufficient to allow people to deal with the loss of false identity. It seems that out of the attempt to express the reality and the implication of such an experience, the rudiments of genuine common language could emerge.

All of this makes sense if Thomas Merton is the catalyst. One can imagine his half-startled, wry amusement at such an idea, but with perhaps an acknowledgement of its justice. For this was a man who had trouble all his life with identity, trying on one and then another, passionately believing that each one was the real one, until it let him down and something else showed through. And then there were all the identities that were pinned on him by others, in which at times he had believed and at times had created, anyway. Perhaps in the end his extraordinarily wide appeal grew from the painfully acquired ability to let go the struggle for identity, and yet live in one or another as it was required, seeing, therefore, some value, however paradoxical, in each. For it is only when the ultimately unreal, even if just and adequate, identities are known as merely tools that people can speak to each other as children of God. If the tools are good tools they give confidence and enable people to meet one another and work together with proper pride and with joy, as people do who are committed to some undertaking which absorbs their energy and devotion. Their language is then the language of their common work and dedication, they meet each other with pleasure and fellowship and—yes—love, and all the identities they bring to this are somehow both relativized and cleansed. (People who need to cling to oppressive identities to survive cannot do this, anyway.)

Identity and language—they go together because language is forged from common experience, and our chosen or inherited or imposed identity dictates the kind of experiences we can have and the things we can say. So the relativizing of identity and the shedding of false identity makes possible the undertaking of work which is liberating, hard, and absorbing, as some began to discover at the Abbey Center Conference. Part of the paradox is that the undoing of false identity is *itself* the work that is necessary, and the sharing of that work begins to create the stumbling words of a new language.

This is a frightening undertaking because it can only go forward if there are no preconditions, no reserved and untouchable areas. If we redefine "problems," if we will not settle for given language, where will it all end? What will become of family, of Church, of nation, even of self? This work is probably the most important that human beings can undertake, as many mystics have known, but they were always regarded as eccentric if splendid, which left the rest of us in safety. Now we are no longer safe, there is nowhere left to turn but back to the beginning, and the Word, and an open-ended search, not for individual enlightenment but for a possible—just possible—salvation for all.

Monastic Values in an Alien World: One Person's Experience*

(Concluding Remarks at the Abbey Center Conference)

Rembert Weakland, O.S.B.

Any conference of this sort could well become just theoretical and abstract. If one would but discuss what monastic values are like and how they should inform the culture of the future, it would have a certain value in itself. But, to make the conference fruitful, one would also have to see these values embodied in people and not just represented in abstract concepts. It is people who carry with them values and who, by the way they live and act, build their values into the fabric of a new culture.

This quest of how monastic values leave the monastery and go into the world, as it were, was not for me personally a purely theoretical matter. It was not one where I could wait for an answer as I just sat back and watched. When I was taken from the monastic milieu to become a bishop, I had to ask that question in the concrete. What part of my monastic training and values would go with me into the new kind of ministry I had been asked to accept? I had to ask the question of how to keep the integrity of the first fifty years of my life intact, as I faced the new tasks I was asked to assume. Such a question was not theoretical but very practical for me.

A conference such as this one awakened again old struggles and old dilemmas. I will try to recall them now and share them with you. Perhaps in the story of one person's quest some general lines can be found for others and even for the future culture itself.

* This essay was presented during the October 22–25, 1993 conference sponsored by The Abbey Center For The Study Of Ethics And Culture, Inc. at the Abbey of Gethsemani, Trappist, Kentucky.

61

The question I asked myself at first was, of course, what monastic practices, what externals if you wish, do I want to take with me, to keep as a bishop. At first I admit that I concentrated on externals, elements like the Liturgy of the Hours with most of its parts recited daily and squeezed in at the right time, a sense of community that resembled the one I had left behind. I did not consider wearing the monastic habit because I felt that the priests and even laity of my diocese might think I was going to make monks out of them. I can truly say I was only interested in myself and my own transformation, not in leading others to any kind of monastic spirituality, but I did not want to give a false impression. In fact, I did just the opposite: I tried on purpose not to impose any kind of monastic values on them and was very careful in talking about my monastic background. Later I learned that they wished for me to share insights of my monastic spirituality and enjoyed stories of the monastery.

But I soon learned that transferring such externals into a new atmosphere would not work, as quaint and romantic as it all seemed. It was, however, artificial and heavy and seemed to give one a kind of spiritual indigestion. So, for example, if I had had a long and exciting confirmation ceremony, it did not seem helpful to recite Vespers afterwards to maintain a sense of monastic continuity. Night after night in May there would be a celebration of some sort, generally Mass celebrated with extravagant solemnity because the bishop was at the parish, a rare occasion for them that demanded many extras. Adding my monastic practices on top of that became too perfunctory for me. Also, it may have seemed "romantic" to remember how things were in the monastery during Advent or Lent—seasons I had loved there—but I realized with my schedule as a bishop I could no longer duplicate those past experiences, as grateful as I was for having had them.

After a bit I gave up such heaviness and had to rethink what my monastic values really were. That was a troublesome period of searching for meaning in two worlds that did not seem to coalesce. Then I found myself going back to the *Rule* of Benedict and specifically to the Prologue and the very beginning of the *Rule*. I realized that there was a deeper level to the monastic "thing." One could call it the "search for God." Benedict asks if the novice is truly seeking God. That must come first. He then points out in the Prologue a listening process for each day. The monk must be listening for God's presence throughout the entire day. That is done in the Liturgy of the Hours, but it is also pursued through all aspects of the monastic observance. I had to apply that idea of a search for God and of listening to God's voice to my own particular circumstances. I could no longer listen with the monks and to the abbot, but I could continue, I soon found out, to listen to God's voice in other ways.

As a bishop I knew I had to listen to the voice of God as the Holy Spirit spoke to the faithful of my diocese. I had to listen to my priests at the Priest Council meetings, to the Pastoral Council and to all the laity, to all those many who came to meetings and who sought to speak with me or who wrote to me about their cares and anxieties, their joys and concerns. I had, in other words, to create new listening posts, or rather to recognize them in the day's routine that was now mine.

My listening during prayer also had to change. I had to listen to God's voice during those many confirmations, church dedications, ecumenical prayer services, and the like. These new moments of prayer were not as systematic and as liturgically correct and proper as they would have been in the monastery, but they were what God was giving me as a bishop. They were not neat and ordered, but they were real to me and vital to my spiritual life.

So, for example, if I had a long ceremony in a parish, a youthful and exuberant confirmation, let us say, I no longer felt a need to say Vespers. It was better, I realized, to reflect prayerfully on that first event and let its spirit pervade my prayer life. If we were praying before a meeting, as boring as the meeting appeared to be and as unenthusiastic as I may have been to attend, or even as amateurish as the composed prayer may have seemed to me, I realized that it was important for me to be present fully to that prayer and not to worry about a proper monastic midday prayer.

The breviary became a flexible skeleton to fill in where the programmed and often unbalanced liturgical life of a bishop had vacancies or blank spots. Strangely enough, however, it became even more important to me than when I was living the monastic routine.

In addition, I had to rediscover my music. It may seem strange, but music is now more important than when I was in the community. It is not that I play that much, but the little I do is life-giving. Listening to music, like reading good literature, is something one finds time for less often but savors even more than ever. Somehow God speaks there too.

I also saw that it was not necessary for me to create a false community around me as if it were a pseudo-monastery. People had their own lives to live and would move on. Change had to come about. But I did learn how important return visits to my monastery were. Sinking those roots again, even if only occasionally, seemed to be enough, or at least all that I would be permitted.

I found that one had to find new support groups that fit the new vocation, that they had to be among all age groups and especially among couples my age and with my general Church background and spiritual history. These friends are important for major feasts and for those moments when one knows that there is need for sustaining powers other than one's own.

Somehow one changes from just having fellow monks on the same search to recognizing all one's fellow Christians on the same larger quest. I wish I had been able to recognize that fact when I was a monk. I believe I would have looked upon my confreres in a different fashion.

One area that I have not solved yet is that of poverty. It is not clear to me how my monastic background should enter into a more simple lifestyle. Benedictines usually live in big buildings that are well appointed and that have a sense of architecture and of the plastic arts that satisfies. They do not have a history of penury nor of ugliness as a substitute for poverty. The right use of things is emphasized rather than the non-use. This question as a bishop has troubled me for a decade and a half. Perhaps before I retire I will solve it. Since my life is so full of appointments and engagements outside of the house and since the house and office are not the center of my activity, I do not pay that much attention to them. They are oases that help sustain me in the larger task that I must accomplish.

I have also realized that often I used "community" as an excuse for not taking care of my own needs, as most people must do. I have decided to learn to do much of my cooking when I can, to work outside on the grounds, and so on. I think such independence is also very Benedictine. My schedule prohibits me from doing these chores in a sufficient way, but the intent is there and sometimes even the action.

Perhaps the hardest adaptation has come in the area of *lectio divina*. I do not find that I can open up for myself the large periods of time that I had found in the monastery. In my new world I realized that one had to learn to pray more like Benedict says, short prayers from the heart and not in many words. I would hate to say that one has to learn to pray quicker, but there is a certain need to take advantage of the many moments of silence that do occur in a day and hope they add up to something more substantial in the long run. I have found that easier than I thought I would.

To sum up this experience, I would say that I have learned that the monastic quest is one of searching for God and not of the externals of the monastic routine and that each person must do that search in one's own environment and circumstances. That search involves the monastic means of prayer and work, of community, of poverty, and personal prayer, all adapted to the new world. What changes is often the balance and the particular means that one can use. But the search, indeed, goes on and gives unity to one's life and to life around oneself.

God Will Be Their Light: Reflections on the Abbey Center Conference*

Francis Kline, O.C.S.O.

Since what follows are my impressions of the Abbey Center Conference which took place at the Abbey of Gethsemani in October 22–25, 1992, the reader stands forewarned that objectivity may be lacking. Is this what really happened during those crystalline days in the Kentucky autumn? A news report of the event would be concerned with the list of those present, the topics discussed, and the format of the conference, and I will include a skeletal description of such. Since the conference was intentionally structured to be inconclusive and open-ended, a mere news report would betray the conference.

The problems of the world were not solved. In fact, the participants felt, at times, as frustrated as every other group or institution feels when it tries to get something going on a rational, humanly integrated level. And yet, something did occur which defies objectivity and clean articulation. So, I have chosen to go impressionistic, to follow my feelings and to express my fantasies about that seminal weekend. My guess is, though, that some, if not many, who were there will be able to identify the event at Gethsemani by what I write. And even if my impressions do not square with theirs, still, there will be enough common ground to stimulate their own recall and to get them to write their own report for others to read.

The Abbey Center for the Study of Ethics and Culture was born in June 1988. Inspired by Jane Norton's vision of gatherings of signifi-

* This essay was presented during the October 22–25, 1993 conference sponsored by The Abbey Center For The Study Of Ethics And Culture, Inc. at the Abbey of Gethsemani, Trappist, Kentucky.

cant or concerned people discussing pivotal issues, the Abbey Center Board, up to ten people of divergent backgrounds, but all of whom were attracted by the idea of meeting at the monastery, held numerous planning sessions about the large conference to be sponsored by the Abbey Center in October 1992. We produced a mission statement, set up trial one-day conferences in various institutions (mostly universities), and began to rouse the interest of distinguished persons. After several false starts and much refining of the idea, we determined to invite four anchor persons who would dialogue certain issues in front of an audience (who would also participate) made up of people who had taken part in one of the ten one-day conferences. But what to discuss?

We engaged Joe Engelberg of the University of Kentucky at Lexington to moderate the discussions along the lines of his highly successful Integrative Studies Method. The topic could be history, religion, politics, truth, or whatever. A text is read and distributed—a gnomic text, usually poetry or something poetic—which immediately situates the topic in its most basic form, and to which other topics can easily relate because of the utter simplicity and clarity of the statement. The following is an example:

> To pursue integrative thought
> we need to consider
> that to every statement
> there exists a domain
> over which the statement
> may be said
> to be true,
> and a domain over which
> it may be said
> to be false.
> Integrative study
> focuses
> on the domain
> over which a statement
> is true.

Joe always insisted in his own groups that no professional labels interfere, no posturing pollute what anyone had to say. Rather, what was said had to come from one's own experience. Encyclopedic knowledge was undervalued here. Personal wisdom gained from the school of hard knocks made one shine. Because Joe's integrative method was approved by the Abbey Center Board for use during the conference, the personalities of the participants themselves remained in the forefront of the discussions. Many topics came up for consideration, such as the formation of communities and the history of communities. But ultimately, these were subordinated to the leading persons in those communities. The conference rarely got theoretical. The personal witness and the individual achievement were always prominent.

Archbishop Rembert Weakland. Archbishop Rembert Weakland easily dominated the conference. To overestimate his gifts and his integration of them across a varied and brilliant career would be difficult. He moves with ease through pastoral work, spirituality, economic issues, music, art, and literature, while maintaining a sharp eye on the gospel tone (or lack of it) in the city and nation.

Having been invited as an anchor participant of the conference, Weakland spoke often and well, enlightening all of us with his insight. He has been described as the keenest intellect among the American bishops. Predictably enough, he was uncomfortable with the Integrative Studies Method because it seemed to him so out of focus. At a preliminary planning session he had raised the question, "What is the goal of the conference?" He related to Joe Engelberg's texts only insofar as they introduced a workable topic whose discussion might possibly bring a reasonable conclusion. Without any hesitation, he persuasively structured the crucial discussions of the third day around a list of seven topics:

1. Shifting worldviews: From the anthropocentric to a more environmental/ecological consciousness.
2. Impact of technology on the human person.
3. Shifting relationships between women and men.
4. Tensions between individual and community.
5. Spiritual awareness in contemporary culture.
6. The contribution of monastic and contemplative life to the human community.
7. Plurality in the modern world.

Without a clear agenda to guide him or anybody else, Weakland, nevertheless, found the mind of the group, if not its heart, and consistently lent the clarity and energy of his own thought to the proceed-

ings. He was well received and admired by everyone. One must
consider the calibre of the gathering to appreciate the archbishop's contribution to the conference. For even among such invigorating people,
he stood out as a giant. People may be well known in our society because they seek to be. They sniff out those issues and plant themselves
in places to speak about them where they know they will get cover-
age. But the archbishop is not one of these. His gifts are of such a quality, and his use of them so straightforward, that our Church and our
educated public must know of such a one.

Rosemary Haughton. Though Marian Wright Edelman and Edmund Pellegrino were invited to the Conference as anchor participants,
they could not come, the former due to Washington political commit-
ments (we were about to elect a president) and the latter due to ill
health. We depended, therefore, all the more heavily on Rosemary
Haughton to mend the breach in our damaged inner circle.

Rosemary came to the conference with the reputation of having
authored several books of penetrating theology. Coming not from an
academic institution, but from Wellspring House, a home-shelter for
victimized women and families in Gloucester, Massachusetts, and before that, from an experimental community in Scotland, and before
that, from her large family household in Yorkshire, she brought to
the conference some vigorous thinking not conceived in an ivory tower.
How rock-hewn the marriage is in Rosemary's life between experience
and conclusion, we were to learn only later. At the beginning of the
conference she carried herself with energy and an immediate grasp
of the problems the conference tried to tackle.

From the start, Rosemary and the archbishop assumed the role
of partners in the enterprise. Though they both tend to be analytical,
she was neither threatened by him nor cowed. It was so refreshing
to watch two pros complement each other, as if they had been doing
this sort of thing for years (which they probably have in their respective circles). She, too, showed considerable frustration at the aimless
commencement of things, but that did not deter her from rolling up
her sleeves, as it were, and doing some gritty work in order to make
things happen. A natural magnet for the discontented elements of the
conference, she voiced her concern not for herself only, but for those
she immediately came to represent.

Though Rosemary is a natural leader, she did not assume the
same kind of commanding role in the conference the archbishop did.

She wasn't interested in that. I noticed that she usually went for an alternative view, not meant to dislodge or redirect the trend of things, but to aid, abet and otherwise enrich the scenery along the road. Her comments on the Dudley Street Community in Boston, as well as her caveats on the Mondragon phenomenon in Spain, both voiced very smartly, indicated her independent spirit. She may be politically correct in her views, but if she is, she arrived there on her own, and not because she was following the lead of others.

One could not help but remark on the antiphonal work of Archbishop Weakland and Rosemary Haughton. Not only did they tend to see different aspects to the same problem, but they enlarged the views of the other conference participants on almost every question by expressing their own plausible arguments. Instead of thinking that one was wrong and the other right, you thought that the question needed further study before you yourself could make a judgment, unless, of course, you also knew the given situation at depth and had already formed an opinion. The richness of views forced us to think.

The complexity of issues such as the maintenance of identity through rapid social change, the place of religion as catalyst or block to social reform, and the paradox of shared common experience within a framework of broad cultural diversity, all served to present few if any solutions to any of the long list of topics brought to the three-day conference. We tried to clarify the question and the problem before attempting any solution. Frequently we broke through to a wisdom of sorts, which itself defied any close systematic thinking. We were forced to conclude, tacitly, that there exists at this time, no structure of belief, no bedrock conviction about the makeup of society (for example, should we continue to tolerate the gap between the rich and the poor?), no one interpretation of the history of our Western culture that most of us are willing to endorse. The plethora of meanings attached to our experience of the world today is simply too heavy for our accustomed constructs to support. To be an entrenched conservative today involves one in such inextricable difficulties of class stratification and privilege as to be downright embarrassing except for the most obtuse. And to be a runaway liberal with never a thought to turn back to see what I have just set irrevocably on fire is less and less possible. The stakes have become too high. Stymied at both ends of the scale, we find it more and more difficult to block the inevitable tide of fragmentation.

Yet, the willingness to come together to address these impossible issues, and to stay together for the weekend without demanding clear answers or breaking up into mutually hostile camps, says much more about the cultural climate of hope than the personal virtues of the participants. We experienced, but were not able to identify, a more prior substratum, a more bonding faith (in what, we could not say). This unspoken assent to what is now forming but not yet able to be labelled emerged in the only way it could—by personal witness. In the individual journeys of those who were willing to speak, we heard stories similar to our own. Sometimes, we had to admire the courage of another while we acknowledged failure. At other times we applied a spot of mercy to our guilt-ridden hearts when we lived in the shortcomings of another's shoes. We hesitated. We resisted this phenomenon of sharing because we were too sophisticated to succumb to hero worship. But by Saturday afternoon, in the small groups, the conviction kept growing that the agonies and the wonders of our particular crucifixions were, if not universal, then common enough to be owned and trusted. We began to trust one another's experiences, and admit that they, in some way, were our own. A culture forming? A metaphysics aborning? A child's attempt to pen the word humanity?

Among the witnesses which moved me the most were:

E. Glenn Hinson. His abortive struggle to remain a moderate, if not liberal, voice at Louisville's Southern Baptist Theological Seminary is well known. (He now teaches at a new Baptist seminary in Richmond.) Glenn spoke often and well, always in balanced phrases with a halting delivery. Here was a living example of how hard one must work and to what extent one must suffer to remain in the liquid marrow of the bone, and not in irredeemable ossification. Polarization of a violent and strident kind is a frequent product of our current crisis of identity. People defend and maintain absurd positions from the past, which may or may not have been legitimate then, and sweep away every other consideration, including truth, in order to clear space around their new idol. Everyone must worship there, or they are figuratively hacked to pieces. Not a few Churches are guilty of this most unchristian behavior. The only response that includes God in the picture is the kind Dr. Hinson offered—a still, small voice of reason and heart. It is only too easily extinguished, and all the more precious for those who can strain to hear it amidst all the din.

Beverly Anne LoGrasso. From Cleveland, and working in social justice programs for the diocese, Beverly brought a feminist corrective to almost all the proceedings. Her accent and her voice were irresistible to me, a hopeless Easterner with an ear for vocal timbre and the relish with which regional accents maul vowels. One had to enjoy her sound or perish, since she spoke up often. Still, her consistency and earnestness, and her penchant for thinking out loud were fresh and appealing, at least to me. She was another example of the patience of woman. When shall we hear and understand?

Janet Guerin. A graduate of Spalding University, Janet is very articulate black woman from Louisville. She, too, brought a corrective to the discussions—this time, not the feminist perspective, but the challenge to professor types to speak in something clearer than academese. Like aviator control, she constantly appealed to the group to come out of the fog and land. But she was so bright and perceptive, that her taunts, good natured as they were, veiled a Socratic lesson: if your theses are so arcane that only specialists can understand them, keep working until you can communicate simply. Otherwise, stay in your research center. The group heard her and did not take itself too seriously. The lessons we did learn could not have been learnt without her.

Lawrence Cunningham. From Notre Dame, Larry had wonderful stories to tell about his experiences in Florence and elsewhere. It's not so much what he said, as who he is, that counted. He is a brilliant writer and teacher, a veritable mine of information about just what you happen to want to know at the moment. His booknotes for *Commonweal* illustrate my point. The love of monasticism over many years has made of Larry an acute observer of the church scene. For he seems to make of monastic life a buoy in an otherwise open sea. He refers to it quietly, but with the glow that a golden lamp has in dim light. Larry brought to the conference's attention the value that the monastic life enjoys in his own estimation. The presence of the conference itself at the Abbey of Gethsemani, enfolded as it was around the monastic schedule, spoke more about the monastic influence on the participants and on their ideas than any formal address could have done. For one so centrally placed in the Church, Dr. Cunningham's ongoing tryst with monasticism has its own significance. As the conference progressed, the monastic theme became more and more pronounced.

John Miller. Pastor of the First Presbyterian Church at Hilton Head Island, John brought to the conference his own concerns about the mainline Protestant Churches and the pieces of them which keep breaking off to the right in obscurantism. Not that the heavy lunges by the Vatican against the flank of more progressive thinkers in the Roman Church disturb him any the less. John, too, is a frequent visitor to monastic retreat houses, has come to do theology around the Psalter, and is altogether intrigued by the quaint stance, but deadly accurate aim that monastic life brings to the Christian bow. He is eager to learn more about this unrecorded tribe of monks and responded to the invitation to the conference with the eagerness of a safari hunter. (He also is a serious and dedicated fan of Archbishop Weakland.)

Richard Getty. A psychologist of some renown in the South, Richard gave one of the most impressive interventions that I heard at one of the small-group meetings. We had identified the fields of interest where we wished to direct our energies. Richard and I both chose the group which would discuss the contribution of monastic and contemplative life to the human community. What Richard said amounted to a poetic and altogether humanistic definition of the human person, replete with fantasy and imagination intact together with the boldest kind of science. He had kept silent until now. But here was rare energy, just sitting there, waiting for the moment to speak—and, everyone listened.

Geralyn Wolfe. President of the Abbey Center Board of Directors, and the dean of Christ Church Cathedral in Louisville, Geralyn has been from the beginning of our enterprise a prophet and a lawgiver. She could put ready hands to fix up a mess. But she could also make us lift up our eyes to distant hills in true inspiration. Her description of the parish in South Philly where she worked so hard to build a community was, at that point, therapeutic for her in the current struggle to be all things to all in Louisville. Pioneers like Gerry need the support and the uplift of others to lift up their arms if they are to pray and point the way for the rest of us. But one wonders, will she herself cross the Jordan?

Barbara Thomas. As one of the principal architects of the Abbey Center's Mission Statement, Sister Barbara is a much sought after spiritual leader and administrator in her large congregation, the Sisters of

Charity of Nazareth. She nevertheless consistently gave great chunks of valuable time to Abbey Center business. I came to believe in her belief. I was not surprised then to hear her give a brilliant and emotionally moving description of her vision of the new world she sees emerging from the confusion of our present situation. In fact, the Abbey Center project itself is her sacrament of the new awareness and the reformed consciousness which alone can propel the best of the past into the future. Her love of Gethsemani and what it stands for, even though it has disappointed her through the years of renewal and experimentation, has been rejuvenated. Gethsemani and the monastic life have proven to her their ability to adapt and to include, to reach out open arms to those who only need a welcoming gesture. So strong is her belief that she carries around her a great aura of power for goodness and confidence in the human family.

By now, in this list of personalities, it will have become clear that while individual issues were tackled and brought to new understanding, the most important thing about the Abbey Center Conference was the people themselves and how they interacted. In this sense, the conference was unique and unrepeatable. What board members like Tom Mullaney had been saying all along came true: the conference is the people themselves. They will bring their own reforming and repentant selves to the meetings. It is not what we say or conclude to, but what we experience together that is important. And so it was.

In the end the witness of humbled and hard-working personalities showed how our world is actually making it through this present crisis of identity, and how these people, as leaders in their various institutions, are bringing about slow and unheralded change. While we have very little to show on paper, major shifts are taking place in our culture with a definite preference toward a more respectful integration—an integration that allows larger and larger numbers of the human family to share in the benefits of an expanding culture.

Even as St. Gregory the Great wrote the *Dialogues,* a work about the saints and miracles of the sixth century Italian South for a people depressed and dispirited by the chaos of the invasions, so we, too, find ourselves turning to models of promise and distinction in an otherwise discouraging scene full of personal failures and betrayals. This, I believe, is the way to interpret Fr. Matthew Kelty's wonderful, entertaining and endearing verbal portrait of his friend Thomas Merton on

Saturday evening. This, too, is the way to view the autobiographical testimonies of Rembert Weakland and Rosemary Haughton on Sunday morning at the conference's closing. It seemed the only response to make after the long list of problems and challenges and unresolved questions that were unearthed and experienced during those days. The archbishop described the by now classic journey of the gifted and charismatic person having to switch fields of interest and service not once but several times. Rosemary Haughton's sharing, however, delivered a shattering wound to all present. For her story about personal and institutional betrayal and bankruptcy is a paradigm for our time. All that is left to her is her faith in herself and the Gospel she believes in. A more towering twentieth-century miracle cannot be imagined, and yet it is all the more horrible and untouchable because no one of us would want to share her pain. The conference ended, not in euphoria, but in sober confirmation that the cultural crisis has hit home, and that the only heroes around are the wounded ones. But then, is there any other way to Christ's resurrection?

In Search of a Context for
the Merton-Suzuki Dialogue

Roger Corless

The meeting between Thomas Merton and Daisetz Teitaro Suzuki is legendary, almost an icon. Two venerable truth-seekers, one emerging from the stout walls of a medieval Christian monastery, the other appearing from behind a majestic stand of peaceful cryptomerias, recognize each other as "fellow citizens"[1] and set the dialogue between East and West in a transcendental context, beyond the accidents of history and culture.

In the summer of 1991 I went to Japan in order to discover more about this meeting.[2] I imagined that I would interview a few people who knew D. T. Suzuki, find out how, when and where he contacted Christianity, and which Christians he met, inspect the library in his former home, the Matsugaoka Bunko in North Kamakura (now officially a museum), so as to list the Christian books I found there, and return to the United States with a clear portrait of "D. T. Suzuki's understanding of Christianity" to supplement our already fairly detailed knowledge of Merton's understanding of Buddhism.

I was able to do both less and more than I anticipated. There was much less on Suzuki's contact with Christianity than I had supposed, and contacts with informants sometimes proved impossible to set up; but as I searched, I unearthed mysteries, half-truths and innuendoes which indicated that beneath the meeting of two eminent

1. The phrase is Merton's. See *Zen and the Birds of Appetite* (New York: New Directions, 1968) 138.

2. I gratefully acknowledge the support of the director and staff of the Nanzan Institute for Religion and Culture at Nagoya, who welcomed me as a visiting scholar during June and July 1991.

and apparently open-minded persons were many layers of ambiguity and hidden agendas. To sort all this out would require a book, or at least an extensive monograph. What I will attempt here is something much less ambitious—the raising of a number of questions and a public rumination on where my research on this topic might take me next.

What is Christianity?

Suzuki was not backwards in coming forwards to express his opinion of what Christianity is all about. What he meant, however, was not always clear. Consider the following:

> As long as God is content in himself he is non-existent; he must be awakened to something which is not himself, when he is God. God is God when God is not God, yet what is not God must be in himself too. And this—what is not himself—is his own Thought or Consciousness. With this Consciousness he departs from himself and at the same time returns to himself. You cannot say that Thought is by Being and that Being has its basis in itself; you must say that Being is Being because of Thought, which is to say, that Being is Being because Being is not Being.[3]

In a letter to Merton, dated March 31, 1959, Suzuki was somewhat more intelligible:

> I am trying to write my understanding of Christianity. Some of the ideas I have are:
>
> We have never been driven out of Eden;
> We still retain innocence;
> We are innocent just because of our sinfulness;
> Paradise and original sin are not contradictory;
> God wanted to know himself, hence the creation;
> When we know ourselves we know God;
> etc. etc.[4]

When I showed this quotation to Mrs. Mihoko Bekku, who was Suzuki's secretary for many years (when she was Miss Okamura), she

---

3. D. T. Suzuki, *Living by Zen*, ed. Christmas Humphreys (New York: Samuel Weiser, 1972) 12.

4. Robert E. Daggy, ed., *Encounter: Thomas Merton & D. T. Suzuki*, (Monterey, Ky.: Larkspur Press, 1988) 12-13.

exclaimed, "That is exactly what Dr. Suzuki thought," and began to explain the "etc. etc."[5] One of the "etceteras" was the resurrection. Why did not Christ resurrect immediately? Why did he wait three days? This, said Mrs. Bekku, was a question which Suzuki asked Merton when he met him, and Merton tried to answer him, but could not do so to Suzuki's satisfaction. From a Zen point of view, Suzuki had said, spiritual life should come immediately from spiritual death; bodily resurrection was not the point.

Further, Mrs. Bekku felt that Suzuki was probably thinking of three of his favorite Biblical passages—Exodus 3:14, John 8:58, and Genesis 1:3.[6] The Hebrew of Exodus 3:14 (אהיה אשר אהיה), which is in incomplete or dynamic mode (the so-called "imperfect tense") is usually interpreted on the basis of the LXX, which uses the Greek present tense (Ἐγώ εἰμι ὁ ὤν), from which we get the static English statement I AM THAT I AM (according to the King James version which, said Mrs. Bekku, was the translation Suzuki usually read). In 1957 Erich Fromm met Suzuki and told him about the difference when the Hebrew was read rather than the English. "I am becoming I am becoming" (as, Mrs. Bekku said, Fromm had translated) seemed preferable to Suzuki because it fitted the Zen experience better. Similarly, he liked the saying of Christ in the Fourth Gospel "Before Abraham was, I am" (John 8:58) because of its Zen feel.

As for Genesis 1:3 ("And God said, Let there be light: and there was light"), Mrs. Bekku said that when Suzuki read these words he asked, "Who was there to witness this act?" He often asked Christians about this, but none could answer. His own answer was *"I was there!"* This was the Zen answer.

Suzuki gave an extended commentary on his interpretation of Genesis 1:3, in which, further, he identified the Hebrew טוב ("good") with the Chinese *miao*[a] ("fine" in the senses of, as in English, both "subtle" and "marvelous," and used in Buddhist texts to translate Sanskrit *sat*[*] in compounds such as *saddharma*, true, real, full or "good"

---

5. Interview with Mrs. Bekku and Dr. Masao Abe in the Palace Side Hotel, Kyoto, June 19, 1991.

6. These passages occur again and again in Suzuki's writings. The importance of Exodus 3:14 and John 8:58 to Suzuki's thinking was independently stressed to me by Dr. Eshin Nishimura in an interview which he kindly granted me at his temple, Kōfuku Zenji, in Notogawa (Shiga Prefecture), later that same day.

Buddhism), in a 1965 interview with Richard De Martino (who was his secretary prior to Miss Okamura):

> . . . in the Old Testament Book of Genesis it is written that God commanded, "Let there be light," and there was light; and the light was separated from the darkness. God saw this light and said that it was "good." Now this "good," in my view, is a "good" that precedes the differentiation between good and evil. I disagree with those Western thinkers and theologians who would maintain that this "good" is the good of good-and-evil. In my understanding, as a "good" that is "before" or "prior to" all dichotomous discriminations—including that between good and evil—this "good" is what would be characterized in Buddhism (and, coincidentally, in Taoism) as *miao*[a]. From such a vantage point, looking upon this "Let there be light!" as a Zen injunction or a Zen command, it would mean: "Dispel—or Awaken from—your delusion!"; or, "See—or be at—the time 'before' heaven and earth were divided into two!" Indeed, if re-interpreted as a Zen challenge, this fiat could be reformulated as: "Be with God in His workshop 'before'—or 'prior to'—His saying 'Let there be light!' "[7]

Examples could be multiplied, but enough has been quoted, I believe, to show that Suzuki approached Christianity not so much as a curious enquirer as a "Zen" interpreter. (Just what he meant by "Zen" we shall examine shortly.) If we realize this, we are not too surprised when we see him identify the Christian God with the Buddhist *nen*[b], the dimensionless present moment of enlightenment:

> . . . when Christians stand all naked, shorn of their dualistic garments, they will discover that their God is no other than the Absolute Present itself.[8]

Merton, for his part, does not seem to have protested these (as we must call them) distortions of the Christian message. It is particularly odd that, as far as I can find out, Merton does not insist on Suzuki taking the cross seriously. The cross is spectacularly missing from Suzuki's interpretation of Christianity—and for good reason—he found

7. "Reflections on Zen and the West," originally published in Japanese in the *Asahi Journal* 7:11 (March 14, 1965). Translated, edited, and annotated by Richard J. De Martino. Privately circulated manuscript.

8. *Living by Zen*, 65.

it disgusting.[9] Mrs. Bekku said that Suzuki was repelled by the image of Christ crucified, especially by the roadside crucifixes which he saw in Germany, with blood realistically streaming down—and in Spain and Mexico it was even worse! When he asked people about them, they said, ''They make us feel grateful.'' But, he thought, how could one be grateful for blood? Surely there must be a sadomasochism in the psychology of such cultures?

In Shintō, and therefore Japanese culture in general, blood is regarded as polluting, so that the biblical notion of blood as purifying is largely inaccessible. An intelligent Japanese man to whom I was trying to explain the Mass studied my missalette with interest, but gave out a yelp and dropped it in alarm when he came to the words *kore wa watashi no chi no sakazuki* (''this is the cup of my blood''). Even Japanese Christians tend to be uncomfortable with the Blood of Christ. The retelling of the life of Christ by the modern Japanese Catholic novelist Shusaku Endo manages to finesse the crucifixion and portray Jesus largely through Taoist images of strength-in-weakness.[10]

It is perhaps significant that the Christian teacher with whom Suzuki felt most at home was Meister Eckhart.[11] The Meister has a lot to say about Zen-compatible things like divine sparks, nothingness, and paradox, but the cross is conspicuous by its absence. I raised this point with Matthew Fox,[12] and tried, without success, to sell Mother Julian of Norwich to him as a greater *Christian* mystic than Eckhart, because Julian sees the blood, and lots of it (''The copiousness [of the blood] resembles the drops of water which fall from the eaves of a house after a great shower of rain, falling so thick that no human ingenuity can count them''[13]) and she sees it as both horrifying and healing.

9. The problem of the absence of the Cross in the discussion of Christianity by the Kyoto School is examined by James Heisig in ''East-West Dialogue: Śūnyatā and Kenōsis,'' *Spirituality Today* 39:2 (summer 1987) 137–47, and 39:3 (autumn 1987) 211–24.

10. *A Life of Jesus*, trans., Shusaku Endo, Richard A. Schuchert, S.J. (New York: Paulist Press, 1973).

11. Eckhart was chosen as the Christian referent in Suzuki's *Mysticism: Christian and Buddhist* (New York: Harper; London: Allen and Unwin, 1962).

12. Interview at the College of the Holy Names, Oakland, Calif., December 19, 1991.

13. Chapter 8 of the long text: see Julian of Norwich, *Showings*, trans., Edmund Colledge, O.S.A., and James Walsh, S.J. (New York: Paulist Press) 188.

What is Zen?

I have presented evidence, partial though it must be at this stage, that Suzuki expressed a greater interest in interpreting Christianity in "Zen" terms than in understanding Christianity on its own terms and that Merton did not seriously object to this procedure. Indeed, if, in this light, we re-read *Zen and the Birds of Appetite*,[14] especially the dialogue between Suzuki and Merton in the appendix, we might be persuaded to believe that Merton was even eager to *accept* a "Zen" interpretation of Christianity.

But what, after all, did Suzuki mean by "Zen"? He uses the word as if it referred to an unproblematically unitary tradition of transhistorical, transcultural, translogical, and indeed altogether transcendental, yet deeply personal, experience of non-duality. Anyone familiar with the rich variety of lineages and sub-lineages in Buddhism in general, and in Zen (and its variants in China, Korea and Viet Nam) in particular, must wonder at this approach. Yet, in the West, for many years, his interpretation went unquestioned. Merton called him "the chief authority on Zen Buddhism."[15]

There seem to be two ways of contextualizing Suzuki's interpretation of Zen as transcendental experience: personal, and political.[16]

On the personal side, Suzuki's father was a medical doctor who was a Confucian scholar and an adherent of Rinzai Zen, and his mother was a follower of a sectarian form of Shinshū (True Pure Land Buddhism, founded by Shinran [1173–1262]) called *hijihōmon*[c].[17] Hijihō-

---

14. See n. 1.

15. Thomas Merton, *Mystics and Zen Masters* (New York: Farrar, Straus and Giroux, 1967) 207.

16. My reflections on Suzuki's personal life are an expansion on an intriguing remark by Professor Hisao Inagaki that Suzuki's great interest in direct religious experience may have come from his mother, "who belonged to an obscure, heretical group of Shin Buddhists who emphasized direct experience of Amida Buddha." (Interview with Professor Inagaki at the Kyōto Dai-ni Tower Hotel, Kyoto, July 17, 1991.) However, the views expressed here are entirely my own.

17. See Suzuki's own remarks on this (where it is spelled *hijibomon*) on pp. 14–15 of *A Zen Life: D. T. Suzuki Remembered*, ed., Masao Abe (New York: Weatherhill, 1986). He calls it, rather vaguely, an "esoteric strain of Pure Land Shin Buddhism," recalls "a kind of *hijibomon* 'baptism' " which he underwent when nine or ten years old, and admits that ". . . I may have been influenced by my mother's involvement with *hijibomon*."

mon, literally "Secret Buddhism," is classified by Shinshū as a heresy (*i-anjin*[d], literally "un-peaceful mind," "peaceful mind" being a technical Shin term for orthodoxy), with the following characteristics:[18]

- it spreads in secret, in a cell-type organization, which helps to preserve its secrecy;
- it holds its ceremonies at night, meeting in storehouses;[19]
- it is very critical of the establishment, especially of Shinshū, · and calls for its downfall;
- the members elect laypersons as leaders, to whom they are fiercely loyal, disregarding the official Shinshū priests;
- the members interpret doctrine freely, according to their own inclinations, e.g., they say that one can become a Buddha in this very body, and that this world, just as it is, is the Pure Land.

Professor Taitetsu Unno of Smith College described the method of initiation as follows:[20] The neophyte is covered with a blanket and taken, at night, inside the storehouse, where s/he hears the chanting and is told of the wisdom-light of Amida Buddha. Suddenly, the blanket is removed, and the abrupt experience of physical light precipitates (it is hoped) an equally abrupt experience of the wisdom-light of Amida. Thus, contrary to the orthodox teaching of Shinshū, which defers enlightenment until after death, one feels oneself to be a Buddha right now, in this very world.

The tradition started under Hōnen (1133–1212, Shinran's teacher), and Shinran disowned his son Zenran for similar practices. Later, both Kakunyo (1270–1351) and Rennyo (1415–1499) wrote against it. However, the somewhat remote location of the sect, mostly in Noto Peninsula on the north shore of Honshū, and its popular appeal, made it difficult for the authorities to eliminate it.

18. "Hijihōmon," *Nihon Rekishi Daijiten* (Encyclopedia of Japanese History), Tokyo, 1975, vol. 8, p. 186, cols. 4–5. I am indebted to Fr. Jan Van Bragt of the Nanzan Institute for this reference.

19. The storehouse (*dozō*[e]), sometimes called in English a godown, is the structure in the traditional Japanese house where treasures are kept. Built of stone, and separate from the main dwelling (which is wooden), it has no windows, and is thus an ideal structure for secret meetings.

20. Personal communication, Buddhist Study Center, Honolulu, August 8, 1991.

The features of the sect which are important for our discussion are its concentration on immediate experience, and its objection to doctrinal and institutional control as irrelevant, or even an obstacle, to this experience. Suzuki, who was born near the Noto Peninsula, seems to have been deeply influenced by these characteristics. He interpreted, dare we say, the Zen of his father in terms of the experiences of his mother. And, it may be that here we have also the clue both to his attraction to Eckhart, and (although it was not at first his idea) his willingness to spend long hours translating Swedenborg.[21]

Again, if Suzuki was attracted to the *hijihōmon*ᶜ experience but, perhaps, wary of its heretical reputation, it might explain why he occasionally claimed that there was no "mysticism" in Zen. According to Fr. Heinrich Dumoulin, Suzuki understood "mysticism" as an Eng-

21. Suzuki translated Swedenborg's *Heaven and Hell* (1910), *New Jerusalem and its Doctrines* (1914), *Divine Love and Wisdom* (1914), and *Divine Providence* (1915). (Curiously, *Heaven and Hell* is not included in the *Suzuki Daisetsu Zenshu* [Collected Works of Daisetz Suzuki].) He also wrote *Suwedenborugo* ("Swedenborg") (1913) which the *Zenshu* says "relies heavily on" (ōku yotte) *Emmanuel Swedenborg: The Man and His Mission* by B. F. Barrett (Philadelphia: The Swedenborg Publishing Association, n.d.). Benjamin Fiske Barrett (1808–1892) was a well-known editor of Swedenborg's works but, although the *Swedenborg Researcher's Manual* by William Ross Woofenden (Bryn Athyn, Penn.: Swedenborg Scientific Association, 1988) records that the Swedenborg Publishing Association was "an independent publishing body founded by Barrett" (197) it makes no mention of the book which Suzuki supposedly used, and I have been unable to find any other reference to it. Mrs. Bekku gave this account of the circumstances under which Suzuki undertook the translation of Swedenborg's works: "Dr. Suzuki spent one Christmas holiday period in London, translating Swedenborg. He was helped by a [Swedenborgian?] minister who knew Latin. The minister would translate the Latin into English and Dr. Suzuki would translate the English into Japanese. 'I worked so hard on that, Mihoko-san' he said. He remembered the gaslight and the dark streets and the cold. He used to wrap himself in a blanket. They used a room in Great Russell Street upstairs from Probsthain's [an Oriental bookshop opposite the British Museum]. The room was still there many years later when Dr. Suzuki visited. 'That's just like the English' he said." A picture of the young Suzuki appears facing p. 352 of the *Transactions of the International Swedenborg Congress, held in connection with the Celebration of the Swedenborg Society's Centenary, London, July 4 to 8, 1910* (London: The Swedenborg Society. 3rd ed., 1912), with the caption "DAISETZ TEITARO SUZUKI, Translator of *Heaven and Hell* into Japanese, A Vice-President of the International Swedenborg Congress."

lish translation of *mikkyō*[f], Esoteric Buddhism.[22] "Esoteric Buddhism" may have sounded dangerously close to "Secret Buddhism."

From the political perspective, it should be noted that Suzuki was writing at a time when Buddhism in general had fallen into disrepute in Japan. It was seen as "corrupt, decadent, otherworldly, anti-social, parasitic, superstitious, and utterly inimical to Japan's aspirations for scientific and technological advancement."[23] In their own defense, Japanese Buddhist intellectuals borrowed and adapted the distinction that was beginning to be made in Europe between the pure essence of religion (what came to be known as spirituality) and its corrupt expression in history and culture. This "New Buddhism" (*shimbukkyō*[g]) was characterized as " 'modern,' 'cosmopolitan,' 'humanistic,' and 'socially responsible.' "[24]

If, then, there was a pure, essential, spiritual Buddhism, where could it be found? Not in doctrines and institutions, clearly, for they are all too culture-bound (and by this move, the New Buddhists stole the thunder of their accusers), but in the innermost heart of those who have experienced true awakening. Various phrases like "No dependence on words and letters: direct pointing at the human heart" could then be selected from the Zen tradition and made to seem consonant with what we might call the psychological monism of Otto, Schleiermacher, and (especially important for Suzuki) William James. The fact that traditional Zen, while admittedly spoofing the Buddhist tradition unmercifully, always remains firmly within it, insisting on proper authentication of a teacher's lineage and being, in fact, a conservative "back to *bodhi*" reform movement, was ignored in favor of packaging it as a non-doctrinal, pan-human awakening to reality-as-it-really-is.

It was perhaps because Merton accepted Suzuki's transcendental interpretation of Zen that he felt it might provide the needed stimu-

---

22. Interview with Father Dumoulin at Sophia University, Tokyo, July 19, 1991.

23. Robert H. Sharf, "Occidentalism and the Zen of Japanese Nationalism." Paper delivered at the American Academy of Religion Annual Meeting, Kansas City, Mo., November 24, 1991, 1. The paper is being revised for publication, and versions of it are scheduled to appear in *History of Religions* for August 1993 and in a book, being edited by Donald Lopez, with the working title *Curators of the Buddha: Orientalism and the Study of Buddhism*.

24. Ibid., 2.

lus to revive the contemplative tradition in Christianity.[25] What Merton did not seem to realize is that Zen Buddhism is *Buddhism,* and to practice it sincerely entails, as with any other form of Buddhism, the giving up of belief in the Christian (or any other) God.

What is Japaneseness?

Suzuki's discussion of what he calls Zen is intimately bound up with his defence of "Japaneseness" (*nihonjinron*[h], literally "discussions of Japanese humanity"). Japaneseness is a topic of such endless fascination to the Japanese that bookstores today regularly have a *nihonjinron*[h] section. The axiom which, being an axiom, is not open to discussion, is straightforward: the Japanese people, and the Japanese language and culture, are unique. The debate is more complex: what *exactly* is it that is unique?

It is usual to say that Japaneseness became a subject of enquiry during the Meiji era (1868–1912), but it seems to me that it can be said to have existed, perhaps under different names, or even without a name, long before that. My suggestion is that Japaneseness is the true "religion" of Japan, and that it has been the true religion of Japan ever since the archipelago was united into a nation. This has something to do, in my opinion, with the survival of Shintō, or perhaps it is the survival of Shintō that has ensured the survival of Japaneseness.

Shintō has most of the features of what we used to call primitive religion, and which we now call tribal, preliterate or (the term I prefer) pre-Axial. That is to say, it is local, pro-cosmic, and celebratory. It has no notion of a profound break between nature and humans, or humans and deities. It gives unity not to those who believe in its doctrines but to those who feel that the *kami* (deity) is their Parent (*oyasama*). The only way in which Shintō differs from other pre-Axial religions (such as the religions of ancient Greece or Egypt) is that it is still living.

25. In my article "Fire on the Seven Storey Mountain: Why Are Catholics Looking East?" *Toward an Integrated Humanity: Thomas Merton's Journey,* ed., M. Basil Pennington, O.C.S.O. (Kalamazoo: Cistercian Publications, 1988 [Cistercian Studies Series, no. 103]) 204–21, I suggest that Merton went through a number of stages, slightly ahead of, and more lucidly than, the Catholic Church as a whole, and that when he met Suzuki he was at the "Romantic Orientalism" stage (see 211–15).

Japaneseness then might be seen as a modern form of the pre-Axial split between tribe members, who alone are called "human," and the rest of the world, who are, if not enemies, certainly strange and sub-human; of war against such non-tribe members; and of a monistic or quasi-monistic identification with nature.

All of these values are discussed by Suzuki as "Zen" in his *Zen and Japanese Culture* (Princeton N.J.: Bollingen Series, 1959) and even more clearly in his *Japanese Spirituality* which, published in Japanese in 1944, has only been available in English since 1972, and in America since 1988.[26]

Suzuki makes a distinction between spirit (*seishin*[i]), which is the opposite of matter, and spirituality (*reisei*[j]), which is "non-discriminatory wisdom."[27] He then sees spirituality as something which awakens after a people has "proceeded a certain degree up the cultural ladder"[28] and concludes that "Zen typifies Japanese spirituality."[29] But it is not alone, for Shinshū is also thoroughly Japanese, although "it is necessary to distinguish distinctly between Shinshū the Shin Sect, which is a group entity, and Shinshū experience, which is the foundation of this group."[30] (Do we hear in this statement the echo of mother's *hijihōmon*[c]?) Japanese spirituality is superior to that of India and China, for only in Japan has Pure Land Buddhism advanced to term as a "transcendental experience" whereas "the Chinese Pure Land school of fifteen hundred years ago is the same as the Pure Land school of today."[31] As for Zen:

> Zen traces its source to the Indian thought of the southern tradition. It materialized within the northern tradition as seen in the Chinese people, where nurtured by a northern temper, it possessed a quite positive and practical nature. Going eastward across the sea, it touched the southern tradition as present in the spirituality of the Japanese people. Japanese spirituality thus on the one hand accepted the practical, logical nature of the Chinese people; but more than that, it perceived in Zen what should be

26. Daisetz Suzuki, *Japanese Spirituality*, trans., Norman Waddell (New York: Greenwood Press, 1988).
    27. Ibid., 15.
    28. Ibid., 16.
    29. Ibid., 18.
    30. Ibid., 19.
    31. Ibid., 20.

termed the intuitive nature of the Indian people as well, with its southern character. . . . This explains why Zen sympathized so directly and deeply with the mentality of the Kamakura warrior class.[32]

We are treading on dangerous ground. With these words, the gentle mystic begins to turn into the mighty warrior who will die for the *kokutai*[k], the Spirit of Japan which can never be wrong.[33] It is from this perspective that Suzuki can make what Robert Sharf calls "occidentalist" statements as, for example, his characterization of "East and West" in "Lectures on Zen Buddhism."[34] Suzuki hangs his argument on two poems—a haiku by Basho, and a stanza from a poem by Tennyson:

Basho—
When I look carefully
I see the *nazuna* blooming
By the hedge!

Tennyson—
Flower in the crannied wall,
I pluck you out of the crannies;—
Hold you here, root and all, in my hand,
Little flower—but if I could understand
What you are, root and all, and all in all,
I should know what God and man is.

From these two short pieces of literature, which we are asked to regard as typical of East and West, Suzuki derives two opposite worldviews:[35]

32. Ibid., 23.
33. Suzuki was accused of this by, especially, Takeshi Umehara who, in an article in the August 1966 issue of *Tembo*, wrote that the placement (in *Zen and Japanese Culture*) of the chapters "Zen and the Samurai" and "Zen and Swordsmanship" immediately after "General Remarks on Japanese Art Culture" ". . . speaks to us of a certain tendency towards militarism in [Suzuki's] thought, the same militarism that Japan has embraced since the early Meiji period." Quoted by Daisetsu Fujioka in "Suzuki Daisetsu," *Nihon Meisō Retsuden* (Biographies of Eminent Japanese Buddhist Clerics), Tōkyō: Shakai Shisōsha, 1968. For an English translation of this biography, see *Dharma World* 19 (March–April 1992) 34–38.
34. D. T. Suzuki, Erich Fromm, and Richard De Martino, *Zen Buddhism and Psychoanalysis* (New York: Harper, 1960) 1–10. I am indebted to Professor Jamie Hubbard for reminding me of this passage.
35. A similar point, also using the "crannied wall" poem from Tennyson,

I have selected these two poets, Basho and Tennyson, as indicative of two basic approaches to reality. Basho is of the East and Tennyson of the West. As we compare them we find that each bespeaks his traditional background. According to this, the Western mind is: analytical, discriminative, differential, inductive, individualistic, intellectual, objective, scientific, generalizing, conceptual, schematic, impersonal, legalistic, organizing, power-wielding, self-assertive, disposed to impose its will upon others, etc. Against these Western traits those of the East can be characterized as follows: synthetic, totalizing, integrative, nondiscriminative, deductive, nonsystematic, dogmatic, intuitive, (rather, affective), nondiscursive, subjective, spiritually individualistic and socially group-minded, etc.[36]

This is a strange list, but we are clearly meant to take ''the East'' (i.e., Japan) as having ''proceeded a certain [further] degree up the cultural ladder,'' that is, as more mature or, as one might say today, more ''together,'' and that this maturity is marked by an ability to handle paradox without qualms, and to leave nature alone, admiring it rather than dominating, managing, and insisting on understanding it fully.

Well, let me screw up my courage and say flat out that this is nonsense. It is a bad joke, as anyone who has been to Japan realizes as soon as s/he steps off the plane. Not only is Japan a serious technological rival of the West, causing CEOs in Detroit to tremble, the very ''Zen'' approach to nature which Suzuki praises is a manipulation of it. ''Raw nature'' says Donald Richie in a brilliantly perceptive article, ''is simply never there.''[37] ''Natural'' nature is, in Japan, always arranged, brought into the anthropomorphic circle, created. Unkempt nature is nonexistent, invisible, ignored. The hand that stunts the *bonsai* is the same that rapes the mountain for yet another underground shopping mall. If we are to compare East and West, we cannot do it like this.

The complexity of the issue is emphasized by an article in *The Japan Times* on bird watching.[38] There is, apparently, no indigenous

---

but a different haiku, is made by Suzuki in his essay ''Kirisutokyō to Bukkyō'' (Christianity and Buddhism) *Zenshu*, vol. 22, 272–75.

36. Ibid., 5.

37. Donald Richie, *A Lateral View: Essays on Contemporary Japan* (Tokyo: The Japan Times, Ltd., rev. ed., 1991) 13.

38. Mark Brazil, ''Wild Watch,'' *The Japan Times*, July 28, 1991, 13.

Japanese tradition of bird watching, and when, under western influence, a society for it was formed, it had to be called "*Wild* Bird Club" (*yacho no kai*) since the word "bird," all by itself, implied a caged or cooked bird, i.e., an anthropocentrically managed bird, not just a bird-bird. Having read the article, it occurred to me to wonder whether it was not, after all, "evil" Cartesianism which, by firmly dividing observer and observed, has allowed the West to view nature-in-itself, to propose that nature has its own inalienable rights, and so to lead the world in ecology and what Raimundo Panikkar calls "ecosophy."

Where to go Next?

Suzuki's maverick and fiery student Ryōmin Akizuki expresses his doubts about the possibility of true dialogue:

> In our Zen-Christian Colloquia in the past several years, I have been impressed by the fact that Christian participants have been more enthusiastic than Zen participants to learn from the other religion, and I have been secretly afraid that the Zen participants have been attending the Colloquia to teach others but not to learn from others, and that, while the Zen participants appear contented and satisfied with their religion, the life of Zen is running dry.[39]

Dialogue requires that those on both sides should both speak and listen. I have, I believe, to my dismay, uncovered preliminary evidence that Thomas Merton was a good listener but that D. T. Suzuki was not. Merton, I think, genuinely wanted to learn from Suzuki, so that he could write about how to put his own house (the Catholic Church) in order, but Suzuki, it appears, wanted to learn only in so far as it would assist him to become a better teacher of Japaneseness to the West, so as to assist it in its evolution towards true spirituality. According to Mrs. Bekku, the *real* religion would help humanity free itself: Zen was the best skillful means (*upāya- kauśalya*) to bring about this freedom, Shin was second best, and Christianity. . . . Mrs. Bekku wanted to say in closing that Dr. Suzuki really admired Christianity and that those who say he disliked it are wrong.

---

39. Ryōmin Akizuki, "The Zen-Christian Dialogue in Me," *A Zen-Christian Pilgrimage: The Fruits of Ten Annual Colloquia in Japan 1967–1976* (The Zen-Christian Colloquium, 1981; typeset by Paul Island typesetters [Hong Kong] Ltd.) 45–50.

In order to continue this research, the following needs to be done:

- the translation into English of the few works on Buddhism and Christianity by Suzuki which are scattered throughout the *Zenshu*
- access to the Matsugaoka Bunko[40] for long enough to catalogue the books and examine marginalia, in order to acquire some notion of Suzuki's exposure to Christian materials
- the writing of a complete, fully researched, and unbiased biography of D. T. Suzuki (there are at present not more than three or four short and rather hagiographic accounts) in order to set his thinking in proper historico-social context
- an examination of the nature and extent of Suzuki's involvement in western occultism (Paul Carus in the U.S.A.; René Daumal in Paris; translating Emmanuel Swedenborg), and the influence it had on him
- a rigorous enquiry into the interaction between those central to the Kyōto School, such as Kitarō Nishida, and those on the periphery, such as D. T. Suzuki, with a fearless investigation of the extent to which the School either supported or undercut Japanese militarism and nationalism through its particular understanding of *nihonjinron*[h] and *kokutai*[k]
- a re-examination of Merton's writings in the light of all the above

When this has been done we will be ready, as Professor Nishimura has suggested, to move into the "post-Suzuki age" beyond the conflict of East and West and into true dialogue.[41]

---

40. Such access is notoriously difficult. When letters of introduction (in Japanese) failed to produce any results, I resorted to the "dumb foreigner" trick and simply turned up: however, the curator had gone to Kyōto, and I was only able to see the outside of the Bunko and visit Suzuki's grave.

41. "Posuto-Suzuki no Jidai," a *geppo*[l] or monthly flyer which Professor Nishimura wrote for inclusion in *Nihon no Meicho* ([Selections from] Famous Japanese Authors), vol. 43 (Kiyozawa Manshi and Daisetz Suzuki), Kyoto: Chūō Kōron Sha, 1984.

GLOSSARY OF CHINESE CHARACTERS

a 妙

b 念

c 祕事法門

d 異安心

e 土蔵

f 密教

g 新佛教

h 日本人論

i 精神

j 靈性

k 団体

l 月報

Otherness Has a Face . . .
and It Is Not a Pretty Face*

Roberto S. Goizueta

The last decade of the twentieth century has witnessed a historical process hailed widely as the twilight of collectivist ideologies and the consequent triumph of individual freedom. We are assured that, from Moscow to Managua, the hand of history has written an epitaph for the grand socialist experiment. Yet an eerie uneasiness pervades the celebration. The columns of menacing Soviet tanks that we saw day in and day out in our news programs not long ago have been replaced by columns of the hungry, homeless, and unemployed, not only in the former socialist states, but in our own country and in countries as distant as Somalia. These are the spoils of our victory. Nevertheless, the presumptive triumph of western ideals has been accompanied in some circles by a fashionable jingoism, now justified—or so we are told—by the inexorable march of history itself. If the Soviet utopia is no longer the inevitable end of history, then the American utopia must be. After all, we have won the Cold War.

One intellectual alternative to this triumphalistic jingoism is that represented by poststructuralist postmodernism, with its emphasis on cultural and epistemological relativity. Rejecting the universalism, conceptualism, and rationalism of modernity, poststructuralist postmodernity often turns to aesthetics as an antidote to the totalitarian tendencies of modern ontologies and epistemologies. In the "postmodernist

* This paper was presented at the January 9–12, 1993 "Scholar's Retreat" sponsored by The Abbey Center For The Study Of Ethics And Culture, Inc. at the Abbey of Gethsemani, Trappist, Kentucky.

merger of life and art,''[1] aesthetic otherness and indeterminacy are put forth as alternatives to rational certitude and instrumentality.

While this process of aestheticization, where life itself becomes the aesthetic object, the *objet d'art* par excellence, emerges from a subversive impulse in postmodernity, the link between that intuitive, liberative impulse and concrete human suffering often remains ambiguous in or, indeed, altogether absent from the discussion. Where indeterminacy is the sole value, how does one take a stand? Some, like John Caputo, insist that one must take a stand on the side of the oppressed.[2] Yet, as Mark Kline Taylor has observed, ''Caputo does not say *how* this 'taking a stand' is consonant with the celebration and valuation of the flux.''[3] This observation is echoed, in more general terms, by Terry Eagleton: ''Any post-structuralist theory which desires to be in some sense political is bound to find itself caught on the hop between the normativity which such politics entail, and its own full-blooded cultural relativism.''[4] Poststructuralists are hard pressed to answer the question: What is the *relationship* between solidarity with the oppressed, on the one hand, and indeterminacy, or aesthetic experience on the other? The consequences of this lacuna, argues Andrew Bowie, will not be limited to the academic world in which the discussion is carried on:

> A major problem that radical aesthetic theory needs to confront in our century is the fact that, if one has lost metaphysical, or collectively binding criteria for the judgement of the products of subjective spontaneity, there is no sure way of distinguishing in advance the aesthetically significant from the politically reactionary. In the twentieth century aesthetic issues become dangerous, they cost lives and affect politics in ways which are not always immediately apparent.[5]

1. Ferenc Fehér, "What is Beyond Art? On the Theories of Post-Modernity," *Reconstructing Aesthetics,* eds. Agnes Heller and Ferenc Fehér (New York: Basil Blackwell, 1986) 67.
2. John D. Caputo, *Radical Hermeneutics: Repetition, Deconstruction, and the Hermeneutical Project* (Bloomington, Ind.: Indiana University Press, 1987) 264.
3. Mark Kline Taylor, *Remembering Esperanza: A Cultural-Political Theology for North American Praxis* (Maryknoll, N.Y.: Orbis, 1990) 39.
4. Terry Eagleton, *The Ideology of the Aesthetic* (Oxford: Basil Blackwell, 1990) 385.
5. Andrew Bowie, *Aesthetics and Subjectivity: From Kant to Nietzsche* (Manchester: Manchester University Press, 1990) 256–57.

It is thus not altogether clear that, for all the talk of otherness and difference, postmodernity is truly capable of embracing cultural otherness and promoting a genuine community of "others." The suspicion remains that much postmodern thinking is but the adolescent child of modernity, rebelling wildly against its parent, yet unable and unwilling to recognize how that very rebellion masks a profound dependence.[6] Those very lines of hungry and unemployed people unmask the illusion that modernity has been transcended; the faces of the poor, the hungry and unemployed, the victims of triumphalist jingoism, all bear the unmistakable imprint of modernity. Their histories of suffering are not forgotten. The underside of modernity per-

6. So, for instance, Eagleton compares Locke, one of the great figures of modernity, with Jean-François Lyotard: "John Locke, father of English liberalism and devout racist, held in his doctrine of anti-essentialism that no particular feature of reality could be said to be in itself more important than any other; and it follows from this that there is no more reason why an individual's colour of skin should not be regarded as an essential feature of her, than why it should. Lyotard's divorce of the descriptive and the normative is exactly in line with this tradition of thought" (Eagleton, 400). Likewise, Russell Berman accuses postmodernists of the same epistemological insularity and aversion to criticism that characterize modern culture: "it is postmodernist eclecticism, the consequence of the avant-garde attack on bourgeois normativity, that precludes systemic criticism. The system can point to the artificial negativity of its internal opposition as proof of its own viability and the impossibility of an autonomous position outside the network of present practices. The cultural theory of postmodernism provides the affirmative descriptions of that which is merely given. Although it may carefully sketch power structures and practical strategies, its rejection of emancipatory autonomy precludes any systematic critical project. Once concepts of truth are treated solely as vehicles for the establishment of an exclusionary discourse and taste becomes only a ploy to establish social distinction, the utopian potential of the autonomous artwork is lost from sight." *Modern Culture and Critical Theory: Art, Politics, and the Legacy of the Frankfurt School* (Madison: University of Wisconsin Press, 1989) 51–52. In a discussion of reader-response theory, Berman also observes that postmodernist relativism can mask an underlying elitist conservatism, resulting in an "authoritarian cynicism": "as Stanley Fish, one of the leading reader-response advocates, repeatedly insists, the result of the theory is not a dissolution of critical or textual authority but a recognition of the constant 'authority of interpretive communities,' i.e., established university critics. . . . No interpretation is permanent, but every interpretation must respond to established norms (because an autonomy outside of established norms is inconceivable) . . . Fish's antitraditionalism turns into a cynical defense of established criticism simply as established. The authority that once adhered to innovative modernism is transferred to the critical guardians of culture within the academic literary institutions" (ibid., 129–130).

dures as the spoils of its victory. Consequently, any epistemological paradigm—by whatever name—that is incapable of "distinguishing in advance the aesthetically significant from the politically reactionary" necessarily remains trapped within the dialectic of modernity. Such a paradigm would represent, in the words of Frank Lentricchia, "the critic's doomed attempt to retreat from a social landscape of fragmentation and alienation."[7]

Comprising a disproportionately large segment of the hungry and unemployed, the victims of North American jingoism, and the underside of modernity, U.S. Hispanics are among those groups which have the ability and, indeed, the responsibility to challenge the reigning interpretations of the present historical juncture. To do so, we seek to retrieve our historical experience, our memories of suffering, our intellectual history, and our spirituality as sacraments of a liberating God, a God whose symbol of victory is the cross. In that light, we can refuse to accept simplistic and, indeed, monstrous readings of history while contributing, from the richness of our own history, to the construction of a truly "beautiful" community, an aesthetic community of others.

One source from which U.S. Hispanics can draw both to critique the dominant ideological alternatives and to help construct new alternatives is our experience of "the mestizo community," the beautiful community, as the locus of popular religiosity and spirituality, the place where we encounter the crucified Christ, and, hence, the birthplace of our liberation. Community is the common root out of which emerge our aesthetics, our understanding of the beautiful, and our ethics, our understanding of the good and the just. For U.S. Hispanics, community is the place where our *mestizaje* (the historical mixture, or confluence, of races and cultures) is most immediately lived out. This is where we struggle every day to forge our identity, for it is where our most cherished values, the values of family, friendship, beauty, and celebration, are brought into direct confrontation with the seemingly contradictory values of the ambient culture. In order to engage effectively the challenge represented by what Virgilio Elizondo has called our "second *mestizaje*," our North American pilgrimage, U.S. Hispanic theologians seek to make explicit the epistemological foundations of

7. Frank Lentricchia, *After the New Criticism* (Chicago: University of Chicago Press, 1980) 186.

our understanding of community as an ethical and aesthetic historical reality. Such an aesthetic-ethical community, thus understood, becomes in turn the locus of our spirituality and theology.[8]

Aesthetics and Community

Central to our culture is an aesthetic understanding of life and community. A strikingly common feature of the Latin American philosophies regnant in the first half of this century is their epistemological *a prioris*, or the epistemological paradigms informing these philosophies. Put simply, the Cartesian "I think, therefore I am" is replaced, in these philosophies, by "We feel (or love), therefore we are." This, indeed, is one of the most consistent and fundamental differences between the post-Enlightenment European and Latin American philosophical traditions—at least prior to the emergence of theologies and philosophies of liberation. If one can hazard such a sweeping generalization, post-Enlightenment European philosophy has tended to accord epistemological priority to reason, while Latin American philosophy has accorded a similar priority to affect; the former has sought meaning, whereas the latter has sought beauty.[9] These paradigms have themselves been challenged, however, by western postmodernists, on the one hand, and Latin American liberation theologians on the other.

8. For a discussion of "second *mestizaje*" see Virgilio Elizondo, *Galilean Journey: The Mexican-American Promise* (Maryknoll, N.Y.: Orbis, 1983) 9–16.
9. E.g., José Vasconcelos, *Estética*, in *Obras completas* (México, 1961) 3:1111-1711, *El monismo estético*, and *Filosofía estética*, in *Obras completas* 4:9-92, and 4:817-954 respectively. (It is sometimes forgotten that Vasconcelos' notions of *mestizaje* and *la raza cósmica* are, for him, not primarily socio-political categories but above all aesthetic categories); Alejandro Deústua, *Estética general* (Lima, 1923), *Estética aplicada, lo bello en el arte: la arquitectura* (Lima, 1932), *Lo bello en el arte: escultura, pintura, música* (Lima, 1935), and *La estética de José Vasconcelos* (Lima, 1939); José Pereira da Graça Aranha, *A esthetica da vida* (Rio de Janeiro, 1920); Antonio Caso, *La filosofía de la intuición* (México, 1914), *La existencia como economía, como desinterés y como caridad* (México, 1919), and *Principios de estética* (México, 1925). This whole tradition is absent from modern and postmodern Western aesthetics. Consequently, contemporary European and North American philosophers remain blind to the fact that much of what is today considered novel and post-modern was, in fact, already being discussed at length in Latin American philosophical circles eighty years ago. For example, in his otherwise brilliant work *The Ideology of the Aesthetic* Terry Eagleton does not cite a single Latin American thinker.

While an extensive analysis of this epistemological difference is beyond the limited scope of this paper, it is possible to uncover the particular experience of community that is reflected in the aesthetic epistemological paradigm of key Latin American philosophers, while proposing how a critical retrieval of a Latino aesthetic, in the light of the more recent insights of Latin American liberation theology, might inform U.S. Hispanic spirituality and theology, as well as the larger society.

Perhaps the most significant influence of Latin American liberation theology on U.S. Hispanic theology has been the praxis-based epistemology which underpins both. It is the most important debt we owe to our Latin American colleagues, one which we are attempting to repay through the very process of developing a theological reflection grounded in the praxis of our U.S. Hispanic communities. Yet the epistemology that underlies Latin American theologies and philosophies of liberation is itself—at least implicitly—both a development beyond and a critique of the aesthetic epistemologies so prominent in Latin American philosophy in the first half of this century and themselves representing, in turn, an important critique of European rationalist epistemologies grounded in the Cartesian *ego cogito*. The increasing appreciation of the role of ideology in perpetuating social injustice has been accompanied, in the writings of liberation theologians, by a radical critique of theologies and philosophies that are not grounded in the ethical-political struggle against that injustice. Understandably, a casualty of this epistemological shift has been the rejection of both (European) rationalist and (Latin American) aesthetic foundations for theology, since, as ahistorical, both appear to prescind prematurely from that struggle. The aesthetic critique of rationalism itself did not go far enough insofar as it too seemed to presuppose an ahistorical experience of otherness that obscured concrete, sociohistorical conflict, thereby making possible the degeneration of aesthetics into but another bourgeois ideology incapable of supporting sociohistorical liberation struggles.

While the Latin American turn to ethical-political praxis and away from aesthetics has represented a crucial stage in the development of Latin American philosophy, I will suggest in this paper that the U.S. Hispanic context, U.S. Hispanics' experience of community, and the challenge represented by our "second *mestizaje*" call for the development of a third epistemological paradigm, one that is not identified exclusively with either of the paradigms we have inherited from our Latin American intellectual forebears. In short, while the aesthetic paradigm of early twentieth-century Latin American philosophy represented an important stage in the development of a properly Latin American epistemology, and the ethical-political paradigm of the liberation theology and philosophy of the second half of this century represents an important second stage in that development, the next century will demand from U.S. Hispanics another paradigm incorporating the advances of both the aesthetic and ethical-political, which are a part of our intellectual history, while responding to the challenges of our second *mestizaje*.

This paper first traces the outlines of a Latin American aesthetics of community by examining, in a necessarily cursory fashion, the work of the great Mexican philosopher José Vasconcelos. It then indicates how liberation theology represents a key critique of that aesthetics, and suggests how U.S. Hispanics might understand our own experience of community, and the popular religiosity rooted in that experience, as a reflection and further development of these two traditions. Such an analysis of aesthetics, ethics, and community—and their interrelationship as revealed in the popular religiosity of an oppressed people— might contribute, in some small way, to our common attempts to answer the question currently being posed to and by postmodernists: What is the relationship between ethical-political action, on the one hand, and aesthetic experience, on the other?

José Vasconcelos and a Latin American Aesthetics of Community

In his *Monismo estético* (1918), José Vasconcelos issues a clarion call for a new philosophical paradigm in Latin America: ''I believe that we are entering the era of the aesthetic philosophies, philosophies grounded no longer in pure reason, nor in practical reason, but in the mystery of aesthetic judgment. It is in the *special pathos of beauty* that I look for the unifying principle, capable of participating in the three forms of action, intellectual, moral, and aesthetic. . . .''[10] The advantage of the aesthetic over both the rational and the ethical, argues Vasconcelos, is that the ''aesthetic pathos'' reflects the unitive, even if amorphous character of human experience itself, whereas reason and

10. Vasconcelos, *Obras completas*, 4:16.

ethics can achieve such a unity only through the imposition of an artificial framework, whether rational or ethical. In his *Filosofía estética*, for instance, Vasconcelos writes that "every rational operation begins by decomposing its object into its most simple elements, but since it cannot join together again the pieces thus created through analysis, one is forced to leap outside the real object decomposed by reason and replace it with the concept. . . ."[11] Likewise, "all ethics implies the study of a norm imposed on that which in life is loose, ungovernable, chaotic, in order to transform it in accord with a redemptive end or aspiration."[12] The aesthetic pathos sublates reason and ethics, synthesizing these in a "return" to experience, an experience that is paradoxically both amorphous and holistic; it is holistic and unitive precisely because it is amorphous and, thus, indivisible in reality. Insofar as ethics presupposes discreet acts with particular redemptive ends, it presupposes a disintegration of human experience as an end in itself. Just as the ethical moment sublates the rational, so too does the aesthetic sublate the ethical:

> Just as the objects observed by the mind confirm our ideational representations and their relationships, the same objects, submitted to ethical judgment, provide intuitions of usefulness or uselessness. . . . Consistent with their experiential criteria, ethical values possess a more concrete reality, richer in substance, than that of ideas . . . yet ethical values are themselves surpassed by an aesthetic moment and a moment of conformation when these values become abstract. Thus, the ancient Platonic-Socratic trilogy, Goodness, Truth, and Beauty, as identical, corresponds to a gradation that proceeds as follows: Truth, Goodness, and Beauty, in ascending order.[13]

In his *Estética*, Vasconcelos argues that this tripartite ascension from the rational to the aesthetic, via ethics, represents "the yearning for communion with the divine nature."[14] It likewise represents a return to concrete experience, which is always holistic, or unitive. If European and North American postmodernists find in aesthetic experience a mediation of difference and otherness, Vasconcelos empha-

11. Ibid., 4:833-34.
12. Ibid., 3:766.
13. Ibid., 3:776.
14. Ibid., 3:1137.

sizes the unitive character of that experience. He does acknowledge and insist that this unity is always a union of others. Yet Vasconcelos gives proportionately less attention to the ambiguous character of this unity in contrast to its synthetic character. The practical result is an ahistorical unity that mirrors the poststructuralist ahistorical otherness. It is thus no coincidence that, for all his talk of a Latin American *raza cósmica* (cosmic race), Vasconcelos remained a Hispanophile who saw Latin America as basically an extension and development of Spanish civilization.

It is in the context of his aesthetic epistemology, then, that one must read Vasconcelos' seminal work on *mestizaje, La raza cósmica* (1925). In this book he articulates systematically his understanding of community as the realization of an aesthetic of *mestizaje*. For Vasconcelos the reality of the mestizo community is understood and appreciated most immediately not through social, political, or even cultural categories, but through aesthetic categories. Indeed, the very words that he uses in his aesthetics to describe the aesthetic transcendence of reason and ethics, *un salto de espíritu* ("a leap of the spirit," or "a spiritual leap") he now uses to describe the transcendent character of the mestizo community, which represents a leap of the spirit beyond homogeneous communities.[15]

The mestizo community supersedes the exclusivist, homogeneous community precisely by virtue of the former's synthetic, that is, aesthetic character. The homogeneous community imposes uniformity either through direct, coercive force or rationally-derived social, political, and economic institutions; the mestizo community represents an aesthetic synthesis, wherein unity is achieved not through domination but through love, or empathy. The mestizo community thus transcends the subject-object dichotomy that underlies exclusivist communities and leads to domination. Defined by an empathic fusion of cultures and peoples, the mestizo community rejects the possibility of setting itself up *in opposition* to other communities, as subject to object, which it can then dominate. This fusion synthesizes the cultures and peoples into a whole, which nevertheless preserves the integrity of the particulars, just as the unitive, aesthetic experience reflects a fusion of subject and object.[16] To realize its very essence, the mestizo

15. Ibid., 2:908.
16. Along with others, Abraham Maslow defines the aesthetic experience as "an identification of the perceiver and the perceived, a fusion of what was two

community seeks an ever greater inclusivity while eschewing both totalitarian domination and atomistic self-sufficiency. According to Vasconcelos, only such an aesthetic experience of community safeguards genuine intersubjectivity, since only in an empathic fusion can the other be related to as an "other," that is as a subject to whom I am inescapably related, or "fused," rather than as merely the object of my knowledge or action. This empathic fusion is what Vasconcelos calls love, the very essence of community. Because this love is the fundamental, constitutive characteristic of the model, mestizo community, it is the very definition of community itself; Vasconcelos replaces the Cartesian *cogito, ergo sum* with *amamus, ergo sumus.*

Liberation theology: The Ethical-Political Praxis of Community

Latin American liberation theology represents not only a critique of individualist rationalism, a fact that is by now common knowledge, but also a critique of aesthetic communitarianism, a fact much less adverted to in the secondary literature.[17] Though implicit in the theological method of liberation theologians, such a critique is made explicit, for instance, in Enrique Dussel's *Philosophy of Liberation:*

> Semiotic, poietic, or poetic beauty finds exposition in the system of the *proyecto* of liberation of the oppressed. . . . That is why its exposition is ugly according to the rules and canons of beauty currently in force; but it is an innovation of the formal coherence of signs and is therefore procreation of the beauty of a new order. The apparent ugliness of the countenance of the oppressed, the withered face of the farmer, the hardened hand of the laborer, the rough skin of the impoverished woman (who cannot buy cosmetics), is the point of departure of the esthetics of liberation. It is entreaty that reveals the popular beauty, the nondominating beauty, the liberator of future beauty. Estheticism is the dominating ideological imposition of the beauty admired by the cultures

---

into a new and larger whole—a super-ordinate unit." *Toward a Psychology of Being* (Princeton, N.J.: Van Nostrand, 1962) 74; see also John H. Haddox, *Vasconcelos of Mexico: Philosopher and Prophet* (Austin, Tex.: University of Texas Press, 1967) 47.

17. Insofar as liberation theology diverges fundamentally from earlier Latin American philosophies of aesthetics, it also diverges from postmodern aestheticism.

of the center and of the oligarchical classes (imposed by the mass media). It is the ideology of beauty.[18]

While not explicitly about aesthetics, an analogous observation is made by Gustavo Gutiérrez in his book *We Drink from Our Own Wells*, where he discusses the post-Vatican II tendency among some First World Christians to replace abstract Cartesian rationalism with a " 'celebration' of the human body in cultural expressions—for example, some modern dances and other bodily forms of expression that are used in eucharistic celebrations."[19] Far from affirming aesthetic synthesis and otherness, the appreciation and celebration of beauty as an antidote to rationalism can function as a denial of historical conflict and suffering, thereby legitimating that very conflict and suffering: Gutiérrez suggests that the crucial question for the Christian is not "Is my body beautiful?" but rather "Is the body of the poor person beautiful?"[20]

The 1992 riots in Los Angeles, for example, were the inevitable consequence of our society's radically different answers to these two questions. We spend billions of dollars each year on makeup, plastic surgery, health spas, health foods and clothes to assure ourselves that *our* bodies are beautiful, while we systematically ignore and desecrate the bodies of the poor. Los Angeles is the paradigm of the "beautiful" community constructed on the backs of the poor, who are in turn relegated to that paradigm of ugliness, the ghetto. South Central Los Angeles is Hollywood's alter ego. Indeed, it is no accident that the riots took place in the very shadow of Hollywood, the capital of North American aestheticism, and Beverly Hills, the home of our leading aesthetes, the beautiful people.

Liberation theologians thus contend that, by virtue of their ahistoricity, a fundamentally aesthetic epistemology and the attendant aesthetics of community overlook the concrete socio-historical, and hence ethical-political character of both beauty and community. That

18. Enrique Dussel, *Philosophy of Liberation* (Maryknoll, N.Y.: Orbis, 1985) 124–25. The text quoted here also alludes to the importance of the ongoing feminist and womanist critiques of aestheticism, an analysis of which is, unfortunately, not possible in this short space.

19. Gustavo Gutiérrez, *We Drink from Our Own Wells: The Spiritual Journey of a People* (Maryknoll, N.Y.: Orbis, 1984) 102.

20. Ibid., 102–03.

is, they overlook the fact that, like reason, beauty and community are always mediated by social, cultural, political, and economic structures and institutions—in short, by ethical-political praxis. Without attention to that mediation, an aesthetic philosophy remains hopelessly abstract. As Latin American liberation theologians have reminded us, beauty and community have a history.

An aesthetic epistemology that privileges either the unitive and synthetic, or the undifferentiatied and indeterminate character of human experience must be grounded in the concrete historical experience of unjust suffering and the struggle against that suffering; both aesthetic synthesis and aesthetic otherness must be grounded in socio-historical otherness. In short, if it is to be liberative, aesthetics must be mediated by the preferential option for the poor. Insofar as the option for the poor mediates an aesthetics of community, the experience of unjust suffering prevents us from dehistorizicing, and hence romanticizing community as the realization of an aesthetic unity of others. An aesthetics of community divorced from ethical-political praxis thus functions as a realized eschatology, with similarly disastrous—in Bowie's words, "politically reactionary"—consequences. The real suffering of the poor, the marginalized, the women is ignored in the face of a dehistoricized community that, as such, will be either explicitly totalitarian by virtue of its homogeneity or implicitly totalitarian by virtue of its inability to take a stand and consequent silent complicity with the status quo. Genuine intersubjectivity is replaced by dysfunctional relationships—all in the name of preserving the beautiful community. And the end is not beauty but death.

An aesthetics of community must thus be born out of the history of suffering. "If one wants the supreme joy of beauty," writes Rubem Alves, "one must be prepared to cry. Sadness is not an intruder in beauty's domains. It is rather the air without which it dies."[21] The pain is an everpresent reminder that the unitive, holistic character of the aesthetic experience reflects a union for which we were born, but which we do not yet possess: "Beauty is sad because beauty is longing. The soul returns to one's lost home. And the return to the "no longer" is always painful. . . . We want to return to beauty, because of the (sad) love story which it tells; because it is the place of

---

21. Rubem Alves, *The Poet, The Warrior, The Prophet* (London: SCM, 1990) 114.

our truth: our lost home. . . ."[22] The Russian philosopher Nicholas Berdyaev writes that "all the beauty in the world is either a remembrance of paradise or a prophecy of a transfigured world."[23]

What is more, we are incapable of remembering paradise unless we are committed to a transfigured world. Only then can aesthetics be truly revolutionary and subversive. "Beauty has its own dialectics," continues Berdyaev, "and Dostoievski has something to say about it. He thought that beauty would save the world. But he also says: 'Beauty is not only a terrible but a mysterious thing. Here the devil struggles with God, and the battlefield is the human heart.' The devil wants to use beauty for his own end.' "[24] In his *The Ideology of the Aesthetic*, Terry Eagleton reminds us that the aesthetic is always ambivalent vis-a-vis history: "If it [i.e., the aesthetic] offers a generous utopian image of reconciliation between men and women at present divided from one another, it also blocks and mystifies the real political movement towards such historical community."[25]

Any premature affirmation of the aesthetic character of community denies human suffering and, in so doing, denies the possibility of authentic, concrete otherness, or intersubjectivity, as constitutive of community. Latin American liberation theologians remind us that the preferential option for the poor makes possible and safeguards the very mestizo community which Vasconcelos wants to affirm. The option for the poor is what makes it possible for a community to obey John Caputo's imperative to "keep the conversation moving."[26]

Liberation theologians remind us that, as Alves writes with such poignance, "beauty has its place in the human heart, which is the centre of the body. The body [especially that of the poor person] is the instrument which sings it."[27] When we countenance the destruction of human beings in their concrete, physical, socio-historical existence, we make authentic intersubjectivity impossible . . . thereby

22. Ibid.
23. Quoted in ibid., 128.
24. Quoted in ibid., 132.
25. Eagleton, 9; "It is unwise," warns Eagleton, "to assume that ambiguity, indeterminacy, undecidability are always subversive strikes against an arrogantly monological certitude; on the contrary, they are the stock-in-trade of many a juridical enquiry and official investigation" (ibid., 379–80).
26. Caputo, *Radical Hermeneutics*, 261.
27. Alves, *The Poet, The Warrior, The Prophet*, 132.

preventing the emergence of that aesthetic community which is always mediated by the body, especially, as Gutiérrez insists, by the body of the poor person. In short, any aesthetics that prescinds from a solidarity with the concrete, physical, socio historical poor can only be a demonic aesthetics. The memory of paradise embodied in the organic unity of the aesthetic community must be mediated by the memories of suffering embodied in the broken lives of the poor and outcast.

The Mestizo Community: Toward a Liberating Aesthetics

In their insistence on the methodological centrality of ethical-political praxis, liberation theologians counter the ahistorical tendencies not only of post-Enlightenment western rationalism but also of aestheticism. If Vasconcelos holds before us the mestizo community as the ideal and model of empathic fusion, liberation theologians insist that any such fusion has a concrete history, a history of violence and conquest. The mestizo community as an ideal remains rooted in the history of the mestizo community as a vanquished community. Otherness has a face . . . and it is not a pretty face. Dare we gaze upon it? Dare we kiss the parched skin? Orlando Espín has written of the ambiguous history of our mestizaje, which emerges out of centuries of political, cultural, racial, and economic exploitation:

> Some Latino groups are the result of the rape of their ancestors by the conquering Spaniards, while others are the outcome of willing *mestizaje*. There are Hispanic communities that trace their roots to the violence of the *encomienda* and others to the violence of the African slave trade. Many were here when the United States either militarily conquered and illegally expropriated their land last century, or bought it without the people's consent to sell. Still others came to the country because they had become the losing victims of political and economic struggles in other lands. But in all cases, the Latino cultural communities are here as the result of vanquishment, of having become the losing victims of someone else's victory.[28]

Furthermore, this experience of vanquishment divides our own Hispanic communities, which are hardly immune to the evils of sex-

28. Orlando Espín, "The God of the Vanquished: Foundations for a Latino Spirituality," *Listening* 27 (Winter 1992) 74.

ism, racism, and classism. Our ability to heal these internal divisions is undermined by an aesthetics of community that, neglecting the history of *mestizaje*, idealizes the experience of *mestizaje*: for example, we cannot ignore the fact that the experience of *mestizaje* has been very different for Hispanic women than it has for Hispanic men. Likewise, the history of *mestizaje*, as a history of vanquishment, prevents us from neglecting the close links between cultural and ethnic violence on the one hand and political and economic violence on the other.

If an aesthetics of community can lead to a premature, and therefore ahistorical resolution of sociohistorical divisions, such an aesthetics remains, nevertheless, a necessary component of a U.S. Hispanic spirituality and theology. Emphasizing the synthetic and indeterminate character of human experience, an aesthetic epistemology prevents the instrumentalization of ethical-political praxis. That is, the aesthetic appreciation and celebration of the mestizo community as an end in itself—as, for example, celebration or "play"—prevents us from viewing community as primarily or exclusively an instrument of social change; aesthetics prevents ethical-political praxis from being judged exclusively by what Vasconcelos calls its "usefulness or uselessness."[29] In turn, to judge praxis exclusively in terms of usefulness or uselessness would be to reify the "distinction between actor and act, agent and 'effect' " thereby instrumentalizing human praxis and community.[30]

The end of liberating praxis is the creation of a society in which all human persons will be treated as ends in themselves, i.e., a society in which human persons are no longer treated as means to some external end, whether that be economic productivity or social change. Vasconcelos reminds us that community is never an object to be

29. See n. 9. As I have explained elsewhere, an aesthetics of community would not "deny the productive and transformative dimension of the arts, e.g., poetry, drama, dance, worship, music, but would ground that dimension in the intrinsic end of artistic performance." "Theology as Intellectually Vital Inquiry," *Proceedings of the Catholic Theological Society of America* 46 (1991) 64.

30. Dana R. Villa, "Beyond Good and Evil: Arendt, Nietzsche, and the Aestheticization of Political Action," *Political Theory* 20 (May 1992) 276. In this article, Villa argues that the performance model of praxis developed by Nietzsche and Arendt in their critiques of the Platonic instrumentalization of action "enables them to conceive action as self-contained, as immanently valuable in its greatness or beauty" (ibid.).

molded, fashioned, and transformed, however desirable the end product; rather, community is fundamentally an aesthetic *performance,* an intersubjectivity to be lived and celebrated.[31] In other words, community is a byproduct of genuine love, where empathic fusion does not erase but preserves concrete human otherness. This is the ideal of the mestizo community, a new community that emerges out of the confluence of races and cultures but where the historical particularity of those races and cultures is respected and affirmed.

Though U.S. Hispanics are rediscovering the power of that ideal as a liberating force in the lives of our communities, we also remember that the aesthetic, mestizo community which Vasconcelos described does not yet exist. The victims of history, including those within our own communities, bear witness to this disquieting fact. Indeed, it is in the interest of the dominant culture to idealize the United States and, more specifically, U.S. Hispanics as a model, mestizo community, for such idealization effectively severs the causal link between the history of conquest and the history of *mestizaje. Mestizaje* can become a cultural ideal to be pursued without socioeconomic consequences.

As evidence of our desire to create a "mestizo community," we might then be tempted to extol the virtues of Mexican-American fiestas, African-American music, and Native American rituals without exhibiting the slightest concern about life in the barrios, ghettos, and reservations throughout this country. Those beautiful cultural expressions become unhinged from the histories of suffering and conquest in which they were born. Uprooted from their integral and historical link to the oppressed communities' struggle for liberation, i.e., ethical-political praxis, those aesthetic expressions become mere commodities to be consumed in the search for multiculturalism—i.e., the postmodern self-as-montage.[32] Our solidarity with the poor would then no longer de-

---

31. Hannah Arendt defines freedom precisely in terms of such an aesthetic performance (as opposed to the "making" of an aesthetic object, in the process of which human action is instrumentalized). She contends that the meaning of freedom "as inherent in action . . . is best rendered by 'virtuosity,' that is, an excellence we attribute to the performing arts (as distinguished from the creative arts of making), *where the accomplishment lies in the performance itself* and not in the end product which outlasts the activity that brought it into existence and becomes independent of it" (quoted in ibid., 279).

32. Walter Benjamin has argued that the instrumentalization of art in moder-

mand a commitment to economic justice but merely an "openness to multicultural perspectives." We can throw on our *serapes* and rest content in our "option for the poor." In a world where poverty seems more intractable than ever, multiculturalism offers a seductive and all-too-easy alternative to the option for the poor.[33]

Likewise, in the midst of a "second *mestizaje,*" we U.S. Hispanics are appropriately concerned about affirming and preserving our community and family values in the face of an individualistic society. Yet these efforts will be fruitless unless we can examine how, in the North American context, so-called family values, or the values of "community," have legitimated the privatization of religion and morality, thereby serving to rationalize the very individualistic economic system which we find so alienating.[34] Just as aesthetics and community mean different things to conqueror and victim, so too does the notion of family values. The family values of Rigoberta Menchú, who witnessed the cold-blooded murder of so many of her relatives, are not the family values of Dan Quayle. Our family values are not their family values; our unity is not their unity, nor is our otherness their otherness. And what separates them is precisely history itself.

The struggle by Latinos and Latinas to create a mestizo community thus demands that we integrate these two important currents of our intellectual history: aesthetics and liberating ethical-political praxis. Yet that integration must not be understood as a "balancing" or "tension" between the two; the process of "balancing" is always a con-

---

nity, through techniques of mechanical reproduction, results precisely in this severing of the intrinsic relationship between a work of art and its socio-historical context, in which the now-objectified "work" of art had initially been a performance, or ritual; "The Work of Art in the Age of Mechanical Reproduction," in *Illuminations* (New York: Schocken, 1955) 217-51.

33. On the dangers of a dehistoricized multiculturalism that remains blind to the political and economic dimensions of culture, see Daniel Lazare, "The Cult of Multiculturalism," *The Village Voice,* May 7, 1991, 29-31.

34. As Russell Berman argues, "family values" play an important role in the alliance between apolitical, postmodern aestheticism and late capitalist consumerism: "The atomistic individual [of modernity], denied any inherited mechanism of self-identification, finds a helping hand in the world of commerce which proceeds to organize private lives in aesthetic terms: the life-style as the new colonial dumping ground for industrial overproduction. The atomized life that has been denied an authentic social context (family, community) becomes the object of commodified aestheticization." Berman, *Modern Culture and Critical Theory,* 88.

ceptual process, since what are balanced are always two concepts or ideas. Rather, aesthetics must be grounded in the ethical-political praxis of liberation, or the preferential option for the poor. From the perspective of the victims of history, aesthetics is forced to shed its political innocence, and otherness takes on flesh and blood. Yet, as the mediator of an aesthetics of community, the struggle for liberation remains open to transcendence, to indeterminacy, and attentive to the intrinsic value of human praxis as an end in itself, irreducible to any single historical project.

U.S. Hispanic Spirituality

The popular religiosity of U.S. Hispanics reveals a spirituality that unites ethical-political praxis and aesthetics insofar as it celebrates life—specifically the communal life—but does so in the very midst of the daily confrontation with the purveyors of death. That spirituality, centered largely though certainly not exclusively on the symbols of the cross and Mary, has functioned as a source of self-empowerment precisely inasmuch as it has presumed an intrinsic and necessary connection between the aesthetic celebration of life and the struggle for liberation. One might even go so far as to say that in that connection lies our very identity, an identity expressed in our popular religiosity.[35] Given the urgency of the liberation struggle, and given the seeming incapacity of aesthetic models to address social problems, the aesthetic dimension of popular religious expressions and devotions has not always been given adequate attention by liberation theologians in Latin America, with the result that, at times, popular religosity has been either instrumentalized in the service of political liberation or simply ignored outright. This lacuna has been corrected in recent years.[36]

35. As Robert Schreiter observes, "celebrations frequently serve to reaffirm identity both in terms of who belongs to the group and in terms of how the world is to be perceived." *Constructing Local Theologies* (Maryknoll, N.Y.: Orbis, 1985) 62. In the specific case of U.S. Hispanic popular religiosity, Orlando Espín and Sixto García argue that "it [i.e., popular religiosity] is probably the least 'Angloed' area of any of the Hispanic-American cultures, the least 'invaded' and thus the more deeply 'ours'." "Hispanic-American Theology," *Proceedings of the Catholic Theological Society of America* 42 (1987) 114–15.

36. It must be noted that a number of Latin American liberation theologians *have* recognized the importance of popular religiosity, e.g., Segundo Galilea and

In dialogue with our Latin American colleagues, U.S. Hispanic theologians have contributed to this process of correction. Our experience of community as a celebrative "aesthetic praxis" rooted in a liberating ethical-political praxis is, for U.S. Hispanics, a principal locus for a spirituality centered on the symbols of the cross and Mary.

As the central symbol of our history of suffering, through which we are identified with the crucified Jesus, the cross is neither a way station nor a counterbalance to the resurrection, the central symbol of that empathic fusion which overcomes all division and alienation. Rather, the cross is the place where we experience the resurrection . . . in the midst of our refusal to accept the cross as God's final word. In the midst of vanquishment, conquest, and abandonment, we too continue to struggle for liberation, hoping against hope and crying out "My God, my God, why have you abandoned me?" "The language of the cross," observes Gutiérrez, ". . . is a synthesis of the prophetic [i.e., ethical-political praxis] and the contemplative [i.e, the aesthetic unity of others and Other] and the only appropriate way of talking about the God of Jesus Christ."[37]

The two great symbols "that appear to be central and organizing symbols in Hispanic popular Catholicism," are the crucified Christ and Mary—and these are inextricably related in our spirituality.[38] As Espín and García point out:

> It would be difficult to find a Catholic Church in Latin America, or even in a U.S. Hispanic barrio, without an image of the suffering Christ. The craftsmen and artificers spare no sensibilities in

Juan Carlos Scannone. Others, such as Raúl Vidales and Hugo Assmann, however, have seen it as intrinsically ahistorical. Arthur McGovern notes that "in recent years, . . . many liberation theologians have come to value popular religion more highly and to recognize its positive features. . . . Consequently many recent studies have looked for the positive, potentially liberating aspects of popular religion." *Liberation Theology and Its Critics: Toward an Assessment* (Maryknoll, N.Y.: Orbis, 1989) 90–91. Robert Schreiter makes a similar observation: "In a second period of its [i.e., liberation theology's] development, it became evident that the exclusion of folk religion (religiosidad popular) from consideration in the building up of liberation theology was a mistake." *Constructing Local Theologies,* 43.

37. Gustavo Gutiérrez, *On Job* (Maryknoll, N.Y.: Orbis, 1987) 100.

38. Orlando Espín, "Tradition and Popular Religion: An Understanding of the *Sensus Fidelium,*" *Frontiers of Hispanic Theology in the United States,* ed. Allan Figueroa Deck, S.J. (Maryknoll, N.Y.: Orbis, 1992) 70.

conveying, in wood and paint, the agony and suffering of their blood-covered Christs. . . . Hispanic popular participation in the Paschal triduum traditionally emphasizes the celebration of Good Friday. . . . The Paschal Vigil and Easter celebration, in some instances, are quite anticlimatic to the celebration of Good Friday.[39]

The authors explain that the symbols and popular religious devotions surrounding Jesus' passion "represent the co-suffering of Jesus the Christ with the poor, the hungry and the oppressed of the celebrating Hispanic communities."[40] When read through the lenses of modernity, these practices may be dismissed as morbid and "unhealthy" glorifications of suffering. When read through the lenses of postmodernity, they may be idealized as aesthetic representations of otherness. Both interpretations, however, would be *mis*interpretations precisely because both would abstract the U.S. Hispanic spirituality of the cross from its historical context, wherein the people's persistent cry, "My God, my God, why have you abandoned me?" echoes Jesus' cry on the cross and, in so doing, represents the oppressed community's refusal to accept death as the final word. As surely as Jesus' cry, with its implicit refusal to stop believing in "my God, my God," revealed the utter powerlessness of the principalities and powers in their attempt to crush him, so too does our people's cry on the cross reveal the impotence of the dominant society in its attempt to effect an "aesthetic" unity through coercion and co-optation—or to relativize our suffering by turning it into a disembodied example of "otherness" that can make no ethical-political claims vis-á-vis concrete others. "I AM A PERSON"—no statement is more revolutionary or liberating than this. It was implicit in Jesus' cry on the cross, and is at the very heart of our community's identification with the crucified Jesus.

The crucified Christ of Latino popular religiosity is a symbol whose aesthetic, evocative power is derived not only from its value as a work of art but from its semiotic history within that community and its religious performances. It is this history that lends the symbol its transformative power: "Though many of these images or paintings [of the crucified Christ] may have true artistic value in themselves, the

39. Espín and García, "Hispanic-American Theology," 85.

40. Espín and García, "Sources of Hispanic Theology" (unpublished paper delivered at the Catholic Theological Society of America convention, Toronto, 1988) 10.

religious value is usually conveyed not by beauty itself but by the work's ability to elicit feelings of solidarity and compassion."[41] This solidarity and compassion becomes, in turn, the basis of the community's identity and, thus, of its ability to withstand and resist the imposition of identity from without—the very concern of postmodernists. What makes such solidarity and compassion possible is the community's own experience of crucifixion: "His [i.e., the crucified Christ's] passion and death express his solidarity with all men and women throughout history who have also innocently suffered at the hands of evildoers."[42] Only when viewed within the context of his own history does the cross of Jesus attain ethical-political significance as a symbol of empowerment and liberation; only when viewed within the context of our history as a community does the crucified Jesus attain ethical-political significance as a symbol of hope.

It is not the vivid depiction of Jesus' suffering that induces passivity and resignation. Precisely the opposite is the case: what induces passivity and resignation is the premature dehistoricization of the cross, whereby it is divorced from its own history. I would suggest that the sense of hope and empowerment is much more palpable, for example, in most barrio churches, with their bleeding, contorted images of the Crucified, than in most Anglo, suburban churches with their ostensibly more "hopeful," more "liberating," and more "aesthetically pleasing" images of the resurrected Christ, with arms gloriously outstretched, superimposed on an all-but-invisible cross.

And thus, the second major symbol in U.S. Hispanic popular religiosity is a symbol of hope in the midst of death, the symbol of Mary: "People celebrate the passion events with processions, where parish or community leaders bear the bleeding image of the suffering Christ, followed by the icon or statue of *la Madre Dolorosa* (The Sorrowful Mother)."[43] In the community's religious rituals these images are mutually implicit, for Mary is the mother of the crucified Jesus—and, therefore, the mother of her crucified children.

This is nowhere more evident than in the symbol of and devotion to Our Lady of Guadalupe. In Mary's identification with the poor

41. Espín, "Tradition and Popular Religion," 70.
42. Ibid., 71.
43. Espín and García, "Hispanic-American Theology," 85; see also Espín, "Tradition and Popular Religion," 70–71.

indigenous man, Juan Diego, and in the historical coincidence of the apparition with the emergence of the Mexican people, Guadalupe *is the Mexican people*, the mestizo community that is literally resurrected in the midst of the conquest. Virgilio Elizondo notes this historical relationship:

> I do not know of any other event in the history of Christianity that stands at the very source of the birth of a people like the appearance of Our Lady of Guadalupe. . . . Guadalupe is not just an apparition, but a major intervention of God's liberating power in history. It is an Exodus and Resurrection event of an enslaved and dying people. . . . Guadalupe is truly an epiphany of God's love at the precise moment when abandonment by God had been experienced by the people at large. . . . It is in this climate of the stench and the cries of death that the new and unsuspected beginning would take place. Like the resurrection itself, it came at the moment when everything appeared to be finished. . . . The natives who previously had wanted only to die now wanted to live; dances, songs, pilgrimages, and festivities resumed![44]

Guadalupe represents the birth of the aesthetic, the beautiful, out of and within the history of suffering, out of and within the concrete history of otherness. In the midst of our crucifixion, Guadalupe has affirmed our identity as a people: "Her presence is not a pacifier but an energizer which gives meaning, dignity and hope to the marginated and suffering of today's society. Her presence is the new power of the powerless to triumph over the violence of the powerful."[45] Thus, she affirms the liberating power of the cross as the place where the mestizo community is given birth: "Races and nations had been opposed to each other, but as the mother of all the inhabitants of these lands, she would provide the basis for a new unity."[46]

The ethical-political, liberative power of popular religiosity thus derives from the very fact that, when arising within a history of oppression, the popular religious affirmation of the life of the suffering community as valuable *in and of itself*, i.e., as beautiful, is implicitly

44. Virgilio Elizondo, *The Future is Mestizo* (Bloomington, Ind.: Meyer-Stone, 1988) 59–64.

45. Virgilio Elizondo, *La Morenita: Evangelizer of the Americas* (San Antonio: Mexican American Cultural Center, 1980) 120.

46. Ibid., 64.

and necessarily already an ethical-political act. In the context of conquest and vanquishment, the victim's affirmation of his or her own personhood (i.e., the beauty of the poor person's body) and, therefore, of his or her own life as *intrinsically* valuable is the most basic and most radical of political acts—the single political act without which all political strategies for change are doomed to fail.

In U.S. Hispanic popular spirituality, the mestizo community, aesthetic unity, and the resurrection of a new, mestizo people (Vasconcelos' *la raza cósmica*), are mediated by a history of conquest, the crucifixion of a people, and the struggle for survival in the face of crucifixion. For us the only genuine beauty, the authentic mestizo community, is that born from suffering; more precisely, that born from the faith, hope, and love which endure in the midst of suffering. The epistemological privilege of the victims pertains not only to ethics, politics, and theology but also to aesthetics, not only to our definition of the good and the true but also to our definition of the beautiful. If our philosophical and theological anthropologies can no longer remain deaf to the voices of the non-persons, our aesthetics can no longer remain blind to the countenances of the non-"beautiful." Only they, the "ugly," have the right to define beauty. Only the victims have the right to define the ideal, aesthetic, or mestizo community. Only they can tell us when and where authentic community, the mestizo community, exists. Thus, the aesthetic, mestizo community will be born on the cross, in the ethical-political praxis of liberation, or it will not be born at all.

A Spirituality of Mercy:
Aelred of Rievaulx*

Katherine M. TePas

Characteristics of Our Culture at the Juncture

We are here to reflect together on spirituality at the juncture of modernity and postmodernity. What are the characteristics of our culture at this juncture? What are the questions and concerns of the human spirit? My reflections in these introductory remarks will focus on that culture which I have had the most time to ponder: the youth and academic culture in the United States as it moves toward the third-millennium. Six years of high-school teaching, years of graduate studies at three universities, and my first semester of teaching at the university level have not made me an expert on the postmodern world, but they have given me plenty to ponder.

Two summers ago I was one of a dozen individuals taking an intensive Latin course at a university in the Chicago area. We were all aspiring scholars, united by our common effort to memorize Latin grammar and painstakingly work our way through Cicero's *De amicitia*. In spite of this common ground, we had an underlying philosophical and spiritual diversity that fascinated me. We included a devout Mormon; a young evangelical whose eyes sparkled when he spoke of knowing Jesus personally; a Catholic who appreciated the Jesus story, but not necessarily the person of Jesus; a philosophy professor who did not believe in God but admired the rigorous thought of Catholic philosophers such as Aquinas and Alasdair MacIntyre; and a second

* This paper was presented at the January 9–12, 1993 "Scholars' Retreat" sponsored by The Abbey Center For The Study Of Ethics And Culture, Inc. at the Abbey of Gethsemani, Trappist, Kentucky.

atheist who thought some people had eternal souls, while others, as revealed through their eyes, seemed to be dead already.

One of the most vibrant characters in our group was an impassioned humanist who had rejected, years ago, his Christian upbringing. He still believed in a subtle and awesome mystery which permeated the universe and an almost infinite untapped capacity within each human spirit. This last Latin comrade was deeply concerned about the thousands of youth, especially those in the inner city, who had not even begun to develop their human potential. Many of these never knew the joy of learning because their lives had been sidetracked into patterns of drugs and violence. His concerns were graphically substantiated by the daily news reports on rising gang warfare that plagued Chicago's inner city.

One undeniable mark of this culture at the juncture of modernity and postmodernity is plurality. There is a diversity in ethnic backgrounds, goals, political ideals, patterns of thinking, religious beliefs, and moral practices. This was obvious even in the Latin course. Diversity is sometimes seen as an end in itself. When I asked a bright and pensive college senior what he wanted to do with his life, he responded ''be different.'' When I further inquired for what purpose or reason he wanted to be different, he had no answer. Apparently being different was a sufficiently worthy goal in itself.

Most observers of our culture see no sign that this diversity will decrease in the coming years: different ethnic and religious groups continue to come to the United States and the multi-cultural movement at universities appears to be gaining strength. Ideologies which encouraged a melting-pot culture, such as nationalism, seem to have lost their primacy. The balance has tipped from a focus on ''one nation'' to a focus on the rights and freedom of the individual to do, think, and believe whatever he or she pleases. The lonely isolation of a radical individualism is usually avoided by the creation of a plethora of interest groups, each championing its separate causes. In some areas the walls of ethnic ghettos have been broken down, only to be rebuilt by equally isolated interest-group ghettos.

This diversity and concern for group rights is accompanied by a sensitivity to social justice issues—or at least a great deal of talk devoted to social justice issues. Students are quick to criticize any comment that appears to be unfair or prejudiced, including comments which place one race, one ideology, or one religion above another. They are also aware of the almost incomprehensible suffering endured in far-away, famine-stricken countries and among the homeless in their own cities.

The majority of people I have encountered, however, do very little to help: their right and freedom to pursue their own happiness takes precedence. They may bring a can of cranberry sauce for a Thanksgiving food drive, but, for the most part, they let others worry about the suffering masses. The students seem to assume that if all have the rights and freedom to do whatever they want, then the suffering people can solve their own problems. When discussing whether or not they could morally spend $100,000 on a car, the chorus argued that if they fairly earned the money they had the right to spend it as they pleased. As part of their own academic communities, the students rest secure in their isolation.

In addition to diversity, an awareness of social justice issues, and each person having an overriding concern for his or her own pursuit of happiness, this age also seems marked by an intellectual ambiguity. The willingness to let others believe whatever they please has been accompanied by an absence of rigorous intellectual conversations. A postmodern combination of relativism and perhaps intellectual sloth seems to prevent people from trying to discern which idea or belief might be more accurate. Students rarely speak in terms of truth and tend to react against anyone who claims to grasp a truth: such a claim seems cruel to them because it necessarily condemns someone else's position as false. There is rarely any common hunger to find the truth and hence rarely any desire or ability to dialogue with others to find it. This lack of dialogue further isolates separate interest groups and belief systems.

Moreover, not only do students seem to doubt anyone's ability to discover some ideological truth, they are also beginning to doubt whether physical and social sciences can ever solve the riddles of the universe and the suffering of human society. There is a certain loss of confidence and hope. They have accepted the inevitability of change—change in society as well as change in text-book answers— but they are no longer convinced that with change comes inevitable progress. There were medical breakthroughs in cancer research, but new, more horrible medical disasters such as AIDS appear before the problem of cancer has been solved. The iron curtain finally fell, but brutal civil wars erupted. Germany was reunited and a neo-Nazi movement began. There was a sense of freedom which accompanied the sexual revolution, but free-sex itself became a mandatory ritual—with the young women getting themselves drunk in order to participate.

Such a loss of hope was combined with a certain distrust among those in the Latin course. The humanist did speak enthusiastically of his hope of one day founding a new kind of school which would revitalize students who dropped out of the regular system. Nevertheless, most of the others spoke of his plans as a foolish dream doomed to failure. They did not share his belief in an innate human goodness which lay dormant, waiting to be awakened in rough, uneducated youth. As already noted, one student believed some humans were already walking dead.

Then there was the bitterness that developed in the main area we had in common: our efforts to learn Latin. Those who did well looked down on those who were struggling unsuccessfully to keep up, and accused them of laziness. One student was convinced he could not survive the course and dropped out. Those who continued the struggle looked on those who seemed to do well with relative ease and accused them of a cold-hearted arrogance.

One of the most poignant comments about our culture came from a big-hearted senior who was not part of the Latin course. He and his live-in girlfriend were together raising their two-year-old daughter. They had been faithful to each other for three years and talked of marrying after he graduated. As his graduation drew near, I asked him how the marriage plans were coming along. With a pained expression he said that he was not sure if he believed in marriage any more. I assumed he was going to give me some 1960s-style answer which argued that their love did not need the approval of any authority or the legitimization of some piece of paper. Instead he sighed and explained that he was becoming more and more convinced that all relationships inevitably dissolve into bitter quarrels.

The final characteristic of our culture which I would like to mention is in direct tension with the diversity, the loss of hope, and the seemingly ever present quarrels. It is an unrelenting hunger for relatedness. My students are quick to argue that everyone is radically unique, choosing for herself or himself some personal set of values that will bring happiness. They claim, at first, that there are no universal human values. Upon further examination, however, they all admit that there is still at least one thing that everyone desires: they agree with Cicero that all long to love and be loved.

Thus at the juncture of modernity and postmodernity, a spirituality is needed that can survive and even blaze forth in a pluralistic, ambiguous, and suffering world. A spirituality is needed which can unite people who do not share common values, beliefs, or ways of thinking, people who have retreated into separate interest-group ghettos. A spirituality is needed which can give hope to people who have lost confidence in scientific and social progress; people who have also lost confidence in themselves and one another; people who have lost confidence in the possibility of permanent relationships, yet people who still yearn to love and be loved.

Our culture has been humbled. This, in itself, is not necessarily a problem. The danger with being humbled, however, is that we can slip into despair.

Aelred's Spirituality of Mercy

A wise friend once quipped that there is a simple answer to every problem, and it is usually wrong. With that stated, I will nevertheless propose for your reflection and critique a somewhat simple answer. I hope that the answer I am tentatively putting forth, when combined with the corrections and different approaches of others, may help meet the spiritual needs of the postmodern world. To explore this answer, I will draw extensively from the works of Aelred of Rievaulx. My proposed answer for a spirituality at the junction of modernity and postmodernity is a spirituality of mercy.

Those familiar with Aelred may be surprised that I intend to use his works to reflect on a spirituality of mercy, rather than on spiritual friendship. Yes, he is the twelfth-century Cistercian abbot who is most famous for his treatise on friendship, *De spirituali amicitia*. Mercy, however, was also one of his favorite topics—both God's mercy toward humanity and humans' mercy toward each other—and I believe that his insights on mercy are more relevant to the topic. Let me justify my choice with a brief explanation of how Aelred understood the difference between friendship and mercy.[1]

1. Aelred's term is *misericordia* and his understanding of this term is formed primarily through meditations on Scripture. In the Vulgate, *misericordia* is used in place of the Hebrew *hesed* and the Greek *eleos*. In English translations it can appear as mercy, steadfast love, loving-kindness, or covenant love. It is the steadfast love of God which gave the author of Lamentations hope (Lam 3:22). It is the

Friendship, according to *De spirituali amicitia*, was the original model for all human relationships. Adam and Eve were created to be friends and all humans were meant to enjoy the mutual affection of friendship love. Friendship is also the model of relationships in the heavenly life. In that state of final perfection God will pour friendship upon all, who will pour it upon each other and back upon him. Yet in the time between the original perfection and final glory, friendship cannot exist among all. Jealousy, pride, selfishness, distrust, and a host of other ills have prevented universal friendship. True friendship does not, according to Aelred's thought, require friends to be mirror images of each other. Yet it does require both parties to have attained already a certain level of virtue and to share already a common understanding of life's goal. True friends, according to Aelred, are attracted to each other because of the goodness they see in each other.

Mercy, on the other hand, was not needed in the original peace of the garden of Eden and will not be needed in eschatological glory. It is not needed when love and affection flow easily from all toward all. It is only when humans become divided by bitterness, quarrels, and rivalries that there is a place for mercy. Mercy appears only after mutual love has grown cold and humans are too weak to unite with God and each other. When no other type of love can effectively unite alienated spirits, mercy comes forth and unites them. Unlike friendship love, mercy flows outward toward another without having first to see any goodness in the other.

After examining as best I can the situation at the juncture of the modern and postmodern world, I think that it is mercy, not friendship that is the necessary foundation for a spirituality today. Our culture, taken as a whole, is not ready to begin with friendship. A spirituality which fosters friendship and draws strength from friendship is a later stage. Among ourselves we have too great a diversity in ideals, vision, foundational beliefs, and ways of thinking for friendship. There is also too little trust and too little trustworthiness among rival idealogies for friendship to take root.

If I may so speculate, I think Aelred would have rather spoken

---

covenant love of God in Hosea that initiated the love relationship without having to be loved first, and which longed to restore the relationship when the beloved ceased to love (Hos 2:19). Depending on the context, it is also akin to *agape* and *caritas*.

on mercy if he were with us today. (And, I will frequently let him speak, since I find that my attempts to paraphrase sap too much of the rhetorical beauty and force out of his reflections.) Meditating on mercy seemed to make his soul sing. While he loved God's power and splendor which were revealed through creation, he delighted even more in God's mercy which was revealed in the incarnation.

Only at the incarnation, when God embraced sinful humanity, was the otherwise inconceivable magnitude of God's love fully revealed. Mercy is that ineffable kindness by which God gazes upon the miserable and desires to surrender his power and shed his splendor in order to be with them.[2] Mercy is the love revealed during the Christmas season, the love of Emmanuel, God with us:

> His name is Emmanuel, which means, God with us. With us, indeed, is God. In the past God was above us. In the past, God was against us. But today Emmanuel, today God is with us in our nature, with us in his grace; with us in our weaknesses, with us in his goodness; with us in our misery, with us in his mercy. God is with us through love, with us through kindness, with us through affection, with us through compassion. O Emmanuel, O God with us. How are you, O sons of Adam? God is with us. With us. You were unable, O sons of Adam, to ascend to heaven in order to be with God. So God descended from heaven so that he may be Emmanuel, God with us. He cast himself out so that he may be Emmanuel, God with us. . . . In what manner could he possibly be more with me? Small and insignificant as I am, weak as I am, naked as I am, impoverished as I am. In all things he conformed himself to me, taking up all that is mine and surrendering all that is his.[3]

Thus Aelred dwelt on the love of Emmanuel, a merciful love which not only *is capable* of uniting with those that are separated by sins and weaknesses, separated by radical differences, not only is it capable of uniting with these, it *longs* to unite with these.

2. *Sermo* 31 *"In apparitione domini," Aelredi Rievallensis Sermones I–XLVI: collectio Claraevallensis prima et secunda*, ed. Raciti, Corpus Christionorum Continuatio Mediaevalis 2A (Turnholt: Brepols Editores Pontificii, 1989).

3. *"In annunctatione Dominica," Sermones inediti B. Aelredi abbatis Rievallensi*, ed. C. H. Talbot, Series scriptorum S. Ordinis Cisterciensis, vol. 1 (Rome: Apud Curiam Generalem Sacri Ordinins Cisterciensis, 1952) 91. If there is no published translation of a text, as in this case, the translations in the article are mine.

Mercy is a love which longs to "come down" to the weak and suffering without any of the negative connotations attached to "condescend." Mercy does not appear in splendid dress to pass out food, clothes, donations for the homeless. Instead mercy surrenders its splendor and becomes one of the hungry, naked, and homeless. Mercy is so consumed by its gaze on the other, its concern for the other, that it has no room for thinking of itself as better than the other. It is the refusal, even in the case of an all-perfect God, to be considered as any better than the most wretched human.

Mercy is the self-emptying love of a God who yearns to be with humans in their suffering. Mercy's power, however, is not limited to this coming down to be one with the suffering. Mercy also raises the suffering up: it heals, strengthens, renews, and recreates. Aelred reflected on Christ's passion, observing that: "He who is as bread for us, hungered himself. He who is the fountain, thirsted. He who is strength, wearied. He who is life, died. Yet his hunger fed us, his thirst inebriated us, his exhaustion refreshed us, his death gave us life. This is his work of mercy."[4]

Mercy heals and gives new life because it does more than simply suffer with the other. It actually absorbs others' suffering so they no longer bear its full weight. When mercy unites with sinners it does not act "holier than thou." Instead it mysteriously absorbs the sin and lets itself be treated as "more sinful than thou." Mercy, in its strong and steadfast embrace of sinners, shields them and takes on the scorn and punishment they deserve.

Aelred used the story of Samson and Delilah to meditate on the strength of mercy's embrace. Samson, a figure of Christ, falls in love with the harlot Delilah, a figure of sinful humanity. Rather than abandoning her, he lets himself be caught, bound and ridiculed. As part of sinful humanity, Aelred spoke to Christ, his Samson: "These your chains were certainly mine. Not you, but I was held by these, debased by these, enchained by these. But what is it, my Lord, my Samson, my sun, my light, which finally captured you, finally held you, finally enchained you. You fell asleep in the bosom of Delilah, the harlot. O love wonderfully burning, . . . bringing down the heights, making strength weak, emptying majesty. . . . That Samson was held, that he was bound, that he did not break the usual chains, was not because

4. *Sermo* 12 *"In die sancto paschae"* 20, CCCM 2A.

of weakness, but because of love."[5] In the end Samson dies. Yet in dying he crushes the power of the Philistines who symbolize the powers of sin which had entrapped humans and bound them to suffer eternal death.

Throughout his meditations on the gospels, Aelred focused on Christ's mercy, revealed in his gentleness and compassion toward sinners. "He did not shrink from the prostitute's touch or the publican's table; he took the defense of one adulteress so she would not be stoned and conversed with another that she might somehow after being an adulteress, become an evangelist."[6]

Note again the transforming power of mercy! Mercy is not a blind love which flows out amorphously toward the masses. It fixes its gaze on individuals and sees all their faults, imperfections, and sins. It knows that one is a prostitute, another a publican, another an adulteress. Yet only because it simultaneously recognizes sin and continues to love, can it inspire a change. Here, in a reference to the woman at the well, merciful love transformed an adulteress into an evangelist. This mercy, in Aelred's mind, is so unexpected, so extraordinary, so powerful, that it works a transformation in those who receive it. Merciful love, not the threat of justice, inspires a freely chosen interior change. The woman who was almost stoned for adultery did not give up her adultery because she was almost put to death under the justice of the law. She gave up her adultery because of the mercy which spared her life. Mercy *did* say "sin no more," but without condemning, and it inspired a transformation.

Indeed, as Aelred told the stories of sinners' encounters with mercy, one imagines the transformed sinners beginning their new life bursting with joy. They seem unable to keep both feet on the ground, dancing and leaping and praising God; or as if completely lifted up from the earth, with newly grown wings, soaring like eagles.

For Aelred, mercy was not restricted to Christ's days on earth. It is the steadfast love of God which continues to visit and console humans. It is the way God always first approaches humans. Mercy comes first because it can pierce through humans' hardened hearts and

---

5. "*In die pasche*," *Sermones Inediti*, 98.

6. *Speculum caritatis* 3.5.13. English translation from *Mirror of Charity*, trans. Elizabeth Connor, O.C.S.O., intro. Charles Dumont, O.C.S.O., Cistercian Fathers Series, no. 17 (Kalamazoo: Cistercian Publications, 1990).

closed minds. Through its unexpected kindness it restores hope and gives the strength to change. "By its force of penetration, cutting through all the doors of the mind that have been locked with the bolts of vice, it imprints some kiss of its sweetness on lips still unclean and by its ineffable pleasantness coaxes the straying back, draws the hesitant close, and gives new life to the hopeless."[7]

When Aelred referenced his own conversion, he noted that he too was visited first by God's mercy. He was never very clear about the nature of his sins and did not dwell on the details of his life before he entered Rievaulx. Yet by piecing together comments from his own writings, we know that he was living at a king's court, surrounded by some of the best things that type of life can offer: a circle of worldly friends, physical comforts, prestige. (The same things many Americans so fervently seek for happiness.) Nevertheless, in several of his works he wrote of this period as one of filled with inner suffering:

> Very deep within me was my wound, crucifying, terrifying, and corrupting everything within me with an intolerable stench. Had you not quickly stretched out your hand to me, O Lord, unable to endure myself I might perhaps have resorted to the worst remedy of despair.[8]

> Habits of sensual pleasure oppressed [me]. But you who "hear the groans of the prisoners and free the children of the slain," broke my chains asunder. You who offer your paradise to harlots and publicans turned me, the worst of them all, back to yourself.[9]

> How generous was his grace in following me when I fled, in allaying my fears, restoring me to hope as often as I was in despair, overwhelming my ingratitude with his kindness? I had grown accustomed to filthy pleasures and he drew me to himself and led me on by the taste of interior sweetness. He struck off the unbreakable shackles of bad habit. He rescued me from the world and welcomed me with kindness. I say nothing of the many and great works of his mercy towards me, lest any of the glory which belongs wholly to it should be deflected on to me.[10]

7. Ibid., 2.11.26.
8. Ibid., 1.28.79.
9. Ibid., 1.28.82.
10. *De institutione inclusarum* 32. English translation from *The Works of Aelred of Rievaulx*, vol. I, *Treatises, Pastoral Prayer*, Cistercian Fathers Series, no. 2 (Spencer, Mass.: Cistercian Publications, 1971).

Up to this point, I have been focussing on Aelred's praise of God's mercy toward humans, including himself. Aelred also believed firmly that humans who were filled with Christ's spirit would be inspired to similar acts of mercy toward others. When divine mercy flows through one human toward other humans, it is no longer the case of a perfect being loving the imperfect, but rather an imperfect human loving another imperfect human, one who has received mercy offering mercy to another; one who continues to need mercy loving another who will also always need mercy.

Aelred described the initial experience of God's mercy as a delightful sweetness that allowed a sinner to release his or her grip on all other sources of pleasure. Through mercy God draws the sinner to himself in a comforting embrace. In mercy, God also draws those who are delighting in such an embrace to give up this consolation in order to serve others. Mercy compels those caught up in the joys of contemplation to "come down" and take on the griefs of others. Thus a pastor who is lingering in the consolations of prayer may be upbraided by God's spirit for neglecting those who need his or her correction, counsel, words of mercy, and encouragement. If tempted to complain about having to abandon the sweetness of prayer, Aelred counseled the soul to recall that "Christ died in order that he who lives may not live for himself." Furthermore, this movement toward others can be done joyfully because the soul is not really being pulled away from God: the merciful God travels with those who serve.[11]

The beatitudes promise that those who show mercy will later receive mercy. Aelred, however, noticed that the reverse is also true: those who have received merciful love are often those who most generously bestow it on others. In this way mercy spreads and multiplies itself. St. Paul was a favorite of Aelred's, for in Paul he saw most clearly the mirroring of God's forgiving and merciful love. Why did Aelred think Paul loved so well? Because Paul was forgiven so much. Indeed Aelred believed God forgave Paul's many sins not because Paul already loved much but so that Paul would be able to love much. The immense love God poured upon Paul transformed him so that he not only loved God deeply, but loved others deeply. Paul, more than all the other apostles, was most animated by Christ's self-emptying and suffering love. Paul did not restrict his love to his fellow Jews. Instead

11. *Jesu puero duodenni* 30–31. Translation from *Works of Aelred I.*

he reached out to all: Jews and Gentiles, Greeks and barbarians, the wise and the foolish. While his holiness raised him above all, his humility made him the servant of all.[12]

In contrast to Peter, who used his sword against Jesus' enemies in the garden, Paul more fully understood and imitated Christ's love which restored the ear Peter cut off. Peter had been impatient, without hope, seeing the enemies of Christ as incorrigible. Paul in contrast had hope for these enemies. He had been one of them. Through earnest prayer Paul served those who persecuted, scourged, and stoned him. He maintained an ardent and undying hope for their salvation. Because of this, Aelred argued that Paul could even be called charity itself:

> Oh soul higher than the heavens, more splendid than the sun, more fervent than fire. What is that most sacred breast, if not a resting place for kindness, a vestibule of mercy, a throne of charity? There indeed love resides on its judgement seat, having Paul's body for its tool and his voice as its instrument. Paul accomplished nothing in himself except through participation in God. As it is said of God that he is love, so it is said of Paul that he is love by participation in love.[13]

Through God's mercy, Paul had been transformed from a wolf seeking to devour Christ's sheep to a good shepherd who gave his life for Christ's sheep.[14]

Throughout his hagiographies and histories, Aelred told other stories of the power of mercy. He narrated several accounts of St. Ninian imitating divine goodness by returning evil with kindness, hate with love. Ninian was said to be always overflowing with mercy. When one of Ninian's enemies was blinded, Ninian approached him with humility and affection, gently corrected and then healed him.[15] In another account several thieves tried to steal the animals Ninian was raising for his own brothers, as well as for the poor and pilgrims. During the attempted robbery one of the thieves was gored by the bull. Ninian,

12. *"In natale apostolorum Petri et Pauli," Sermones inediti,* 135.
13. Ibid.
14. *Sermo 1 "In Adventu Domini"* 37, CCCM 2A.
15. *Vita Niniani* 4. An English translation is in "Lives of St. Ninian and St. Kentigen," *Historians of Scotland,* vol. 5 (Edinburgh: Edmonston and Douglas, 1974) 137–57.

''moved by mercy,'' wept and begged God to restore the thief to life. His prayers were answered.[16]

Aelred told similar stories of King Edward the Confessor. Once when Edward was trying to take a nap he observed a poor lad who had noticed that the chest which kept the royal treasury had inadvertently been left open. Edward watched curiously as the small boy searched about for a container, found a small bowl, filled it with large coins from the treasury, hid the bowl in his clothes and crept out. The boy returned, refilled the bowl, and snuck out again. During the boy's third trip Edward realized that the royal steward was approaching. The king broke his silence in order to protect his young thief, warning him to run quickly less the treasurer find him. The steward cried out in anger when he realized that the treasure had been plundered. Edward, as Aelred retells the story, told him, ''Be quiet, perhaps he that took it needed it more than we do. Let him have it.''[17]

The particular strength of mercy is that it can hold another in deep affection and actively serve him or her without having been loved first. Driven by its own nature, it flows out toward those who have done nothing to deserve love and those who otherwise may be unlovable: those who are steeped in sin; those who are vain, obnoxious, fickle, argumentative, and deceitful; those whose are opposed to everything one holds dear. In other words, mercy loves those who have none of the prerequisites for a spiritual friendship.

Yet, as already noted, mercy can also transform. God's mercy inspires hope and virtue where there was previously despair and sin. God's mercy inspires those who have been touched deeply by it to, in turn, show mercy toward others. Moreover, mercy can also create a return of affectionate love toward the one who first showed mercy. Thus, in some of Aelred's stories, sinners who received a saint's mercy become friends of the saint: the mercy not only inspired a change in life and a change of heart, it inspired a reciprocal affection. Aelred noted that Ninian's enemy not only repented and stopped persecuting Ninian after he was healed, but cherished the saint with the deepest affection. Similarly, Aelred told how King Malcolm made a friend out of a traitor by showing mercy. The king had learned that one of his officers

16. Ibid., 8.
17. *Vita Edwardi, Patrologia Latina, Cursus Completus*, ed. J. P. Migne, vol. 195, col. 746B-D.

was intent on killing him. Rather than punishing the traitor, he arranged to be alone with the man during a hunt and confronted him: "If you are able, if you dare, if you have the heart, fulfill what you intended, render to my enemies what you promised." When the would-be traitor falls trembling at Malcolm's feet the king assures him, "Be not afraid; you will suffer no evil from me." Instead of pursuing his original aim to kill the king, the man now promises fidelity and becomes a friend.[18]

Aelred, too, was known for his affection and mercy toward all types of people. In *De spirituali amicitia* he explained that while only a few of his monks were capable of spiritual friendship, he nevertheless loved and felt loved by each of them.[19] It should be noted that these monks were not a homogenous group of cultured men. Twelfth-century England was rough and violent. In his writings Aelred repeated tales of grotesque brutalities in war, of murders, and of mutilations. Aelred's monks grew up in this environment. In an Advent sermon Aelred indicated that some of those at Rievaulx had previously lived the proud life of those born into wealth, others had been notorious for their cruelty, and still others had lived off of plunder, deception, and fraud.[20] In another sermon he revealed the multitude of faults still present among those at Rievaulx: there were monks who complained and quarreled; monks who loved their own will more than God's; those who were slow to work and quick to rest; those who were vain; those who failed to follow the guidelines of the order; those who spoke imprudently and others whose silence simply masked an inner bitterness; those who readily accused others of injuring them; and finally, those who were unable to tolerate others' faults.[21]

Aelred encouraged his monks to show mercy toward each other and himself. He begged those who were "spiritual and perfect" (and one must wonder if any of his monks dared to consider themselves such) to carry those who were crippled by faults and sins. The strong should sustain the weak by their counsels, consolations, exhortations, corrections, and prayers. In this way the maturer monks could be like Peter when he healed the cripple at the temple. With the help of such

18. *Genealogia regum anglorum*, PL 195, 735A-D.
19. *De spirituali amicitia* 3.82-83.
20. *Sermo 1 "In Adventu Domini"* 38, CCCM 2A.
21. "*In sollemnitate apostolorum Petri et Pauli de tribus portis et tribus templis*," *Sermones inediti*, 128–29.

love the crippled brothers would be able to leap up, praise God, and walk cheerfully along with the strong. Moreover, Aelred told his monks that he was as one crippled in both legs, needing especially to be carried by those who were strong.[22]

In an attempt to explain the rapid growth of Rievaulx under Aelred, Walter Daniel (who lived under Aelred at Rievaulx for seventeen years) stressed its reputation for mercy:

> When was anyone, feeble in body and character, ever expelled from that house, unless his iniquity was an offense to the community or had destroyed all hope of his salvation? Hence it was that monks in need of mercy and compassion flocked to Rievaulx from foreign peoples and from the far ends of the earth. . . . And so those wanderers in the world to whom no house of religion gave entrance, came to Rievaulx, the mother of mercy, and found the gates open and entered by them freely. . . . If one of them in later days had taken it upon himself to reprove in angry commotion some silly behavior, Aelred would say, "Do not, brother, do not kill the soul for which Christ died, do not drive away our glory from this house." . . . [I]t is the singular and supreme glory of the house of Rievaulx that above all else it teaches tolerance of the infirm and compassion with others in their necessities.[23]

The last passage I will use from Aelred is a long excerpt from his pastoral prayer. Written during the final year of his life, it beautifully reveals Aelred's own spirituality of mercy: a spirituality which blends his knowledge of Christ's mercy with a desire to show merciful love toward his monks. The prayer illustrates a hope-filled humility, a self-forgetful desire to be with and for others, and a mercy which can create mutual love between those who initially had nothing in common:

> You know my heart, Lord; you know that my will is that whatever you have given your servant should be devoted wholly to their service, and spent for them in its entirety; and I myself, moreover, would be freely spent for them. So may it be, O Lord, so may it be. My powers of perception and of speech, my work time and my leisure, my doings and my thinking, the times when things

22. Ibid.
23. *Walter Daniel's Life of Aelred of Rievaulx* (Oxford: Clarendon Press, 1950) 37.

go well with me, the times when they go ill, my life, my death, my good health and my weakness, each single thing that makes me what I am, the fact that I exist and think and judge, let all be used, let all be spent for those for whom you did deign to be spent yourself. . . . Give me, by your unutterable grace, the power to bear with their shortcomings patiently, to share their griefs in loving sympathy, and to afford them help according to their needs. Taught by your Spirit may I learn to comfort the sorrowful, confirm the weak and raise the fallen; to be myself one with them in their weakness, one with them when they burn at causes of offense, one in all things with them, all things to all of them, that I may gain them all (1 Cor 9:22). Give me the power to speak the truth straightforwardly, and yet acceptably; so that they all may be built up in faith and hope and love, in chastity and lowliness, in patience and obedience, in spiritual fervor and submissiveness of mind. And since you have appointed this blind guide to lead them, this untaught man to teach, this ignorant one to rule them, for their sakes Lord, if not mine, teach him whom you have made to be their teacher, lead him whom you have bidden to lead them, rule him who is their ruler. . . . Teach me to suit myself to everyone according to his nature, character and disposition, according to his power of understanding or his lack of it, as time and place require in each case, as you would have me do.[24]

According to Walter Daniel's accounts of Aelred's relationships with his monks, such prayers were mightily answered.

A Living Example of Mercy at the Juncture

Because mercy does not depend on any previous virtue, similarity, or likeness to attract it, it can initiate and sustain a love relationship between any two persons. If mercy can pierce the shut doors of hardened hearts and minds, we can hope that it could also overcome impasses in dialogue, pierce through ideological differences and melt walls created to defend interest-group ghettos. We may also hope that mercy has the strength to reconcile quarrels and help fragile love relationships grow stronger. Developing a spirituality of mercy, fostering hearts and minds of mercy, seems to be the place to start in the postmodern world. Such a spirituality is simple. Yet lest it also appear hope-

24. *Oratio pastoralis* 7. *Works of Aelred I.*

lessly idealistic, as a foolish dream, I would like to close with the story of a man who is living this spirituality today. It may well be one of those charming acts of God's grace that I met this man during that same summer at Chicago. He is an amazing man who gave me hope when I was disillusioned by the biting criticisms among the Latin scholars and despairing over the apparently unstoppable inner city violence.

Bill Tomes grew up in the white middle-class Chicago suburbs where his classmates considered him a "nerd."[25] In 1980 he stopped into a church to pray. At the time Tomes was in his mid-forties, unsuccessful in attempts to find a wife, and unsure about his career. His fiancée had married someone else when he was out of town. He had already tried two careers which did not quite work and was in the process of trying to discern a third. While praying, he heard the directive, "Love. You are forbidden to do anything other than that." When he asked how he was supposed to love, he was told, "by loving." When he asked what specifically he was supposed to do, he heard only, "I'll lead. You follow."

I met Tomes through my uncle who is a psychiatrist in the Chicago area. Tomes had arranged to meet with my uncle professionally because he was hearing these voices. He feared that he might be hearing God and hoped my uncle would simply determine that he was crazy. Instead my uncle tended to support Tomes' fears. It took Tomes several years before he understood exactly what God was asking. Now, after having given away all his possessions, this graying, white-skinned suburbanite is working in the Chicago housing projects, loving the members of rival gangs. Over the last decade he has come to know thousands of the youth who belong to 125 gangs in Chicago. He also knows each gang's trademarks and special handshakes. He lives by a few simple rules "Love. Don't be afraid. Don't defend yourself. Forgive everyone for everything."

For his work, Tomes is given a modest stipend from Catholic Charities. He enters the projects in early afternoon and rarely leaves before 1:00 a.m. He spends his time with the youth in the apartment hallways, basketball courts, hospitals, jails, and gravesites. His goal is to stop the killing, and when that is impossible he consoles the friends

25. In the following account, personal recollections are supplemented by background information from Jill Boughton, "The Remarkable Story of Bill Tomes," *New Heaven/New Earth* 9 (July 1991) 6–8.

of the victims and speaks at their funerals. The local Catholic cardinal and several at Notre Dame University praise his work. Notre Dame's football team has even allowed him to bring some of the youth down to meet the players and watch practices.

My uncle reasons that the gangs have not killed Tomes yet because he has such deep humility and simplicity, if not even a bit of foolishness about him. His vulnerability seems to elicit a certain compassion and pity in the youth. Tomes explained it more bluntly: "I'm dumb shit. I am no better than them and they know it."

His unconditional love for each person is often reciprocated. In an environment from which few escape and in which many expect to die young, funerals become an odd final glory, a time for a gathering of loyal friends. A ten-year-old assured Tomes that he is so well loved that everyone plans on attending his funeral. Bill has asked that if he is killed, his funeral be ecumenical and on neutral turf so rival gang members can attend. "The guy who kills me," he explains, "is still my brother and should be loved more than anybody else."

In contrast with some others who work with these youth, Bill does not dwell on the rewards of being so appreciated. He is not there for self-aggrandizement or to attain a sense of self-worth. Instead his love for these young men weighs heavily on him. If he was not compelled by the God who is love itself to be with the inner city youth, he told me that he would have quit the work long ago. Why? Because he hates having to see those he loves so much die. The ten-year-old, assuming he would not live long, had also asked Tomes, "Will you come to my funeral?" A merciful love has led Tomes to be with and suffer with these gangs.

When I asked him when he felt closest to God, he responded "When the shooting starts. Then I hear Christ say, 'I am walking. I want you walking.'" Tomes explained that this means he is to walk into the midst of the shooting and toward the one who is firing the gun. It is at these times that he has the most striking sense of Christ besides him (and sometimes hears a whispered "duck right" or "duck left" to help him dodge a bullet). The merciful God travels with those who go out in mercy.

Tomes' love for these gang members is blazing and unambiguous. They have nick-named him "Brother Love." They know he would still love them even if they did not change. While he does not approve of their destructive behavior and longs to see them change, he is not among them to judge them as a representative of the law. Nevertheless, as a testimony to the miraculous power of mercy, his love has inspired some transformations. Some have become Christians, including a few shooting victims whom Bill baptized as they were dying. Others have given up their drugs and gangs in order to find real jobs. Still others have applied to colleges. They have done so in spite of the death-sentence imposed by the gangs on those who leave. Perhaps the most amazing result of Tomes' love is a peace treaty negotiated between rival gangs that has lasted five years. Mercy can multiply and spread itself, creating peace where previously there was only enmity.

A spirituality of mercy thus seems to be the place to begin at the juncture of modernity and postmodernity. Mercy can begin to fulfill the hunger to love and be loved when great diversity, lack of trust and hope, and continuous quarrels seemed to have paralyzed all other types of love. After mercy has softened hearts, recreated trust, and re-enkindled hope, then other forms of love can arise. Such mercy is more than social work. It is a spirituality because it is inspired and animated by the Spirit who chose to be incarnated as merciful love. Some of those steeped in an agnostic and violent world have even found reason to believe in God because of it.

"Although It Is Night":
A Carmelite Perspective on Spirituality at the Juncture of Modernity and Postmodernity*

Steven Payne, O.C.D.

Soon after the beginning of St. Theresa's reform [John of the Cross] was kidnapped by opponents . . ., and disappeared. No one had any idea where he had gone and . . . nobody seemed to care. He was locked up in a cell without light or air during the stifling heat of a Toledan summer to await trial and punishment for what his persecutors seriously believed to be a canonical crime. . . .

The color scheme of John's imprisonment is black and ochre and brown and red: the red is his own blood running down his back. The movement is centripetal. There is a tremendous stability, not merely in the soul immobilized, entombed in a burning stone wall, but in the depths of that soul, purified by a purgatory that those alone know who have felt it, emerging into the Center of all centers, the Love which moves the heavens and the stars, the Living God.

. . . The religious police could not disturb the ecstasy of one who had been carried so far that he was no longer troubled at the thought of being rejected even by the holy![1]

—Thomas Merton

* This paper was presented at the January 9–12, 1993 "Scholars' Retreat" sponsored by The Abbey Center For The Study Of Ethics And Culture, Inc. at the Abbey of Gethsemani, Trappist, Kentucky.
1. Thomas Merton, O.C.S.O., "St. John of the Cross," *Saints for Now*, ed. Clare Boothe Luce (New York: Sheed & Ward, 1952) 251-53. For a discussion of Merton's work on John of the Cross, see "Thomas Merton's Practical Norms of Sanctity in St. John of the Cross," ed. and intro. Robert E. Daggy, *Spiritual Life* 36 (Winter 1990) 195–97.

For almost nine months, from December 1577 until the following August, the Spanish Carmelite John of the Cross lay imprisoned in the Order's monastery of Toledo beside the Tagus river, punished by his own religious confreres for alleged disobedience in their juridical dispute with the followers of St. Teresa's "reform," which John had helped extend to the friars. The physical sufferings he endured are well-known, and have often been described in lurid detail. But far more painful, it seems, were his spiritual and psychological torments: self-doubts about his own behavior and convictions, fears that the "Teresian" project to which he had devoted his life had been crushed (and that he had been totally forgotten by its members), uncertainty about his fate and the intentions of his captors, suspicions of poisoning—and, worst of all, the sense that he had been abandoned by God.[2] John found himself alone, in the dark, stripped of all his former certainties and without any familiar spiritual compass, perhaps with only the distant murmur of the Tagus River for his companion. Yet somehow, in the crucible of John's torment was born some of the most splendid poetry of any period or language: the *Romances*, the initial verses of the *Cántico espiritual*, and the "Song of the soul that rejoices in knowing God through faith," with its repeated refrain, *"aunque es de noche."*

> For I know well the spring that flows and runs
> *although it is night.*
>
> That eternal spring is hidden,
> for I know well where it has its rise,
> *although it is night.*
>
> I do not know its origin, nor has it one,
> but I know that every origin has come from it,
> *although it is night.*
>
> I know that nothing else is so beautiful,
> and that the heavens and the earth drink there,
> *although it is night. . . .*[3]

2. For a recent and reliable account of John's sufferings in Toledo, see Federico Ruiz, O.C.D., and others, *God Speaks in the Night: The Life, Times and Teaching of St. John of the Cross,* trans. Kieran Kavanaugh, O.C.D. (Washington: ICS Publications, 1991) 157–88.

3. *The Collected Works of St. John of the Cross,* trans. Kieran Kavanaugh, O.C.D., and Otilio Rodriguez, O.C.D., with revisions and introductions by Kieran Kavanaugh, O.C.D., rev. ed. (Washington: ICS Publications, 1991) 58–59. Note from the title that the soul in this poem actually *rejoices* in knowing God through

In the final section of this paper, I will return to John, to consider briefly how his rediscovery of God in the midst of such profound anguish and abandonment may offer hope to those coping with the darkness and disorientation of our own times. But I want to begin with a special word of gratitude to the sponsors and organizers for inviting me to this Gethsemani retreat on "Spirituality at the Juncture of Modernity and Post-Modernity." The juxtaposition of topic and location is a happy one, since the monastic community at Gethsemani Abbey offers a living example of how to draw creatively upon the spiritual riches of the past in facing the needs of the present and future.

I should also confess at the outset, however, that I feel poorly qualified to address such a daunting theme, since my expertise tends to be focused in the area of Carmelite spirituality (not usually considered "post-modern"!), and since my editorial work with The Institute for Carmelite Spirituality (ICS) Publications and our journal, *Spiritual Life*, ironically leaves me little time to keep abreast of current scholarly discussions in contemporary spiritual theology.

Still, my own peculiar perspective may provide a useful counterpoint to the other contributions. In the following pages, therefore, after some general remarks on the proposed theme, and some observations on the "spirituality" scene today as it falls within my limited purview, I hope to offer some tentative suggestions as to how the Carmelite tradition, and especially John of the Cross, might address or contribute to the understanding of spirituality in a postmodern context. For if our contemporary world seems to many to be a chaotic "wasteland" of conflicting voices and competing interests, perhaps a spirituality born of the desert is precisely what we need for survival.

What Are "Modernity" and "Postmodernity"?

I'd like to begin with a few thoughts on the general theme of this retreat itself. If my remarks seem naive, obvious, wrongheaded, or even curmudgeonly, I apologize in advance. It may simply illustrate one of the points I want to raise: that it is not clear to what extent the "concerns of postmodernity" have really penetrated the collective

---

faith, rather than complaining of the darkness and confusion—not what one might have expected from John's sufferings.

awareness of Carmelites, those with whom we most commonly minister, and Catholics in general.

What precisely is meant by "modernity" and "postmodernity"? While these expressions are obviously interrelated (*post*-modernity presumably representing something that comes after, or stands in opposition to, modernity) it is no surprise to be told, I'm sure, that the meanings attached to these terms are as varied as those who use them. "Postmodern" architecture may have little relation to "postmodernity" in other fields. Intellectual historians continue to argue whether particular authors and thinkers should be classed as late modern or early postmodern figures. As Richard J. Bernstein has recently noted:

> Anyone with even the most superficial acquaintance with recent debates can scarcely avoid noticing that the terms "modernity" and "postmodernity" are slippery, vague, and ambiguous. They have wildly different meanings within different cultural disciplines and even within the same discipline. There is no consensus about the multiple meanings of these treacherous terms. Furthermore there is the paradox that many thinkers who are labeled "postmodern" by others, do not think of themselves as "postmodern" or even use this expression. For example, when asked to name "postmodern" thinkers I suspect many would include Heidegger, Derrida, Foucault, and perhaps Nietzsche. But none of them ever rely on the term.[4]

Yet, even at the risk of sliding "into a quasi-essentialism where we talk as if there are a determinate set of features that mark off the 'modern' from the 'postmodern' "[5] it is perhaps sufficient to say that today the term "modernity" is generally used in theological circles as a shorthand way of referring to a certain set of principles, ideas, and presuppositions about truth, knowledge, language, morality, the world, and the place of human beings within it—principles and presuppositions "forged during the Enlightenment (c. 1600–1780)" by such thinkers as Descartes, Hume, Kant, Newton, and their intellectual and cultural heirs.[6] Among the characteristics of modernity, the following are often included:

4. Richard J. Bernstein, *The New Constellation: The Ethical-Political Horizons of Modernity/Postmodernity* (Cambridge, Mass.: MIT Press, 1992) 11.

5. Ibid., 200.

6. Diogenes Allen, *Christian Belief in a Postmodern World: The Full Wealth of Conviction* (Louisville: Westminster/John Knox Press, 1989) 2.

1. A belief in the radical autonomy and conscious self-determination of the individual human subject (traceable back to the Cartesian *cogito*).

2. A view of language as merely an instrument used by the autonomous subject to express pre-linguistic thoughts and feelings.

3. A confidence in the capacity of science and rationality to discover, progressively and cumulatively, all objective truth, and to explain all natural phenomena without postulating any God (except, perhaps, the deists' "cosmic watchmaker" who set the universe going).

4. An attempt to ground morality in principles evident to human reason, rather than in divine commands (Kant's categorical imperative).

5. A belief in the inevitability of human progress.[7]

The list, obviously, could be extended. One important but unsuccessful Christian response to such principles came from the group of Protestant theologians now identified with nineteenth century "liberal theology," usually viewed as an attempt to accomodate the presuppositions of modernity, but at the expense of traditional Christian content and truth claims.

Of course, as soon as we begin making these kinds of generalizations about the "modern" worldview, we must immediately qualify them. Any careful reader will find vast differences among the thinkers usually identified with "modernity," as well as surprising affinities between any one of them and certain premodern and postmodern figures. (I am always uneasy when our new students come home to the monastery after two or three introductory philosophy lectures at the nearby seminary, full of loud opinions about the demise of modernity and the bankruptcy of all post-Cartesian thought, before they have actually *read* anything of Descartes, Hume, or Kant; as I sometimes tell our older friars, what I spent years studying in the philosophy

7. For characterizations of "modernity" and "postmodernity," see Allen, *Christian Belief in a Postmodern World;* David Ray Griffin, William A. Beardslee, and Joe Holland, *Varieties of Postmodern Theology* (Albany: SUNY Press, 1989); David Tracy, *Plurality and Ambiguity: Hermeneutics, Religion and Hope* (San Francisco: Harper & Row, 1987).

department at Cornell, they covered in an afternoon under the heading *Errores*.)

It is not altogether clear, either, whether we can really talk about a single, pervasive mindset named "modernity," or whether we are really talking about a cluster of related (but not always identical or even fully compatible) Enlightenment issues and concerns shared primarily among the Western intelligentsia. The Catholicism with which many of us were raised in the 1950s, for example, shared few of the presuppositions identified above. And while ordinary Americans may experience very concretely the negative social consequences of "modernity's" belief in inevitable historical progress, its "culture of separation," or its one-sided emphasis on the autonomous subject (see, for example, Robert Bellah's discussion of the dangers of "expressive individualism" in American culture[8]), in certain other respects modernity's conclusions have never won widespread popular acceptance on this side of the North Atlantic, except perhaps in the halls of academia. Americans remain among the most religious people of any developed nation, at least by such measurable standards as regular church attendance, Bible reading, and personal prayer.[9] Moreover, in some recent controversies over school curricula and "scientific creationism," for example, as well as in the popular "New Age" movement, we now seem to see postmodern arguments and considerations brought to the defense of what many would consider "premodern" world views.

But perhaps this misses the point, since, however widespread (or not) the presuppositions identified with modernity once were, we can at least say that, over the last century or so, they have come under increasing attack. The positivistic dream of pure science as an avenue to uninterpreted, empirically verified "objective" facts, with exclusive claims to all knowable truth about the "world-out-there," has crumbled in the face of such developments as Heisenberg's uncertainty principle and the mysteries of quantum physics. Attempts to base morality on fundamental axioms self-evident to all rational human beings have foundered on the apparent historical and cultural relativity of our ethical

8. Robert N. Bellah and others, *Habits of the Heart: Individualism and Commitment in American Life* (Berkeley: University of California Press, 1985) 142–63, 277–81.

9. George Gallup, Jr. and Jim Castelli, *The People's Religion: American Faith in the 90's* (New York: Macmillan, 1989) 20–21 and passim.

and rational norms. Philosophers and psychologists have increasingly explored the ways in which our experience is linguistically shaped, while the "hermeneuts of suspicion" (Freud, Feuerbach, Marx, Nietzsche, etc.) unmask the various psychological, socio-economic, and cultural forces that systematically distort our interpretation of experience. No longer, therefore, can the embattled subject retreat into the security of an indubitable Cartesian *cogito*, the commentators tell us, since even the self is a social construct, shaped by a shared language, culture, and tradition with embedded systematic distortions. Recent history, moreover, has shattered the myth of inevitable human progress, as we discover that the very heirs of modern culture (in Nazi Germany and elsewhere) are capable of engineering genocide, and that the scientific accomplishments of modernity have confronted us with the possible annihilation of all life from the earth. The presuppositions often identified with "modernity" have been radically challenged, and we find ourselves, so it seems, in a different world, whatever terminology we may choose to describe it.

All of this has been stated more clearly, carefully, and insightfully by others. But even if these are the challenges usually associated with "postmodernity," the responses seem radically varied. Indeed, the very term "postmodernity," since it suggests no positive content of its own, is applicable to any number of perhaps mutually incompatible reactions to the alleged failure of "modernity," just as "postcommunism" can refer to a whole range of different and even contradictory responses to the demise of the former Soviet Union. David Ray Griffin, in his introduction to one of the volumes in his SUNY "postmodernity" series, identifies at least four basic types of postmodern theology: "(1) constructive (or revisionary)," which he seems to equate with some version of process theology; "(2) deconstructive (or eliminative)," associated with Derrida, Lyotard, and others; "(3) liberationist," under which rubric he would presumably include the various black, feminist, Latino (or Latina), Native American, and other liberation theologies; and "(4) restorationist or conservative," a label he awards to George William Rutler, John Paul II, and possibly Richard John Neuhaus.[10] Other authors identify other brands

10. See Griffin, "Introduction: Varieties of Postmodern Theology," *Varieties of Postmodern Theology*, 1–7. Interestingly, there are discussions of John of the Cross from within almost all of these brands of "postmodernity." For a "process" ap-

of "postmodernity," particularly of a hermeneutical orientation. Yet we can see how confusing the terminology has become, when the current pope is counted a "postmodernist," and process theology (with its roots in the metaphysics of Whitehead's process philosophy) is as "postmodern" as the strongly anti-metaphysical bias of some deconstructionists. Certainly one can make a case for calling them all "postmodern" in some sense, but the label may obscure as much as it clarifies.

In any case, the question arises again: to what extent has such "postmodernity," and the alleged demise of modernity, really penetrated to the level of general awareness, particularly to the level of everyday spirituality? I cannot recall the last submission to our journal *Spiritual Life* that seemed even remotely influenced by Ricoeur, Foucault, Gadamer, or Habermas (much less mentioning them by name), and to the extent that any of our articles incorporate process or liberation perspectives, we are barraged with irate letters denying that these have anything of value to offer people today. (The "postmodernity" of John Paul II is apparently acceptable to our readers, however!) At a more academic level, in recent decades I managed to complete both undergraduate and graduate programs in philosophy at Cornell (with a heavily Wittgensteinian orientation at the time) without once hearing the names of Derrida, Lacan, and others, as far as I can recall; it was only at my insistence that I was able to study Heidegger, and then only as part of a directed reading course in *Being and Time*. Even today, while there is greater dialogue between the analytic and continental traditions, Derrida and others seem to be taken far more seriously in departments of theology, literature, and modern languages than in the philosophy departments of the United States (just as Anselm and Aquinas often receive a more careful reading from philosophers than from theologians these days).

---

proach, see Daniel A. Dombrowski, *St. John of the Cross: An Appreciation* (Albany: SUNY Press, 1992); for a feminist perspective, see Constance FitzGerald, O.C.D., "Impasse and Dark Night," ed. Tilden Edwards, *Living With Apocalypse: Spiritual Resources for Social Compassion* (San Francisco: Harper & Row, 1984) 93–116; for an approach influenced by Levinas, see Alain Cugno, *St. John of the Cross: Reflections on Mystical Experience* (New York: Crossroad, 1982); for the "postmodernist" pontiff, see Karol Wojtyla, *Faith According to Saint John of the Cross*, trans. Jordan Aumann (San Francisco: Ignatius Press, 1981).

My own experience is that many philosophers influenced by the analytic tradition have understood their "postmodernity" to mean primarily an end to linguistic positivism's veto on metaphysics.[11] Anglo-American philosophers with or without any particular religious affiliation have taken up again the classic arguments regarding the existence of God, the problem of evil, the possibility of miracles, and so on, with an enthusiasm and battery of rigorous analytic tools that make many scholastics look slipshod by comparison.[12] The ontological argument (which, it should be noted, exercised a tremendous fascination for thinkers as varied as Barth, Hartshorne, and many post-Wittgensteinians) becomes a classic illustration of the intricacies of modal logic.[13] It is ironic, I think, that so many analytic philosophers with nothing obvious to gain from any rescuscitation of "natural theology," and no stake in reviving "the thirteenth, the greatest of all centuries," are nonetheless taking these arguments more seriously than their counterparts in the seminaries and theology departments. If this is a "postmodern" phenomenon—and in some respects it might be described that way—it is one that deserves more serious attention from contemporary theologians, and yet seems worlds apart from Heidegger and the deconstructionists.

In short, there are no clear breaks or sharp divisions between premodernity, modernity, and postmodernity. On the contrary, it seems more and more clear that they continue to coexist side-by-side,

11. Diogenes Allen, for instance, argues that "the breakdown of the modern mentality" now makes it possible to argue once again that one should believe Christianity "because Christianity's true"; see *Christian Belief in a Postmodern World*, 1ff.

12. For examples of this revival of interest in philosophy of religion among Anglo-American philosophers influenced by the analytic tradition, see the articles and bibliographies in *Readings in the Philosophy of Religion: An Analytic Approach*, ed. Baruch A. Brody (Englewood Cliffs, N.J.: Prentice-Hall, 1974); *Philosophy of Religion: An Anthology*, ed. Louis P. Pojman (Belmont, Calif: Wadsworth Publishing Co., 1987); *Philosophy of Religion: Selected Readings*, eds., William L. Rowe and William J. Wainwright, 2nd ed. (New York: Harcourt Brace Jovanovich, 1989); the "University of Notre Dame Studies in the Philosophy of Religion" series; and the journal *Faith and Philosophy: Journal of the Society of Christian Philosophers*.

13. See especially Plantinga's detailed and influential analysis of the ontological argument in Alvin Plantinga, *God and Other Minds: A Study of the Rational Justification of Belief in God* (Ithaca, N.Y.: Cornell University Press, 1967) 26–94; and Alvin Plantinga, *God, Freedom and Evil* (New York: Harper Torchbooks, 1974) 85–112.

even within ourselves, sometimes creating conflict, sometimes a fruitful interplay. One is reminded of Bultmann's famous remark, in "New
Testament and Mythology," that "it is impossible to use electric light
and the wireless and to avail ourselves of modern medical and surgi-
cal discoveries, and at the same time to believe in the New Testament
world of spirits and miracles."[14] I can only say from my limited experience in publications and other ministries what has no doubt been
stated often before: that many people—and not just the uneducated—
not only *can* but *do* so believe, especially when "New Age" trappings
are part of the package. Is this an indication of vestigial superstition
or of intellectual schizophrenia? Possibly, but also possibly something
more. At any rate, postmodernists willing to interpret sympathetically
the "popular religion" of other cultures should presumably extend the
same courtesy to their own heritage.

Some Contemporary Trends in Spirituality

What does all of this mean, then, for spirituality at this particular historical moment? And to what extent are "modernity" and "postmodernity" useful categories for understanding it?

The answer will depend, of course, upon our notion of spirituality itself. Here it is especially important to distinguish between
"prescriptive" and "descriptive" approaches, since there is a tendency
to specify "authentic" spirituality in ways that make our characterizations true *by definition*. Prescriptive definitions stipulate what the matter under consideration "really ought to be," or what "really ought
to count" as instances; a descriptive definition, on the other hand, looks
at how terms are actually used in ordinary practice. One might argue
"prescriptively," for example, that all true instances of postmodern
spirituality must explicitly include ecological concerns or process perspectives, but the fact remains that these elements are often lacking
in much of what would ordinarily be described as spirituality in our
present historical context.

Rather than deciding in advance, therefore, what "spirituality
at the juncture of modernity and postmodernity" should look like, it
may be more useful here to describe briefly certain obvious trends in

14. Rudolf Bultmann and others, *Kerygma and Myth* (New York: Harper Torch-
book, 1961) 5.

contemporary spirituality as we find it. In true "postmodern" fashion, I need to acknowledge that my field of vision is to some extent limited by social class, occupation, religious affiliation, and so on. That is to say, among other things, that I tend to draw my impressions of contemporary spiritual trends from contacts with individuals and groups that explicitly *identify* themselves as interested in "spiritual" matters, from the kinds of books coming out and articles we receive for *Spiritual Life,* from conversations with people in the urban and suburban parishes where the Carmelites work, from second-hand reports from other Carmelites and friends throughout the world—and, more broadly, from whatever rises to the level of media or scholarly attention.

At the same time, although the net is thus cast fairly wide, I realize that my sources are in some respects a self-selected group of people who resonate with what Carmelites do and what we publish (and are therefore, at the very least, usually literate). I would not presume to generalize about contemporary Inuit spirituality, for example, or the "spiritual ethos" shared by the staff of the Apple Computer Corporation, or even the spirituality of the "Nubian Islamic Hebrews" who have their ominous-looking headquarters only a few blocks from our monastery in Washington; in some respects we share the same time and place in history, but in other respects we may be worlds apart, and in any case these are spiritual currents with which I have little direct acquaintance.

Moreover, one might argue that much of what passes for spirituality today is instead actually a distraction or escape from authentic surrender to the transforming power of the Holy Spirit. Without necessarily denying such a charge, my goal here is simply to list and comment briefly upon what would ordinarily be described as some of the major "contemporary trends in spirituality," particularly here in the United States. What are the themes and concerns, in other words, that loom large today in popular movements, workshops, retreats, lectures, and publications in the area of spirituality?

1. First, there is clearly a strong, and apparently still growing, interest in traditional spirituality (from which our own "ICS Publications," with its line of Carmelite classics, has certainly benefited). Whatever else may have changed since the Second Vatican Council, vast numbers of Catholics continue reading Louis de Montefort and the *Imitation of Christ,* listening to tapes of Bishop Sheen, wearing their

scapulars and Miraculous Medals, and saying their novena prayers and "Little Office of the Blessed Virgin Mary"; this same vitality of older forms of piety is also evident among Protestants and other groups, though obviously manifested in different forms. The influx of immigrants in recent years has only reinforced this trend. Sometimes the spiritual expressions of modern and premodern eras are carefully "retrieved," as in Paulist Press's outstanding "Classics of Western Spirituality" series. Sometimes they are almost defiantly "non-retrieved," by more conservative organizations and individuals, as if to say "whatever postmodernity may be, we don't much like it"; such attitudes seem to underlie some of the "fundamentalist" tendencies currently gaining ground in many religious groups. In either case, we are obviously not just dealing with classic texts here, but also with "old time religion" televangelism, pilgrimages, novenas, and so on, as well as the current fascination with apparitions, weeping statues, apocalyptic messages, and other extraordinary phenomena.[15] Even though these are often promoted by use of the latest technology, they typically hark back to an earlier era of spirituality.

2. Publications and prayer groups focused on Scripture and biblical spirituality remain widespread, as a look at any recent religious publisher's catalog, magazine circulation statistics, or diocesan directory shows.

3. Much of spirituality today is influenced by liberation or social justice perspectives of various sorts, and lately by a growing concern for ecological issues.[16] It is a mistake to assume that these are simply "liberal" preoccupations; more than ever, believers all across the spectrum readily agree that any authentic spirituality has social consequences. Both "conservative" and "liberal" groups and publications, after all, lionize Mother Teresa especially for her work with the poor. Disagreements certainly arise over the analysis of the systemic causes of social problems, and thus how persons concerned about spiritual growth should position themselves on such issues as abortion, gay

15. The award-winning weekly newspaper, *National Catholic Register*, now carries a regular supplement, *Mary's People*, on apparitions around the world.

16. See for example Segundo Galilea, *The Way of Living Faith: A Spirituality of Liberation* (San Franciso: Harper & Row, 1988); Gustavo Gutiérrez, *We Drink From Our Own Wells: The Spiritual Journey of a People* (Maryknoll, N.Y.: Orbis Books, 1988); Jon Sobrino, *Spirituality of Liberation: Toward Political Holiness* (Maryknoll, N.Y.: Orbis Books, 1988); and (for a "green" perspective) see the writings of Thomas Berry, C.P.

rights, military intervention in Somalia, or the former Yugoslavian republics, and so on. But it is difficult to find any contemporary spiritual writings or movements that fail to recognize one's duty toward the world and its disadvantaged, however that obligation is perceived and whatever tactics are proposed. Whether that recognition is translated into liberating praxis or concrete action is, of course, another question.

4. There is a continuing flood of new publications and workshops on women's (and, more recently, men's) spirituality.[17] Some of these explicitly incorporate liberation and feminist perspectives; others just as clearly do not, but rather offer a spiritual rationale or devotional sustenance for more traditional gender roles. Whether the more recent "men's movement" is complementary or contrary to feminist goals is still being debated.[18] Meanwhile, however, most retreat centers, spirituality programs, and religious publishing houses now provide a whole line of products and services related to women's and men's spirituality.

5. There is a comparable explosion in Twelve-Step, co-dependency, and recovery-related spirituality. One of the consequent problems is that addiction and co-dependency have come to be defined so broadly that virtually every individual and every group is labeled "dysfunctional," and a new kind of "co-dependency" on the support group itself may be fostered.[19] Alcoholics Anonymous has expressed some reservations about the tendency today to appropriate Twelve-Step spirituality for every individual and social problem. Nonetheless, it is clear that many today have found spiritual guidance from such programs, and from the challenge to "turn one's life over to a Higher Power."

17. See for example Susan Cady, Marian Ronan and Hal Taussig, *Sophia: The Future of Feminist Spirituality* (San Francisco: Harper & Row, 1986); Carol P. Christ and Judith Plaskow, eds. *Weaving the Visions: New Patterns in Feminist Spirituality* (San Francisco: Harper & Row, 1989); Joann Wolski Conn, ed., *Women's Spirituality: Resources for Christian Development* (Mahwah, N.J.: Paulist, 1986); Charlene Spretnak, ed., *The Politics of Women's Spirituality: Essays on the Rise of Spiritual Power Within the Feminist Movement* (Garden City, N.Y.: Anchor Books, 1982).

18. See Kay Leigh Hagan, ed. *Women Respond to the Men's Movement: A Feminist Collection* (San Francisco: HarperSanFrancisco, 1992).

19. See Wendy Kaminer, "Chances Are You're Codependent Too," *New York Times Review of Books* 95 (February 11, 1991) 1ff.; Lynette Lamb, "Is Everyone Codependent?" *Utne Reader* (May/June 1990) 26ff.; David Rieff, "Victims, All?" *Harper's* 283 (October 1991) 49–56.

6. In a similar vein, it is perhaps symptomatic of our times that Baltasar Gracian's seventeenth century "Art of Worldly Wisdom" has recently been successfully repackaged as a "self-help" book.[20] Indeed, "how-to," "self-help," and "healing" books now dominate the non-fiction bestseller lists, and related programs of every sort are springing up everywhere. Not all of these are explicitly "spiritual" in the traditional sense, but can be seen as one contemporary response to existing spiritual needs.[21]

7. Certainly one of the most important trends in spirituality today, for better or worse, is the so-called "New Age Movement," together with various related pop psychologies, holistic health programs, and so on. It is difficult to make any broad generalizations about "New Age" spirituality, since the terminology is used so carelessly by advocates and opponents alike. The "New Age" label has been applied in recent years to everything from transcendental meditation, yoga, "Christian Zen," acupuncture, centering prayer, the enneagram, intensive journaling, guided imagery, spiritual books written from a Jungian perspective, "global" and "creation-centered" spirituality, to crystal-gazing, channeling, witchcraft, satanism, and the light jazz sometimes labeled "New Age music." Alarmists detect in all of this a vast organized conspiracy against the Christian faith[22] (to the point where, for example, any article *Spiritual Life* now publishes on, say, the theme of "divinization" in St. John of the Cross generates a spate of accusations that we are promoting dangerous "New Age" ideas!). I would guess, rather, that what these "New Age" practices and ideas have in common, if anything, is a certain eclecticism and willingness to appropriate from many different sources (albeit not always with sufficient critical discernment) whatever is useful in one's spiritual journey.

8. Whether one regards it as part of the "New Age Movement" or as a distinct phenomenon, there is certainly widespread interest

20. See Baltasar Gracián, *The Art of Worldly Wisdom: A Pocket Oracle* (New York: Doubleday, 1992).

21. St. Mary's Press, for example, has recently begun offering a fine and very successful "Companions for the Journey" series, each entry bearing a similar title of *How to Pray With . . .* some particular saint.

22. See, for example, Randy England, *The Unicorn in the Sanctuary: The Impact of the New Age on the Catholic Church* (Rockford, Ill.: TAN Books, 1991), for a call to arms against the "New Age" that lumps together everything from Teilhard de Chardin and Modernism to Matthew Fox and Silva Mind Control.

today in the spiritual insights to be gleaned from other faiths and traditions, including Eastern religions, Native American spirituality, and so on. Sometimes archaic traditions are selectively pillaged or reinvented in a very anachronistic way (as when, for example, sanitized "wicca" or "druidic" cults are established that the original practitioners would scarcely have recognized); sometimes the very sources of alleged "ancient wisdom" are themselves problematic.[23] Still, today there is an increasing number of even-handed and insightful studies of other religions, and excellent opportunities to acquaint oneself with other spiritual traditions.

9. Finally, there are certain "cottage industries" of spirituality resources focused on particular movements (e.g., Focolare, the charismatics), target groups (e.g., parishes, RCIA, religious communities), individuals (e.g., Thomas Merton, Thérèse of Lisieux, Hildegard of Bingen, Mother Teresa), stages of life (e.g., midlife, aging), disciplines (e.g., centering prayer, spiritual direction), and so on.

This is only a brief, and necessarily incomplete, listing. But when we consider all this, however, what if anything counts as distinctively "postmodern" (or even "modern")? Perhaps those involved in some of the trends mentioned above no longer believe in the inevitable progress of history, for example, but then, neither did the "premoderns." Perhaps the increased emphasis on affectivity and the power of myth and symbol represents a loss of confidence in classical science as the privileged avenue to truth and reality (though in some quarters the "scientism" of the past seems to have been replaced by faith in the unlimited potential of computer technology). Perhaps attempts to develop a "global" spirituality, or to situate Christian uniqueness claims in respectful dialogue with other traditions, might be considered "post-

---

23. The current debate surrounding the authenticity of Forrest Carter's *The Education of Little Tree* (Albuquerque, N.M.: University of New Mexico Press, 1976) or Chief Seattle's oft-quoted speech recalls similar controversies over the reliability of Carlos Casteneda's books on the Yaqui "don Juan" some years ago. See, for example Henry Louis Gates, " 'Authenticity,' or the Lesson of Little Tree," *New York Times Book Review* 96 (November 24, 1991) 1ff.; John Leland, "New Age Fable from an Old School Bigot?" *Newsweek* 118 (October 14, 1991) 62; Jerry L. Clark, "Thus Spoke Chief Seattle: The Story of an Undocumented Speech," *Prologue* 17 (Spring 1985) 58–65; Malcolm Jones, "Just Too Good to Be True," *Newsweek* 119 (May 4, 1992) 68; Richard de Mille, *Casteneda's Journey* (Santa Barbara: Capra Press, 1976).

modern." Certainly, spiritualities incorporating the perspectives of liberation theology and feminism are "postmodern" if those movements are; it may be "postmodern" in some sense, as well, to apply the interpretive categories of codependency and recovery to institutions and groups rather than to individual subjects.

Still, it seems to me that if true "postmodernity" not only accepts but even revels in pluralism, relativism, ambiguity, and the loss of the rational subject, then few of the trends described above are fully "postmodern." On the contrary, the spirituality most popular today seems to represent not so much a celebration of the demise of modernity, but a search for some sense of meaning, truth, and self-identity in the face of an increasingly fragmented (and fragmenting) world. Individuals and communities are searching for something to rely on when all the roadmaps and familiar landmarks have disappeared, and they often seek it in other traditions (often distant in time, place, or cultural mindset). Carmel offers one such tradition.

The Carmelite Contribution

I want to suggest that the Carmelite heritage in general, and John of the Cross in particular (especially in his "dark night" doctrine), can make an important contribution to spirituality at the historical juncture we have just described. Certainly Carmel is not unique in this regard, as Thomas Merton himself clearly showed in his creative retrieval of the Cistercian heritage and other traditions. In fact, Carmelite spirituality might be regarded in some circles as part of the current problem, rather than part of the solution, since (more so than many monastic traditions) it places so much emphasis on the quality of the *individual subject's* interior relationship with the divine. (Recall Leibniz's enthusiastic endorsement of the Teresian maxim, taken out of context, that "the soul ought often to think as if there were nothing but God and itself in the world."[24]) Certainly, in the hands of later manualists, John's and Teresa's narratives of the soul's journey become dissected into increasingly more refined hair-splitting over the stages and degrees of meditation and infused contemplation. Little

24. Gottfried Wilhelm Leibniz, *Philosophical Writings,* ed. G.H.R. Parkinson (London: J. M. Dent & Sons, 1973) 42 ["Discourse on Metaphysics"] and 122 ["New System, and Explanation of the New System"].

wonder, then, that even today the friars continue to get numerous vocation inquiries from those who asssume they are ''called to Carmel'' because they seek a refuge to cultivate their own private experience of God, unmediated and untainted by any contact with products of ''modernity'' and ''postmodernity'' (including the bothersome others in community).

Again, it must be admitted that Teresa and John of the Cross were people of their own times, living in a Post-Tridentine era not usually regarded today as the high point of liturgical or ecclesial spirituality. This is only to admit that Carmelite spirituality is not all-inclusive, and needs supplementing with other traditions.

Still, I believe there are several important areas today in which the Carmelite tradition has a contribution to make. Begun in the late Crusader period at the beginning of the thirteenth century by men from the West living in the East (on the slopes of Mt. Carmel), in a lifestyle reminiscent of the desert fathers, ''hermits in community,'' then driven West by the fall of the Latin kingdom and assimilated to the mendicants, attending the great universities while always retaining a certain ''dangerous memory'' of their eremitical roots, preaching far and wide while longing for the silence and solitude of the desert, Carmelites seem at least one apt model for those today struggling to maintain a sense of spiritual identity in the face of massive social changes, even radical transformations in the externals of their lives.[25]

And the Carmelites confronted this challenge using several tactics. First, despite enormous pressures to adopt a classic religious *Rule*, they held on steadfastly to their own original ''formula of life,'' given by Albert (the patriarch of Jerusalem), and grounded in their own experience, with its emphasis on ''following in the footsteps of Christ'' and ''staying in your cell, meditating on the Law of the Lord day and night and keeping watch at prayer, unless attending to some other

25. For a more detailed history of Carmelite origins, summarized here in a single sentence, see Elias Friedman, O.C.D., *The Latin Hermits of Mount Carmel: A Study in Carmelite Origins* (Rome: Teresianum, 1979); and Joachim Smet, O.Carm., *The Carmelites: A History of the Brothers of Our Lady of Mount Carmel*, vol. 1 (Darien, Ill.: Carmelite Spiritual Center, 1975). Based on dated historical information, but still worthwhile, are Peter-Thomas Rohrbach, O.C.D., *Journey to Carith: The Story of the Carmelite Order* (Garden City, N.Y.: Doubleday & Co., 1966); and Thomas Merton, ''The Primitive Carmelite Ideal,'' *Disputed Questions* (New York: Farrar, Straus and Cudahy, 1960).

duty.''[26] And their choice of biblical paradigms was equally felicitous: *Elijah* (because of their location near his fountain) and *Mary* (patron of their first chapel built at Albert's directive, and thus the "Lady of the the place").

From *Elijah*, the Carmelites inherited a strong sense, still crucial today, of always "standing before the face of the living God," of needing to repeat the Exodus journey through the desert to Sinai/Horeb, and of finding God not in the predictable places or extraordinary phenomena, but in the "tiny whispering sound." As "sons and daughters of the prophets," they recognize as well that this encounter with the divine always imposes an ethical demand to speak out against injustice and expose the false gods of one's own time. Medieval Carmelites, in fact, allegorized the whole Elijah cycle in the First Book of Kings as a paradigm for all those whom God calls (see 1 Kgs 17:2-3) to "leave here, go east" (against sin), and "hide in the Wadi Cherith" (charity), where "you shall drink from the stream" (taste God somewhat even in this life) and be fed by the ravens (in morsels, not with a surfeit of consolations).[27]

The other classic paradigm for Carmelites is *Mary*, from whom they learn an attitude of radical availability to God's will, without counting the cost ("Let it be done to me as you say" [Luke 1:38]). John of the Cross points to Mary as the prime example of someone utterly responsive to the Spirit, free of her own agenda.[28] But at the same time this implies not merely a passive enjoyment of spiritual privileges, but an active engagement on behalf of those in need (e.g., rising up "in haste" to go serve her cousin Elizabeth [Luke 1:39]).[29]

26. See Bede Edwards, O.C.D., trans., *The Rule of Saint Albert* (Aylesford and Kent: Carmelite Book Service, 1973); Michael Mulhall, O.Carm., ed., *Albert's Way: The First North American Congress on the Carmelite Rule* (Rome: Institutum Carmelitanum, 1989).

27. For this allegorical interpretation, see Michael B. Edwards, O.C.D., trans., *The Book of the First Monks (chapter 1 to 9)*, Vineyard Series #3 (Oxford: Teresian Press, 1969). In the time of Sts. Teresa and John of the Cross, this book was still regarded (incorrectly) as the earliest rule of the Carmelites, given them in A.D. 412.

28. See *Ascent 3, 2, 10* in *Collected Works*, and Emmanuel Sullivan, O.C.D., "Mary and the Holy Spirit in the Writings of John of the Cross," ed. Steven Payne, O.C.D., *Carmelite Studies 6: John of the Cross* (Washington: ICS Publications, 1992) 109-22.

29. See Elizabeth of the Trinity, "Heaven In Faith," para. 40, *Complete Works*

These two models, and the memory of their origins, guided Carmelites through the vicissitudes of an often paradoxical and uncertain history. If, as Merton observes, "it can be said that the Carmelite spirit is essentially a 'desert' spirit, a prophetic ideal,"[30] then perhaps this tradition can help those today who find themselves negotiating a contemporary social and cultural wilderness, littered with the debris of "modernity." Its essentially narrative structure—telling again and again the story of those who have sought and been found by God—can offer support to those for whom grand theological systems have become problematic. This is a spirituality that speaks of the perennial possibility of inner silence and solitude before the living God, mediated in many ways but able to survive the sucessive deaths of every mediation. This is a spirituality that is at once profoundly contemplative and prophetic, "mystical and political," even if contemporary Carmelites themselves have yet to grasp fully their prophetic role in the contemporary world.

The Teresian and Sanjuanist Contribution

The riches of this Carmelite tradition come to full flower in Teresa of Avila and John of the Cross. Though both describe, perhaps in more detail than any of their predecessors, the wide range of possible "spiritual experiences," both offer a healthy antidote to the modern notion (perhaps grounded in modernity's preoccupation with the experiencing subject) that spirituality and mysticism have essentially to do with generating certain unusual feelings or states of consciousness. This misunderstanding can be found at all levels today, from the academicians who try to decide whether mysticism is "everywhere the same" by comparing phenomenological descriptions of mystic states (divorced from the context of a religious way of life), to the thousands of white-collar executives in stressful jobs who practice a half-hour of "meditation" every day, simply to achieve some state of inner equilibrium in order to become more effective competitors in the marketplace.

For John and Teresa, the goal of the spiritual journey is never merely some private inner bliss, but total transformation in the love

---

of Elizabeth of the Trinity, trans. Aletheia Kane, O.C.D. (Washington: ICS Publications, 1984) 110–11.

30. Merton, "The Primitive Carmelite Ideal," 228.

of God and complete identification with Christ; their spirituality thus is essentially and necessarily relational. Teresa herself was one of the first founders to articulate so clearly the ecclesial mission of a contemplative way of life; Christian spirituality, and the contemplative vocation, ultimately only make sense if they are undertaken for the sake of the Church and world, and not simply for the salvation of one's own soul.[31] Neither saint talks much about "mysticism" as such. They prefer instead to speak of "mystical theology" (which for them means not the study of mysticism but the experiential knowledge of the divine [see *Canticle*, Prologue, 3]), about union with God, about prayer, about contemplation as a "secret, loving inflow of God into the soul" (*Night*, 1, 10, 6). And although both describe the inner joy and peace that comes from finding God, they would be surprised, if not appalled, at the idea that these are somehow the direct goal of one's spiritual efforts. Teresa insists that the transforming mystical union of the seventh of the "dwelling places" of the *Interior Castle* is given not for our own satisfaction, but for the sake of "works, works, works."[32] John likewise continually criticizes those who "seek themselves in God":

> I should like to persuade spiritual persons that the road leading to God does not entail a multiplicity of considerations, methods, manners and experiences . . . but demands only the one thing necessary, true self-denial, interior and exterior, through surrender of self. . . . [Nor does the journey] consist in consolations, delights, and spiritual feelings, but in the living death of the cross, sensory and spiritual, exterior and interior. I will not enlarge on this, though I would like to continue discussing the matter because from my observations Christ is little known by those who consider themselves his friends. For we see them going about seeking in him their own consolations and satisfactions, loving themselves very much, but not loving him very much by seeking his bitter trials and deaths . . . (*Ascent* 2, 7, 7-12).

Both saints, in short, do indeed hold out a final prospect of unshakeable inner peace and joy, yet not as personal achievement but as gift,

31. See *Way of Perfection*, 1, 1-6; 3, 1-10; *Book of Foundations*, 1, 7-8, in *The Collected Works of St. Teresa of Avila*, trans. Kieran Kavanaugh, O.C.D., and Otilio Rodriguez, O.C.D., vols. 2, 3 (Washington: ICS Publications, 1980, 1985).

32. *Interior Castle*, seventh dwelling places, 4, 4-6, in *Collected Works of St. Teresa*, vol. 2.

the fruit of self-transcending love. And both saints insist these are attained, not by anesthetizing ourselves to the world's pain, but by suffering courageously the cost and consequences of that love.

More generally, I believe John and Teresa can be helpful in grappling with the apparent "postmodern" loss of confidence in the Cartesian ideal of the autonomous rational subject, fully conscious and in control of its beliefs and behavior. For both mystics, human beings are essentially relational. Recall that in Teresa's master symbol of the soul as a crystalline castle of seven progressively more interior "dwelling places," God dwells permanently in the center as the sustaining source of the whole edifice, whether we are aware of (and respond to) this divine presence or not; we would not be the creatures we are without that presence. Similarly, John of the Cross insists that "the soul's center is God" (*Flame* 1, 12), so that the human subject cannot exist or be understood except in relation to the divine, the term of its fulfillment, which (as John so forcefully stresses) transcends any human thought or feeling. In this sense, the human person is radically "de-centered" into mystery, into the unknowability of God. Thus the contemporary spiritual search for complete "self-possession" and control of one's own life is ultimately doomed to failure, precisely because we are constituted by this unlimited capacity for the infinite we cannot grasp or define, what the scholastics would call an "obediential potency" for participation in the very inner life of God:

> One should not think it impossible that the soul be capable of so sublime an activity as this breathing in God through participation as God breathes in her. For, granted that God favors her by union with the Most Blessed Trinity, in which she becomes deiform and God through participation, how could it be incredible that she also understand, know, and love—or better that this be done in her—in the Trinity, together with it, as does the Trinity itself! . . . Accordingly, souls possess the same goods by participation that the Son possesses by nature. As a result, they are truly gods by participation, equals and companions of God (*Canticle* 39, 4–6).[33]

But it is perhaps in relation to the so-called "hermeneutics of suspicion" and his own teaching on the "dark night" that John has

---

33. See also John's comments on the "deep caverns of feeling" in *Flame*, 3, 18–26.

most to contribute to the "postmodern" dialogue. As Merton again observes:

> [John of the Cross] is the Father of all those whose prayer is an undefined isolation outside the boundary of "spirituality." He deals chiefly with those who, in one way or another, have been brought face to face with God in a way that methods cannot account for and books cannot explain.[34]

John takes to its most radical conclusions the ancient principle that God infinitely transcends everything finite, including all human methods, thoughts, images, and feelings, however exalted. He is likewise a brilliant diagnostician of the myriad forms of human evasion and self-deception possible even in the most seemingly sublime religious matters. In the *Ascent of Mount Carmel* and *Dark Night* treatises, for example, he takes us through a detailed taxonomy of natural and "supernatural" experiences, and shows how easily apparently holy people can end up unconsciously twisting religious ideas and feelings to their own self-serving purposes if they begin to mistake them for the divine reality to which they are only meant to lead.

And while he is obviously a sixteenth-century author, not a member of the Frankfurt School, John's teaching can be easily broadened to incorporate whatever is legitimate in Marxist, feminist, and other critiques of religion. Some years ago, for example, Jesuit theologian Michael Buckley noted that John's analysis of the human capacity for projection has an uncannily contemporary ring:

> With Feuerbach, John is sensitive to the humanization which consciousness works upon its God; with Freud, he is acutely aware that the religious movement towards God can emerge either from the desire for satisfaction or from the drive to be morally reassured. In contrast to both, what he elaborates is not a process of assimilation or of psychotherapy, but of the transformation of the person by grace, the gradual becoming God by participation in the divine nature. . . . This continual contemplative purification of the human person is a progressive hermeneutic of the nature of God, the gradual disclosure of the One who infinitely "transcends the intellect and is incomprehensible to it." . . . Whatever knowledge one has does not move into the objectification of God but

---

34. Merton, "St. John of the Cross," *Saints for Now*, 259.

passes through objectifications, contradicts their adequacy, and in faith "reaches God more by not understanding than by understanding." . . . [John insists] that the evolution or personal development of faith must pass through the desert and the cross. . . . What I am suggesting is that the contemporary interest in spirituality may not be of incidental importance or of accidental occurrence, that for the reflective and sensitive mind—one which grasps the conditionality of imaginative and cultural structures, the necessities which issue from a background of which one can only be half aware, the profound limitations of one's knowledge and social situation—for such a person, the alternative may well lie between atheism and contemplation.[35]

To be sure, believers have always known the danger of remaking God in our own image. Modern authors such as Feuerbach, Freud, Nietzsche, Habermas, Durkheim, and feminists, however, have alerted us to the dynamics of projection, and to the complex, subtle, and often previously unrecognized ways that our class interests, patriarchal presuppositions, culture, and even language itself systematically distort our religion. Taking their "hermeneutics of suspicion" seriously might seem to leave us forever trapped in a house of mirrors; each newer, seemingly purer faith-stance we adopt as the old ones are "unmasked" proves to be just a more subtle projection of our own needs and interests.

John would certainly not agree here with those whose proposed solution is simply to move "out of our heads and into our hearts." While the recovery of the affective dimension and the suspicion of modern "rationality" may be an important component of some kinds of "postmodernity," John clearly believes that human affectivity severed from reason is as suspect, and as much in need of redemption, as reason divorced from affectivity. Indeed, for John love of God and neighbor is not primarily a matter of our affections in the superficial way these are often understood today, since our emotions are as often grounded in illusion as our concepts, and we can as easily fall in love with our own good *feelings* of love as with the real persons to whom those feelings are ostensibly directed. Thus, I end up "loving" not the poor as they really are, but my own sentimentalized image of the poor

35. Michael Buckley, S.J., "Atheism and Contemplation," *Theological Studies* 40 (1979) 694–99.

because of the comfort it gives me. For John, our natural capacity for love is constrained by the limits of our concepts and imagination; what our affectivity is drawn to of its own power is not God as God is, but our own image of God, and thus our desires are initially as distorted and misdirected by conscious and unconscious interests as our rationality.

So, for John of the Cross, it is the *whole* human person in every dimension—rationality, feelings, memories, presuppositions, unconscious drives and so on—that needs to be radically purified. Indeed, one important consequence for scholars is that even our own interpretation of John and his spirituality needs a "hermeneutic of suspicion," since it can become an idol. Ironically, those otherwise recognized as brilliant authorities on Sanjuanist doctrine can themselves sometimes display as "inordinate" an attachment to their own exegesis and scholarly reputation as any spiritual "beginner" frantically searching for consolation in prayer. As Gustavo Gutiérrez notes:

> Even here [among theologians] I seem to find a danger of idolatry: our own reflection, no matter how honest, can be transformed into a hindrance. Once again John of the Cross cuts away whatever is infected, whatever impedes the vision of God, with the scalpel of his experience and of his poetry. This makes him important for us.[36]

Despite his own reputation for physical austerities, John would surely have agreed with the wise comment of Teresa's friend Domingo Bañez, evaluating a Carmelite novice master overzealous for penance: "If he is looking for mortifications, here is one in very truth: to believe that he is mistaken."[37] Surely there is a lesson here for many leading "postmodern" figures, who seem to become so defensive when their own ideas and texts are criticized or "deconstructed."[38]

---

36. Gustavo Gutiérrez, "Rereading Saint John of the Cross from a Latin American Perspective," *Spiritual Life* 38 (Winter 1992) 233.

37. Crisógono de Jesús, O.C.D., *The Life of St. John of the Cross,* trans. Kathleen Pond (New York: Harper & Bros., 1958) 67.

38. See for example Thomas Sheehan's criticism of the deconstructionists' attempts to explain away Heidegger's sympathies with National Socialism, in Thomas Sheehan, "The Normal Nazi," *New York Review of Books* 40 (January 14, 1993) 30–35; and the subsequent heated exchange between Sheehan and Derrida in the "Letters" column. On the other hand, one sign of the maturing of the mod-

To sum up, then, John is as willing as any "postmodern" to concede our human incapacity to escape the bounds of our own history, culture, class interests, and so on. Left to our own devices, we would remain trapped forever in an irresolvably pluralistic world of fundamentally relativized values. This is the kind of scenario we see played out all too often today in arguments over "politically correct" speech, university curricula, polarization in the churches. Confidence in the possibility of rational debate has broken down, because all differences are reduced to historically and culturally bound opinions, and disputants no longer agree on any common ground or shared principles from which to start. And so discussion and moral persuasion are replaced by pressure tactics, shouting at each other across an unbridgeable cultural gulf.

Where John parts company with such "postmodernity" is in his conviction that grace is always possible, and can break through the cycle of self-interest and dysfunctionality. Intellect, memory, and will are, indeed, culture-bound and distorted by our past, but they can be progressively purified through God's self-communication in faith, hope, and love. To be sure, each new step along the way is always provisional, with further and more subtle evasions and prejudices to be "unmasked." None of us in this life is ever fully free and loving, or ever in full possession of the ultimate we seek. Yet, to the extent that we open ourselves to the painful and purifying questions and challenges that "postmodernity" and ordinary life today pose, we grow beyond what we once were, our horizons expand, and we travel further on the journey. Faith, hope, and love communicate God only in an obscure manner, says John, but they do not for this reason fail to communicate God truly (see *Canticle* 12, 4). And therefore, like good "postmoderns" (though perhaps for different reasons) we can afford not merely to endure "modernity's" demise, but even to rejoice in it, because we realize that the death of all penultimate certainties merely clears the way for the truly ultimate, for God. ("I am happy with St. John of the Cross among the rocks," writes Merton.[39]) That is why

ern feminist movement is its growing capacity for self-critiques; these run the gamut from the wildly provocative fulminations of Camille Paglia to the more thoughtful critique of "difference feminism" in Katha Pollitt, "Are Women Morally Superior to Men?" *Nation* (December 28, 1992) 799–807.

39. Thomas Merton, O.C.S.O., *The School of Charity: The Letters of Thomas*

John of the Cross can walk fearlessly through the desert and the darkness of his time and ours, singing:

> I know that [the spring] is bottomless
> and no one is able to cross it,
> *although it is night.*
>
> Its clarity is never darkened,
> and I know that every light has come from it,
> *although it is night. . . .*
>
> It is here calling out to creatures;
> and they satisfy their thirst, although in darkness,
> *because it is night.*
>
> This living spring that I long for,
> I see in this bread of life,
> *although it is night.*

Merton on Religious Renewal and Spiritual Direction, selected and ed. Patrick Hart (New York: Farrar, Straus, Giroux, 1990) 33.

Standing on the Edge of the Abyss: A Postmodern Apocalyptic Spirituality*

Tina Pippin

"The Apocalypse is the way the world looks after the ego has disappeared" (Northrop Frye 1982:138).

Sit back, but not comfortably, and watch the enactment of the end of the world. Your guide is the seer who calls himself John. He is going to take you through his visions of the future: the storming of the earth and its powers by the powers of heaven. The fates of the sinful and the righteous and the destruction of the old earth and the creation of the new are all presented as flesh and blood reality. This journey is not for the squeamish. There is war, rape, cannibalism, burning flesh, martyrdom, the burning of the earth, the terrorizing by seven-headed beasts, and the dead coming back to life. Your seat is conveniently placed at the edge of the bottomless pit, the abyss of chaos. But look around—there is a heavenly liturgy and a wedding feast and a beautiful city of hope. John is telling you what your choices are. He is telling you what you have to do to reach utopia. John has the wisdom of the end time: "I warn everyone who hears the words of the prophecy of this book: if anyone adds to them, God will add to that person the plagues described in this book; if anyone takes away from the words of the book of this prophecy, God will take away that person's share in the tree of life and in the holy city, which are described in this book" (Apoc 22:18-19). Any questions?

The New Testament vision of the apocalypse is a fast, scary, cathartic, and hopeful narrative. I want to approach the concept of

---

* This paper was presented at the January 9–12, 1993 "Scholars' Retreat" sponsored by The Abbey Center For The Study Of Ethics And Culture, Inc. at the Abbey of Gethsemani, Trappist, Kentucky.

the Apocalypse as a spiritual resource by approaching the abyss, the bottomless pit, in the text. The narrative motivates the reader to choose the way of heaven through using wisdom to discern the signs of the times, especially the political powers. I want to do a postmodern reading of the concepts of wisdom and the abyss in the Apocalypse by taking a postmodern turn in this journey of the end time.

The abyss is a fantastic poetic, postmodern space. But traditionally the abyss represents the hell to be avoided at all costs. All the enemies, those evil and dangerous political powers that oppress the earth, have been thrown into the abyss, which is an especially good reason to avoid the void. In the Tanak (Gen 1) the abyss is the ocean surrounding the land and also the chaos out of which the world was created. Abyss has an alternate meaning of "intellectual or spiritual profundity"; the dark night of the soul which leads to enlightenment. Parker Palmer uncovers this idea in his discussion about the political meaning of apocalypse: "So apocalypse *may* not be an end but a new beginning, a time when we are invited into the power of the spiritual life. Whether it *will* be a new beginning depends on our understanding of spiritual truth and our capacity to follow its call" (1984:23-24). I contend that traditional (and dominant) readings of the Apocalypse are patriarchal and limit the use of the text as a spiritual resource to a male vision of the end of time, the worship of the throne (phallus), and the distortion and destruction of goddess-based religion and women's power. A rereading of/into the abyss and of Wisdom (Sophia) in the Apocalypse leads to some new interaction with and questioning of the past and the future.

Emphasis on Wisdom and wisdom traditions is a frequent theme in feminist theology. Rosemary Radford Ruether explains: "It is in the hands of Holy Wisdom to forge out of our finite struggle for truth and being for everlasting life. Our agnosticism about what this means is then the expression of our faith, our trust that Holy Wisdom will give transcendent meaning to our work, which is bounded by space and time" (1983:258).[1] By focusing on Sophia the creative process is tapped.

1. Charlene Spretnak (1991:8) uses wisdom traditions from different religions (Buddhism, Native American, neo-paganism, and monotheism) in her postmodern reading. She states: "Because of the resilience of the wisdom traditions, which have survived the rise and fall of countless empires and ideologies, we have the opportunity to reclaim and renew the kinds of sensibilities with which we might cultivate awareness of the sacred process of the unfolding of the person, the or-

Rather than continuing to relate unquestionably to the total ecocide and genocide of the Apocalypse, a reclaiming of Sophia provides a different wisdom about the impending end of the world.

Poet Denise Levertov (1987:59) expresses the anxiety of relying on patriarchal wisdom in a poem entitled, "The Sun Going down upon Our Wrath":

> Get wisdom, get understanding, saith
> the ancient. But he believed
> there is nothing new under the sun,
> his future
> rolled away in great coils forever
> into the generations.
> Among conies the grass
> grew again
> and among bones.
> And the bones would rise.

The crisis and hope offered by apocalyptic literature stirs the imagination—from the violence of war to the peace of the realm of the divine. A headline in *The New York Times* (January 3, 1993) read, "From Creation to Apocalypse in 76 Hours Flat."[2] The Society for Secular Armegeddonism is proclaiming "pre-apocalyptic stress syndrome." Seeking the presence of the divine in the face of apocalypse is difficult. How do we "face apocalypse"? And how do we know what to do in the face of apocalypse? One starting point is with the biblical text and with facing the Apocalypse of John and its "wisdom"— scanning its heaven and peering into its abyss—going from creation to apocalypse to creation to apocalypse to creation—the endless end of the world.

---

ganic community, the Great Family of All Beings, and the cosmic whole. In the absence of such orientation, many lives may well become focused by default on becoming the Number One consumers in the global shopping mall, while many other lives will continue to be shaped by hunger and privation."

2. The article discussed a marathon reading of the Bible in a Washington, D.C. church. The pastor comments, "I'd be happy if people simply got literary pleasure out of this, or a lesson in ethics. . . . It's not like we're overburdened by morality these days. Especially in Washington."

Apocalyptic Wisdom: Discerning the End of Time

The tension between chaos and creation is central in the Apocalypse of John. This tension and the resulting ethical dualism call the hearers/readers of the book to patient endurance and testimony. The connection of wisdom traditions in the Mediterranean (especially North Africa) and in Mesopotamia (manticism) with apocalyptic is found by scholars in the context of the ethical. The value system and the ethical demands of choosing good over evil are at stake. The point is not to find an evolutionary link of prophecy to wisdom to apocalyptic, but there are connections between apocalyptic and wisdom in the Apocalypse of John.

Jonathan Z. Smith makes the connection between wisdom and apocalyptic by examining the *Babyloniaka* of Berrossus, a priest of Marduk (290–280 B.C.E.) (1975:132). Smith is interested in the author of this text, a priestly scribe of an elite, well-educated class. Of these mantic scribes Smith notes, "They hypostatized the scribe and scribal activities in the figure of Divine Wisdom. They speculated about hidden heavenly tablets, about creation by divine word, about the beginning and the end and thereby claimed to possess the secrets of creation" (1975:135).[3] Thus, two main "influences" of the wisdom tradition (which can also be said about the prophetic) are the role of the seer/sage and the passage of time (beginnings and endings).

The seer of the Apocalypse of John claims wisdom—the knowledge of the mysteries of the heavens as revealed to him. John is told to "write in a book what you see and send it to the seven churches" (Apoc 1:11). John fearfully faces the mysteries and reports (accurately, of course) what he sees. According to Kurt Rudolph, "wisdom was originally a practical matter, namely 'insight' into certain connections existing in human life and in the world and modes of behavior derived from this insight and put into the service of instruction and education. . . . A person's wisdom depends on what he or she has seen and thereby come to know" (1987:393). In the Apocalypse seeing (and hearing) is believing, and believing is seeing (and hearing). Experienc-

---

3. On the wisdom sage as mantic scribe (and the work of the scribe as a cultic activity), see P. R. Davies (1989:260ff). Davies uses 1 Enoch, Daniel, and Ben Sira as Jewish examples. Davies states, "The plausible *Sitz im Leben* for this erudite yet speculative discourse is an intellectual one . . ." (265). See also John Collins (1990).

ing the secrets of the end is more than cathartic; ethical action is required once one "sees" and "knows" and "hears." The wise have sight (and at least one ear to hear) and will triumph; fools are blind and deaf and will fall.

John Gammie (1990:497) focused on this relationship of "prudentialism to apocalypticism" which developed from a concern for family and king (Proverbs) to include divine election and warnings against idolatry (Sirach and Wisdom of Solomon). Gammie also incorporates Leo Perdue's work with Victor Turner's theory of liminality, noting that wisdom literature focuses on crisis periods or turning points (1990:483).[4] In Turner's studies, through the liminal experience the community participates in a ritual of role reversals, but liminality also refers to crossing individual thresholds in life, such as the entry into adulthood. Apocalyptic literature operates in a liminal zone, representing the ultimate and final crisis of the person and the universe. The Apocalypse crosses *the* major threshold—of the end of the world and the creation of God's new order. Anyone who disrupts God's order (and the final "communitas") is destroyed. Social deviants (Jezebel, the Whore, the Beast, any unbelievers, to name a few) are considered dangerous. In the apocalyptic liminal zone the abyss is the "final" place of those who are impure. The "ritual process" (to borrow from Turner) is set by God in the Apocalypse. Anyone who refuses to play by God's rules is out. And the seer wants the Christian community to know and understand these rules.

"These are the words" begins each of the letters to the seven churches. Wisdom is given through the words and by the Word, the Son of Man, "who holds the seven stars in his right hand" (Apoc 2:1), "the first and last, who was dead and came to life" (2:8), "who has the sharp two-edged sword" (2:12), "who has eyes like a flame of fire, and whose feet are like burnished bronze" (2:18); "who has the seven spirits of God and the seven stars" (3:1), "the holy one, the true one" (3:7), and "the Amen, the faithful and true witness, the origin of God's creation" (3:14). The description of the Son of Man in 1:13-16 is amplified and expanded throughout these messages to the seven churches. The angels announce, John reports, and Jesus Christ (bloody lamb, sword-wielding savior) gives testimony with his awesome and terrifying presence (1:1-2). The words are from Jesus through intermediaries

4. See Leo G. Perdue (1981).

(twenty-four elders, angels, an eagle, and John). These words have power over both believer and unbeliever and over all the earth. The authority behind the words is God.

In the Apocalypse of John there are four major passages associated with wisdom influences: 5:12 and 7:12 (both are hymns), and 13:18 and 17:9. In these passages wisdom is specifically discussed. From discussions of these sections I want to move into a broader discussion of the interfacing of wisdom and apocalyptic in the text through the concepts of ethics, the threat (or threat as perceived by different parties), the Goddess Sophia, and chaos (the abyss) and creation (the New Jerusalem).

Apocalypse 5:12 and 7:12: Hymns to the Throne of Wisdom

> Then I looked, and I heard the voice of many angels surrounding the throne and the living creatures and the elders; they numbered myriads of myriads and thousands of thousands, singing with a full voice, "Worthy is the Lamb that was slaughtered to receive power and wealth and wisdom and might and honor and glory and blessing!" (Apoc 5:11-12). And all the angels stood around the throne and around the elders and the four living creatures, and they fell on their faces before the throne and worshipped God, singing, "Amen! Blessing and glory and wisdom and thanksgiving and honor and power and might be to our God forever and ever! Amen." Then one of the elders addressed me, saying, "Who are these, robed in white, and where have they come from?" I said to him, "Sir, you are the one that knows" (Apoc 7:11-14).

In these hymns from the heavenly liturgy God and the Lamb are the ones worthy to receive wisdom. Wisdom dwells with God. The throne and the heavenly choir of elders, angels, and four living creatures sing praises on the bestowing of wisdom and other attributes on the Lamb and the one who sits on the throne. Thus, the Lamb and God possess wisdom, and wisdom in turn comes from the throne. The throne is the place of highest wisdom.[5] Power, might, wealth, bless-

5. Elizabeth Johnson notes that "the more transcendent is God's wisdom, and the more it is hidden in heavenly mysteries, the more the author locates hope for meaningful life in the disjunctive future" (1989:207). On the throne as central see Elisabeth Schüssler Fiorenza (1991:120): "Revelation's central theological query is: To whom does the earth belong? Who is the ruler of this world? The book's

ing, and honor are heaped onto God by the heavenly choir. The choir chants the truth. Participating in wisdom becomes a cultic activity. Heaven is a poetic (and musical) place.

From the throne God is a divine judge. God's actions throughout the narrative are defended. God's involvement in the suffering of the world is justified in the Apocalypse. James Crenshaw relates that "in wisdom thought, creation functions primarily as defense of divine justice" (1976:27). Since God is destroying the evil powers in the process of destroying the earth, God's actions are justified. The tension between destruction (chaos) and creation is heightened by this judgment.

The agents of revelation are the ones who speak (or sing) in the Apocalypse. In 7:13 one of the twenty-four elders poses a question to the seer. John defers to the heavenly authority with his reply, "Sir, you are the one who knows" (7:14). The authority of the ones in the inner circle of heaven nearest the throne of God is emphasized. If one is to possess wisdom, one must imitate the wise ones nearest the throne (the elders singing praise to God; the martyrs under the altar; the two witnesses; Jesus the slain Lamb).

Furthermore, one is also to imitate the seer, John, by respecting the visions and seeking to understand God's revelation. John obediently follows the instructions from the heavenly guides. In Apocalypse 10:8-11 when the angel asks John to eat the scroll, he eats. John reports: "So I took the little scroll from the hand of the angel and ate it; it was sweet as honey in my mouth, but when I had eaten it, my stomach was made bitter" (10:10).[6] The act begins a new wave of prophesy, as it does for the prophet Ezekiel (Ezek 2:8–3:3). So John chews, grinds with his teeth, swallows, and digests the scroll. Lips, mouth, teeth, tongue, stomach, and bowels are all involved in the eating process. John's desire to know all the heavenly secrets leads to a bit of indigestion. Tibor Fabriny notes that the act of swallowing notes absorption or incorporation: "The reader is absorbed by the vision and recreated by it" (1992:76-77) just as John is. This is inspired eating.

---

central theological symbol is therefore the *throne,* signifying either divine and liberating or demonic and death-dealing power."

6. Elisabeth Schüssler Fiorenza states that the bitter scroll symbolizes death (1991:76).

Apocalypse 13:18: The Threat of Monsters

This calls for wisdom: let anyone with understanding calculate the number of the beast, for it is the number of a person. Its number is six hundred sixty-six (Apoc 13:18).

The monster in the Apocalypse is the political state. Rather than worshipping the Son of Man, the whole earth worships the monsters (13:4). The dragon and the beast of the earth and the beast of the sea are like the four beasts of Daniel 7; here the different national powers are combined into one imperial power with different forms. To discern who the beast is requires wisdom, since most of the inhabitants of the earth follow the beast blindly, marking their foreheads or right hands as slaves (13:16).

The number of the beast who rises out of the earth is 666. The believers are to calculate this number so that they know which person is represented. This use of *sophia* is linked to "the specific Christian-apocalyptic sense of esoteric knowledge" (Wilckens 1971:524).[7] The number of the beast remains a mystery, although valiant efforts have been made to decipher the code.[8] John is telling secrets and revealing mysteries, and "anyone with understanding" will know how to live in the world before the eschaton. The sets of opposites—the Son of Man/Lamb with the Beast; the Bride and the Woman Clothed with the Sun with the Whore and the Jezebel—lead the believers to see the different ethical choices. There is also a "confusion of values" (Camp 1985:117-18).[9] The beasts are hypnotic, and the Whore of Babylon is amazingly seductive. She also has a name of mystery on her forehead, "Babylon the great, mother of whores and of earth's abominations" (Apoc 17:5). The Bride is also seductive, in a different way, of course.

The results of following the beasts or the Lamb are made clear. The threat of the earthly political (and economic) power is great until

7. Wilckens states that in 13:18 and 17:8-18 *sophia* "is the knowledge which is reserved for Christian confessors and which enables them to perceive the true meaning and ramifications of the events which were taking place on earth in their day" (1971:524).

8. Paul Boyer (1992:chapter 8) traces the manifestations of 666 in popular culture and the interpretations by conservative Christian groups. The main focus is on the political situation in the Middle East and the European Common Market.

9. Camp is referring to the language in Proverbs 1-9 and the use of seductive feminine imagery for the strange woman.

its overthrow. But the threat of death at the hands of the earthly power is not as great as the threat of chaos. God's threat is bigger. Those who do or follow evil will eventually (very soon) meet the judgment of God. Only those who are not confused but understand the mysteries as explained by John can be counted as insiders in the "utopia of wisdom," a place where everyone shares the special wisdom. All war, death, and famine has ended, and all the enemies have perished. The wisdom of the empire is in tension with God's wisdom throughout the Apocalypse. The two thrones compete for the allegiance of humanity. As Claudia Camp notes concerning Ben Sira: "This sage addresses an educated, well-to-do, but—as far as political, economic, and social matters are concerned—persistently threatened audience" (1990:198). By enacting all these different threats in the narrative, the Apocalypse becomes motivational rhetoric.

The threat is part of the ethical variable of the perception of the situation, according to ethicist Glen Stassen. The threat is measured in terms of its "nature, degree, and linkage with other elements" (Stassen 1980:68). The perception of the threat from different ethical players is important. John sees the imperial threat differently than some of the seven churches (e.g., the Nicolaitans). The imperial power perceives yet a different threat—from colonials who are rebellious—to the attack from God's army. The heavenly powers see the threat from the political power and all who make themselves impure by following it. Readers of the Apocalypse have experienced the threat in their own contexts. How the threat is perceived determines both interpretation and action. For example, Daniel Berrigan and Ernesto Cardenal stress the present threat of the imperialistic policies of the United States and urge the radical ethical action of choosing Christ over "Caesar." In the Apocalypse there are threats from many sides (e.g., the imperial power, seductive, evil women, God's judgment), but only one true promise.

Apocalypse 17:9: Sophia Displaced

> This calls for a mind that has wisdom: the seven heads are seven mountains on which the woman is seated; also, they are seven kings . . . they will make war on the Lamb, and the Lamb will conquer them, for he is Lord of Lords and King of kings, and those with him are called and chosen and faithful (Apoc 17:9 and 14).

The great Whore who thinks to herself, "I rule as a queen" (18:7), is discerned and destroyed. The angel gives a detailed explanation of the mystery of the Whore. The believers are called to come out of the Whore and to enter the Bride, the New Jerusalem.[10] Again, the choices are participation in the new creation or in chaos, the destruction of the earth. The Whore is dethroned, as the beast was. The Lamb alone rules in the new heaven and earth.

In Proverbs 1-9, Wisdom as personified as a woman is a counselor, lover, and administrator of divine justice, and she is given the power of indirection, where women's intellect is praised (Camp 1989:274-281). Wisdom is a goddess—a wise goddess who passes her wisdom on to wise men. Wisdom (*sophia*) is Maat,[11] Aphrodite, Astarte, the Queen of heaven, and the daughter of the Father God (Gnosticism). By the Apocalypse there is a return to the King God, the King of kings and Lord of lords. Wisdom is displaced from the throne, or at least co-opted into the Son of Man figure and the Woman Clothed with the Sun and the Bride. The Woman Clothed with the Sun is the mother of the Messiah (Mary), and her astrological surroundings of a "moon under her feet, and on her head a crown of twelve stars" (12:1) resemble Wisdom. The Bride of the Lamb becomes the city of the New Jerusalem; otherwise she might be a queen and co-monarch. However, in medieval artistic representations the Bride is often crowned as a queen but is known only in relation to her husband.

So what happens to Sophia in the Apocalypse? Is she part of Jesus and God, since wisdom is bestowed upon them? In the first and second century c.e. Jesus is portrayed as Sophia, from the wisdom sayings of Jesus (in Q and Gnostic gospels) to extracanonical apocalyptic literature. The main story line is that Sophia is rejected on earth and returns to heaven. In the Similitudes of Enoch 42:2, "Wisdom went out in order to dwell among the sons of men, but did not find a dwelling; wisdom returned to her place and took her seat in the midst of the angels."[12] Is Sophia the Bride or the Bride and the Spirit (Apoc

10. See the discussion of gender and misogyny in Pippin (1992).
11. The Egyptian goddess Maat "symbolized truth, justice, and order in cosmos and society". . . . This order "existed and is known and with an unbroken confidence in the act-consequence connection. Modesty, uprightness, self-control, subordination, silence, are virtues of the wise." Maat is eventually replaced by the sun god Re (Rudolph 1987:396).
12. See the discussion of Jesus as Sophia in James M. Robinson (1975) and

22:17)? Is the Bride the consort made legitimate? James M. Robinson relates that the Holy Spirit "is feminine in Semitic languages and at times is interchangeable with Sophia" (1975:6). In any event, the powerful Sophia of Proverbs is personified in many figures and thus is disempowered. Susan Cady, Marian Ronan, and Hal Taussig (1986:50) point to "Sophia's muted status in the New Testament," which certainly is the case in the Apocalypse.

Another aspect of Sophia is her antithesis, the Jezebel and the Whore. As in Proverbs 1–9, the counsel of a "strange" woman is dangerous. There is a female threat in the Apocalypse. The sexually aggressive female is the most threatening. Giving in to her seduction leads to death: "and I will strike her children dead" (2:23). Following the dangerous female also leads to the abyss. The abyss or the bottomless pit is female in Greek.[13] The abyss represents the ultimate chaos. The abyss is the female hell mouth (the vagina with teeth), portrayed by the large mouth of the beast in certain medieval representations. In the Apocalypse of Paul 41 the hell mouth is the place of eternal punishment. The angels with Paul say to each other, "Open the mouth of the well that Paul, God's dearly beloved, may look in, because power has been given him to see all the punishments of the underworld. And the angel said to me: Stand at a distance, for you will not be able to bear the stench of this place." There is fire in this well, like the lake of fire and sulfur ("the second death"—20:14) in the Apocalypse of John. Were the seers expressing castration anxiety? What is the effect of pulling the readers/hearers to the edge of the abyss? Do we nervously peer inside the pit?

Conclusion: The Pit and the Throne

> Then I saw a new heaven and a new earth; for the first heaven
> and the first earth had passed away, and the sea was no more.

---

especially, Elisabeth Schüssler Fiorenza (1983:130-40) on "The Sophia-God of Jesus and the Discipleship of Women" and Cady, Ronan, and Taussig (1986).

13. Camp (1991:29-31) shows that the Strange Woman in Proverbs 1–9 is related to Death and Sheol: "The language of death, shades, and Sheol, which have had its origin in the cult of a goddess (so Blenkinsopp) or some other chthonic deity (so McKane), is transformed in Proverbs to articulate a force—defined here as female—that will ultimately split the religious cosmos of Judaism and Christianity into a dualistic moral system in which women can come out on only one side."

And I saw the holy city, the new Jerusalem, coming down out of heaven from God, prepared as a bride adorned for her husband (Apoc 21:1-2).

All chaos is removed to the "outside" in the Apocalypse—the sea, the dangerous women, the evil monsters, all the unfaithful, and death. A new Eden is created as a new paradise with the tree of life restored.[14] Where is the tree of the knowledge of good and evil, the wisdom tree? Where is the wise serpent?

The need for wisdom is in the time before the end of time. "Anyone who has an ear to hear" is given the chance to gain wisdom and discernment enough to make the choice for good and against the powers of evil. Both powers are seductive and mysterious. Paradise is the reward for making the wise choice. But where is Wisdom, the female personification and deity, in the Apocalypse? The Goddess both is and is not in the text; that is, she is not present in the form we know from Proverbs 1-9, as the powerful creatrix, teacher, and judge. She is subdued and passive, deferring to the male authorities (Jesus and God). The Queen of Heaven gives birth to the Messiah (the Woman Clothed with the Sun) and later marries the Messiah (the Bride). Her body is laid out (and marked and measured by the seer) as the heavenly city and the New Creation. Wisdom loses her place in the pantheon. She exists in the future world in a different form; or rather, she has been re-formed. Women are placed either in the pit (as spiritually dangerous and impure and therefore needing to be murdered) or on the throne, where they are worshiped for their "spiritual purity" and confined in their roles.

Do you doubt the wisdom of the Apocalypse? Then fall, fall, fall into the abyss,[15] the bottomless pit, the great endless gulf, the void. The fall is unavoidable. You were on the threshold, at the edge of the opening of the mouth. Were you thrown? Or did you get too close to the edge, straining to peer in? You will fall forever, free-fall in eter-

---

14. Cf. 4 Ezra 8:52: "Because it is for you that paradise is opened, the tree of life is planted, the age to goodness is established and wisdom is perfected beforehand." Anthropologist Bruce Lincoln says that in many cultures the concept of paradise is an inversion of the world: "Of the otherworld, all that can be said is that things there are totally *other*, completely opposed to all of this earth" (1991:29).

15. An alternative meaning of abyss is "intellectual or spiritual profundity."

nal flight. You will be at the opposite end of Heaven, falling further from its salvation with every second. You are in Hell, Sheol, the under-world, the place of darkness, of the dark, dangerous female. You are eternally outside of Heaven, the New Jerusalem, that place of light and material delights, paradise regained. You have found the void, the *tabula rasa*, nothingness, the dark, deep innards of earth. You are in no place (*ou topos*), utopia.

Works Cited

Boyer, Paul. 1992. *When Time Shall Be No More: Prophecy Belief in Modern American Culture*. Cambridge: Harvard University Press.

Cady, Susan, Marian Ronan, and Hal Taussig. 1986. *Sophia: The Future of Feminist Spirituality*. San Francisco: Harper & Row.

Camp, Claudia V. 1985. *Wisdom and the Feminine in the Book of Proverbs*. Sheffield: Almond.

_____. 1990. ''The Female Sage in Ancient Israel and in the Biblical Wisdom Literature.'' In John G. Gammie and Leo G. Perdue, eds., *The Sage in Israel and the Ancient Near East*. Winona Lake: Eisenbrauns, 185–203.

_____. 1991. ''What's So Strange about the Strange Woman?'' In David Jobling, Peggy Day, and Gerald Sheppard, eds., *The Bible and the Politics of Exegesis*. Cleveland: The Pilgrim Press, 17–31.

Collins, John J. 1990. ''The Sage in the Apocalyptic and Pseudepigraphic Literature.'' In John G. Gammie and Leo G. Perdue, eds., *The Sage in Israel and the Ancient Near East*. Winona Lake: Eisenbrauns, 343–54.

Crenshaw, James L. 1976. ''Prolegomenon.'' In Crenshaw, ed., *Studies in Ancient Israelite Wisdom*. New York: Ktav, 1–60.

Davies, P. R. 1989. ''The Social World of Apocalyptic Writings.'' In R. E. Clements, ed., *The World of Ancient Israel: Sociological, Anthropological and Political Perspectives*. New York: Cambridge University Press, 251–71.

Fabriny, Tibor. 1992. *The Lion and the Lamb: Figuralism and Fulfilment in the Bible, Art and Literature*. New York: St. Martin's.

Frye, Northrop. 1982. *The Great Code: The Bible and Literature*. New York: Harcourt Brace Jovanovich.

Gammie, John G. 1974. ''Spatial and Ethical Dualism in Jewish Wisdom and Apocalyptic Literature.'' *Journal of Biblical Literature* 93:356-85.

_____. 1990. ''From Prudentialism to Apocalypticism: The Houses of the

Sages amid the Varying Forms of Wisdom." In John G. Gammie and Leo G. Perdue, eds., *The Sage in Israel and the Ancient Near East*. Winona Lake: Eisenbrauns, 479–95.

Griffin, David Ray. 1989. *God and Religion in the Posmodern World: Essays in Postmodern Theology*. Albany: SUNY Press.

_____, ed. 1990. *Sacred Interconnections: Postmodern Spirituality, Political Economy, and Art*. Albany: SUNY Press.

Johnson, E. Elizabeth. 1989. *The Function of Apocalyptic and Wisdom Traditions in Romans 9–11*. Atlanta: Scholars.

Levertov, Denise. 1987. "Poetry Reading." In *Facing Apocalypse*. Eds. Valerie Andrews, Robert Bosnak, and Karen Walter Goodwin. Dallas: Spring, 49–69.

Lincoln, Bruce. 1991. *Death, War, and Sacrifice: Studies in Ideology and Practice*. Chicago: University of Chicago Press.

McGinn, Bernard, trans. and introduction. 1979. *Apocalyptic Spirituality*. New York: Paulist.

Palmer, Parker J. 1984. "The Spiritual Life: Apocalypse Now." In Tilden H. Edwards, ed., *Living with Apocalypse: Spiritual Resources for Social Compassion*. San Francisco: Harper & Row, 23–38.

Perdue, Leo G. 1981. "Liminality as a Social Setting for Wisdom Instructions." *Zeitschrift fur die Alttestamentliche Wissenschaft* 93:114-26.

Pippin, Tina. 1992. *Death and Desire: The Rhetoric of Gender in the Apocalypse of John*. Louisville: Westminster/John Knox.

Robinson, James M. 1975. "Jesus as Sophos and Sophia: Wisdom Tradition and the Gospels." In Robert L. Wilken, ed., *Aspects of Wisdom in Judaism and Early Christianity*. Notre Dame: University of Notre Dame Press, 1–16.

Rudolph, Kurt. 1987. "Wisdom." In Mircea Eliade, ed., *The Encyclopedia of Religion*. Vol. 15. New York: Macmillan.

Ruether, Rosemary Radford. 1983. *Sexism and God-Talk: Toward a Feminist Theology*. Boston: Beacon.

Schüssler Fiorenza, Elisabeth. 1983. *In Memory of Her: A Feminist Theological Reconstruction of Christian Origins*. New York: Crossroad.

_____. 1991. *Revelation: Vision of a Just World*. Minneapolis: Fortress.

Smith, Jonathan Z. 1975. "Wisdom and Apocalyptic." In Birger A. Pearson, ed., *Religious Syncretism in Antiquity: Essays in Conversation with Geo Widengren*. Missoula: Scholars, 131–56.

Spretnak, Charlene. 1991. *States of Grace: The Recovery of Meaning in the Postmodern Age*. San Francisco: Harper.

Stassen, Glen. 1980. "Critical Variables in Christian Social Ethics." In Paul D. Simmons, ed., *Issues in Christian Ethics*. Nashville: Broadman, 57–76.

Wilckens, Ulrich. 1971. "Sophia." In Gerhard Friedrich, ed., *Theological Dictionary of the New Testament*. Vol. 7. Grand Rapids: Wm. B. Eerdmans, 496–526.

"Not Himself, but a Direction": An Interview about Thomas Merton with John (Jack) H. Ford

Conducted by George Kilcourse
Edited by David King

George Kilcourse: How and when did you first meet Thomas Merton? Had you read much of Merton's work before that meeting? What were your impressions of him and of his work?

Jack Ford: I think I would talk about my encounter with Merton at two different times. To begin with, I, like everybody else that I knew, had read *The Seven Storey Mountain* and that was the thing I guess that attracted me to him, to Gethsemani. I started going out to the monastery after World War II. Ironically enough, it was a non-Catholic with whom I went to the monastery for the first time to meet Merton. I had been taking the Leader's Great Books Course here in Louisville, and there was a fellow named William Hobick who was in that course and, one day, said he was going out to Gethsemani and would I like to go along? I had been to Gethsemani only several times before, with other people, but this was an invitation I accepted because he said he was going to see Thomas Merton. And I thought, well that's impossible, but I'll go along. I think at that time I had a rather distorted and elevated notion of Gethsemani itself. I thought it was a holy place different than the way it really is holy. There was a kind of image people got who read things like *The Seven Storey Mountain* that everybody was wearing a hairshirt and fasting excessively and being tormented in the name of the Lord. I think it was later that you found it was a place of joy, and that this was very important.

This old brother led us back to the old house; there was no guest house at that time, but it was a big room with two or three beds. It was wintertime, and you had to put your hand on the radiator to realize that there was anything like heat in anybody's mind. But Merton came in, and I approached him with a great deal of awe, waiting for him to levitate and that sort of thing. I really did, I had this very exalted and distorted notion of what the Trappist life was about and who Thomas Merton was. So, I remember just getting on my knees asking for his blessing. I'm not sure that's what I was supposed to do, but it was a very uncomfortable experience, I'm quite certain, for him; and in retrospect it's a very uncomfortable experience, so far as memory is concerned, for me.

Then there was a space of years before I really got to know Tom again, and that was when Dan Walsh came to Bellarmine. It was through Dan that I really got to know him, and then later on we developed a relationship on our own. But without Dan, I think there would have not been the relationship for a lot of us in Louisville, especially Bellarmine College. I think that it was through him—he was the conduit to Gethsemani and Merton. And so when I did get to know Merton that second time, I think I knew a real person better, and not an image, and I think we built a friendship based on a more solid understanding of him, and of Trappist life, and the Church in general.

Kilcourse: Any particular impressions of him when you got to know him that second time, just as a person?

Ford: It was significantly different. I think that I was not simply in awe. I always had great respect for him, but never a saccharine kind of awe. But I think the thing that's always struck me about Merton was his capacity to relate to people, and people of all levels. I don't think that I ever, in all of this time—and when I knew him at the beginning he was just beginning to grind out his writing, as he became famous and was corresponding with people throughout the world who were prominent, from Pasternak to Maritain, to Dorothy Day—I never sensed a bit of arrogance in the man. I think that he had not a pseudo-simplicity but a genuine simplicity that came through, and I don't think I ever saw that change.

Kilcourse: You became quite involved in the plans for the hermitage. Could you recollect how that came about and what developments punctuated Merton's vision of the hermitage and its coming-to-be?

Ford: I think that Merton occasionally, as I remember at least, became restless. And the schedule at Gethsemani was so unbelievably demanding, and he had, from time to time, health problems. I think the most remarkable thing about this man is—and it's been said time and time again—that he kept the life that he did. He was faithful to all of the monastic rules. He was an effective teacher of the novices, a leader of the novices. I don't just mean directing; he was a *leader* of the novices, and yet at the same time he sat down at the typewriter and produced material the way he did. If he didn't have anything else to do but that, it was remarkable that he did it. So I think that there was this need to find some space and some time to do some of these things. If you remember in *The Seven Storey Mountain* and other places, he said when he went to Gethsemani that he didn't want to become a writer. That changed. I believe since he did see that was going to be his vocation, that he would want to do that as best as he could. I don't think this was a purely selfish reason or that he simply wanted to be away from the monastery itself.

We were sitting on a hill out there one day, and talking, he was always talking about what might be over the next hill, and he said he'd like to have a hermitage. One of the other things he said he'd like to have was a little building next to it where seminars could be held. And we talked about it for a while, and it occurred to me then that the Ford Foundation was doing some rather creative things, and I thought, well, with his name and the ambition that he had for that shelter and getting people to come from all over and talk, that it might be very productive in many ways.

So I mentioned this to a good friend of mine, Art Bec Var, who was in charge of design for General Electric. He got one of his staff, and we went out there and again sat on the hill and played a rather unmerciful joke on Merton. We brought all this good food, and I think we even had a bottle of wine, and we unwrapped a little package of cheese and gave it to him, but he soon got beyond the cheese. Anyway, they later returned and had this beautiful design of a building, and since it was going to be outside in the beautiful surroundings of the abbey, they designed it in glass. And so in this whole thing you would have been in the woods but inside talking.

Merton got very excited about it. The only thing that he objected to was that it was all glass, and he still had this thing about what was going on at Fort Knox. In those days you could hear the guns going off at Fort Knox, but he thought how horrible if we had an atomic war. He could just see that glass flying into people. But again, it was kind of funny now, and it was funny then to me, that he would stop and worry about how in the world he's going to die, or how in the world he's going to be preoccupied.

Things were moving along and we finally got word from Abbot Fox that he couldn't have the seminar building. But it was a leverage because it was going to be hard to say "no," "no." He could more easily say one "no" and one "yes." Well, he didn't have to, but he did. He said you can't have the hermitage built, but we'll build it for you, and you'll have to put the seminar building off. At the time Merton wrote a letter to Art Bec Var, which was lost until the last few years when he went to a book when he started talking about remembering the guest house and the letter fell out. And the letter said, in effect, that Merton hoped that someday there would be some seminars at Gethsemani and that people would come.

I had an embarrassing thing happen in connection with that. I always was very respectful of the monks, but in jest I wrote a letter saying I was very disappointed we were not going to have the seminar building, and I asked do you think we ought to do the abbot in in a vat of monk's cheese. He called me the next day, rather genuinely excited, and he said, "My God, don't you realize he reads the mail?" (*laughter*). So after that, there was no more attempt at humor! Shortly thereafter, the hermitage was put together. I think the brothers did most of it, but it turned out to be very nice, and I think Merton was very happy. I thought in a way, though there was never another building there, that there was activity from there that was going to be lively.

Just by way of a digression, I remember when I heard that he was going to go to the hermitage, I felt that this was going to be good-bye forever. He went to the hospital for a physical, and Gladys and I went down to see him, and I offered to give him a kitchen shower. But I was sad because I felt I would never see him again. I went out to Gethsemani a short time later and said something to one of the brothers. I said, it's really kind of an uncomfortable feeling telling him goodbye because I'll never see him again; and the brother, I can't remember who it was, just smiled and said, "You'll find that Father Louis is a very gregarious person." As a matter of fact, I saw him much more after he got into the hermitage, but I think that's kind of interesting. He really did get away, but at the same time he opened himself up to do things that his vocation was demanding he do. I don't think this was a luxury he sought, but I think it was something he saw as related to his vocation

Kilcourse: When several of Merton's celebrated visitors came to the Abbey and later the hermitage, you accompanied them. Who were the most memorable visitors? What do you recall about such meetings with Merton?

Ford: Well, I guess that there were four or five. The first was Father Ford, who had baptized Merton, if I remember correctly, when he was at Columbia, I can't remember the name of the church. . . .

Kilcourse: Corpus Christi.

Ford: Corpus Christi, that's right. And he had not seen Merton, since he had been at Gethsemani. So I met him but I did not get involved in the conversation, I just left him there and stayed for a while, and then he came back with me. But it was a great event for him, and I'm quite certain it was for Merton.

The next one was Rosemary Haughton, who was then living in England and beginning to write extensively, had some beautiful stuff out. She was on a lecture tour in this country, and he had called and asked if Gladys and I could meet her, and keep her overnight, and bring her out the next day to the monastery. Rosemary at that time was pregnant, I mean very pregnant. I joked with him later on, "eleven months pregnant," because I could just see her getting in the woods out there and having to rush her to the hospital. But it didn't turn out that way, it turned out very well, and we were there for awhile. I think we had a picnic. We excused ourselves and they had a chance to talk. We brought her back, and I stand in awe of the fact she got on the plane to go and give a lecture someplace else. How she'd been doing this I don't know. But she also raised the windows in our house because she couldn't stand the heat—English you know. Very wonderful person, and I believe I've mentioned to you before, George, when we had a seminar out there recently, that it was about twenty-five years to the month that she had been out there.

I guess the most memorable visit for me was the time that I took John Howard Griffin out. John had his leg in a cast at the time. He had severe diabetes, like Merton sometimes in ill health of a variety of kinds. Father Murphy from Toronto was there and John Howard

Griffin, and Jacques Maritain, and Dan Walsh, and Merton and myself. And there was a fellow named Penn Jones who came with John. He was a retired general in the army. And Kennedy's death had been, maybe a year before, and Penn Jones was on this kick about a plot, and he had written a book. I have a copy of the book still, I think, but he was saying that there was some hanky-panky going on in this whole business of the assassination. Years later there was a movie made called "Executive Decision," and I was sitting there watching the movie, and after it was over, the credits came on and he was given credit for part of the research in the movie itself. I brought Penn Jones and John Howard Griffin back to wait at the house for awhile, and I kept Griffin for a little bit after that. Maritain himself was there with shawl, and this was spring, but it was warm and he was out there with that shawl. Some young woman, I should've mentioned her name but I don't remember, who was kind of a nurse taking care of him. I would like to say that very profound conversation went on, and maybe it did after I left (*laughs*). That night I think Maritain and Father Louis had a chance to go on in French and talk to one another. But that was just a very nice sociable day, and I think Griffin took some pictures of that encounter that have been floating around for years. Very, very pleasant.

I guess at one time or the other, maybe we took people out, but those would be the most significant. I remember taking our children out for some picnics.

Kilcourse: You earlier mentioned Joan Baez's visit?

Ford: Joan Baez, that was a going-the-other-way visit. Joan Baez had gone to Gethsemani with her husband to meet Merton, and I think was a bit shocked, for some reason or other, about Merton. She went out there perhaps with some of the idea that I had when I went for the first time, expecting him to come out and levitate, and I don't know what else. In any case, she found a real down-to-earth human being. They had rented a car, and again, I think, with the profundity of mind that Merton had—he didn't always look at practical things—he got in the car to take her back to the airport, and after he got there he realized he didn't have a way back to Gethsemani, so he called the house, and I got him. Then the problem got to be whether he'd spend the night or go back. I taught class the next morning so he had to be back. Anyway, he went back that night. So that was a reverse trip.

Kilcourse: In *The Seven Storey Mountain* Merton gives a vivid description and account of Dan Walsh and his influence as a philosopher and teacher. You chaired the department of philosophy at Bellarmine College when Dan began teaching there. What was he like as a teacher? As a colleague?

Ford: I think *The Seven Storey Mountain* pretty well described Dan when Tom said here was a self-effacing, elfish kind of man who was sitting there talking about St. Thomas at Columbia University. Dan was teaching at Columbia and Manhattanville and while at Manhattanville, of course, he met the Skakels and the Kennedy girls, and also Tommie O'Callaghan from Louisville was there at that time, and he got to be a very good friend of Tommie's. Right after Vatican II there was a suggestion that the monasteries realized that their priests should be getting theological and philosophical training that had been pretty much taken for granted. I think what was being suggested was that they'd better update and do this. I have heard that Abbot Fox wrote to Dan and wanted to know if he'd be interested in coming to Gethsemani to do some teaching. In the meantime, I think Dan had had some health problems and was in an accident or something, but he was at a time when he could have used a sabbatical or some rest.

He came to Gethsemani and began teaching there, and within a short time, perhaps within a year, he was teaching at Bellarmine part-time. Dan lived in that old guest house and I'm terrible talking about space, but if you remember there was a cot and a chair and a little table for a desk and a wash basin and little else, and Dan lived in that room for years. Now he wasn't a guest, he was living there. So you would go in that room and it would be so piled up with books and stuff that you couldn't get in. I think for him to have lived like that was rather remarkable. Not that he stayed there all the time. Dan could stay in Gethsemani so long, and then he had to get away. I think the relationship with Bellarmine was good. He came to Bellarmine (and this was before I was the chair) and began teaching and also, then, became the conduit between Bellarmine and Gethsemani.

As a lecturer, I would have to put Dan down as certainly dull. I mean he was nothing other than that. And yet at the same time, if you were patient enough to sit there for ten minutes and listen to him and not look for theatrics, but listen to what the man had to say, then he got to be a great influence on the students at Bellarmine. I don't think there'd be any other way of putting it. And students who were willing to sit and listen for that first few minutes, who began to listen to what he was saying, got to be very devoted to him. Dan had a real following at the college. At the same time, he was getting to be kind of an institution in some respects.

They had a gatehouse at Gethsemani that had (I use the word loosely here) some art objects and religious gadgets (there's no other way to put it) and cheese and fruitcake were sold there too. And Dan had this shopping bag, and he would fill up the shopping bag and he would come in and he would be walking down the hall and see people with whom he was working or liked, and here would come some fruitcake or cheese. I was convinced they were paying him with fruitcake and cheese at Gethsemani for a long time. He was a very, very generous person. He had no car. The whole time that he was here, he never drove. That meant that some of us would be taking him back to the abbey. And when he got back to the abbey, he'd tell you to wait a minute. And he'd go in the gatehouse and pretty soon you'd see him coming out. My children had more rosaries and scapulars and statues of the Sacred Heart than you could shake a stick at! Dan, incidentally, became godfather of our youngest child.

To get back to Bellarmine for a moment, there had been no relationship at all between Gethsemani and Bellarmine College. I think some of us may have gone out there. But after Dan came and began making some contact, several things happened. First, we had faculty retreats start. I was working with a faculty organization that got it started. Actually, Merton gave the first one. So we went out there for about three days, and that was when it was an all male school. And for all practical purposes, except for maybe the librarian, we had an all male faculty, which meant that there was no great difficulty. But this was an exceptional thing, a Merton conference for two days and a half for faculty. We had great esprit de corps.

Kilcourse: How many people were involved?

Ford: I'd be afraid to guess. I guess we had maybe forty people. But there was a thing about Bellarmine College at that time, where people did not get divided so much among departments, but they really shared in the teaching experience. You took great pride in the fact that the chemistry department was doing such and such if you were in the philosophy department, and they were taking pride in what we were doing, and I think all of that is coming out of the fact that there was a spiritual integration going on as well as an intellectual one.

Dan had an effect on the faculty that way. He amused a lot of people, but this was the kind of amusement that you get from a grandfatherly type person, which he would never want to be. Dan would not, I think, desire to be a grandfatherly type, but I think that's the way he was looked at. Many students loved him and admired him and imitated him. He didn't get involved to a great extent in department activities. Dan was a very lonely person. I don't want to say a loner. That would be incorrect, but he was a lonely person whereas he had a great many friends, but I don't know if Dan had intimate friends or not. As I say, I question that, I don't know, but he was a great force in the college then with his getting Merton to meet with us and for us to feel that. We could go out to the abbey, then at the same time Merton was coming and using the library. I don't think Tom ever taught a class, I don't think he ever lectured a class, but he did use the library at the time, and he got to know people at the college—Fr. John Loftus especially, and Father Horrigan. That's when I think the whole idea of the collection started. Dan would have to be responsible for any relationship that Bellarmine College did have, and consequently has, with Gethsemani.

Kilcourse: I know Dan did read, didn't he, the statement that Merton wrote for the 1963 inauguration of the collection.

Ford: That's right. He did.

Kilcourse: Dan never really wrote much of anything did he?

Ford: No, he didn't.

Kilcourse: A lot of tapes of his things are in the library at the abbey.

Ford: Yes, that's right. I think that some of the students took tapes. I know Tom Bizot was one of his students, and he took practically all of his courses. And in a way you were not taking a course, for example, in metaphysics, you were taking a course in Walsh, that kind of thing. One of the monks told me that when Dan was teaching there (I taught some there a few years back, and I was trying to get some type of book that would be a survey of all Thomistic philosophy) and I had a book, and Father Flavian looked at it and said, "Oh Dan used to use that, except he never opened it" (*laughter*).

Kilcourse: Could you comment on how Dan Walsh became a priest of the Archdiocese of Louisville?

Ford: I think you'd simply have to stress the word surprise. Dan's work at the abbey had been going on for years, and his work at Bellarmine. He didn't do that much in the community. I think he'd attended a couple of dinners with Archbishop Floersh at the time, and of course Dan was a great name-dropper in terms of the Kennedys and so on. But here was this very conservative archbishop who called Dan on the telephone one day, and I happened to be in the office. This was not a call to come down to the chancery, I want to talk to you about something. He got a call on the telephone, and he said to me "The archbishop said he wants to ordain me." And to give you some idea of what my reaction was: "You're getting older, you've been a good layman, and now you want to go be a priest!" He had to decide about this, and it didn't take him long. And I think he went through a brief routine of some presumptuous person taking him by hand through some theology quickly for a matter of weeks.

But a short time later, we're not talking about a year or two later, we're talking about months later, Dan was ordained at St. Thomas Seminary. There was a celebration, and Merton came in for that, and the abbot, as a matter of fact, did too. We had a big party over at Tommie O'Callaghan's and it was quite an event.

I don't think that Dan (and maybe this is not appropriate for our conversation) was ever accepted by the priests in the archdiocese. First, he didn't go through the seminary with anybody. He didn't associate with many priests. He hadn't been to the parishes for Mass or anything. As a result, in later years, he became ill and retired. If he had been lonely before, this loneliness was unbelievably compounded now. After Kennedy had died, I think the two great shocks that finally did him in were when Merton died and then Fr. John Loftus died shortly thereafter, all of these things within a space, what, of months. I was still at Bellarmine when Kennedy died. But then, I think that Merton's death was devastating. They had become friends, intellectual friends. But for Dan now Merton had become kind of an alter ego. I don't know how to explain it. He was really immersed in Merton's life and I mean that in a very positive way. I guess if he had a relative or person close to him it was Merton that he identified with. And as a result, I think

Merton's death was devastating to him. And then, Father John shortly thereafter, a matter of weeks.

So he wanted to quit teaching after that, and did. This is a digression from the priesthood, but not completely. Then he was going to be at Gethsemani for awhile. I don't know how much we want to get into this, but then he got a trailer moved over on Thompson Willet's property and lived there for some months. But again, as a priest he was not anyplace. So actually when he came back to Louisville and got an apartment, why Bishop Maloney, who was very kind and had always been kind, went to see him and encouraged him to ask for anything he might need.

But then even when Father Timothy and I were at Dan's death bed, the question got to be, what do we do with this man who's dead? I put a telephone call in to Bishop Maloney, and he asked what are we going to do, and I said I guess put him in a funeral home for a while then take him to Gethsemani to be buried. And he said, "Wait just a minute, I think we always have the priests of the archdiocese have a Mass together. Could you arrange for him to be here at the cathedral?" So we had a Mass at the cathedral, but very few people showed, very few priests showed. Again I think that what I would stress would be the loneliness, even for the vocation to the priesthood that Dan had.

At the same time, I think he did a lot of good. I remember vividly his coming to Baltimore to visit one time. I wanted him to come up as a priest and teacher, and he got off the bus with a shoebox with his chalice in it and a shopping bag with his clothes. He was going around like pretty much of a vagabond who would be willing to sit down in the next breath and talk about the distinguished people with whom he had dinner, and the Kennedys, and how they would go on a plane to go swimming in Florida.

Kilcourse: A beautiful man.

Ford: Yes.

Kilcourse: Could you describe how Merton has affected your faith and intellectual life? What did Merton's life of prayer mean to you?

Ford: Well, I don't know . . . that's very hard. I think what Merton did was help me remove a lot of intellectual garbage that I had carried around, such as, that there are certain ways that you do things, there are certain paths that if you follow you were going to be a Catholic Christian. And I think what he helped me do as much as anything was to show me the relationship between the faith and the world in which we live. I was raised in a time when social concerns, even though the social concerns were there, were out of the line of vision. You know we've got a lot of good thinking today that people don't pay attention to. But the bishops are at least recognizing the social problems even if they are not tormented by the search for answers. I think that what Merton did for me was to show me the implications and the obligations of the faith in terms of community. This famous scene at Fourth and Walnut for him was something he used for other people to see that talking about the Mystical Body was not talking about something only in the order of grace or grace working through nature, but the implications of these in society. So I think he did that.

In terms of prayer life, he taught me at least what prayer was going to be in the truly contemplative sense of the word. Not necessarily verbalizations, but you could also in prayer let God happen to you as well as going after God. And I think that to see that what you were doing, even though you said these things, I became even more deeply aware that what you were doing was prayer. Meister Eckhart has a line that I think was true of Merton, and he may have known about it, "It's not so much what you do that makes you holy, the idea is that you make holy what you do." I think this is something he did, and did for a lot of us.

I concluded a book review I did on Merton once by saying given the fact that he had the warts that he had, and there were not many, that here is a man who joined his voice in the chorus that had been intoned by a young Jewish woman who simply said "Yes." And I think that that was the most fantastic thing about him, that the "Yes" was a total "Yes." And his legacy enabled others to say that "Yes." If anybody had been a betting person, you would never have guessed that this man who went to Gethsemani would have ever had a chance at making it for a month. But I think this is a testimony to the grace of God. This is another thing I don't think people talk about enough with reference to Merton. There's an old line about when somebody writes a biography of a saint you always see how good the saint was, but when the saint writes an autobiography you always see how good God was. And I think there's not enough about the demonstration of God's love for this man, and the grace he gave to him for him to do what he did. Because you read, especially in Mott's book, where this was a spoiled, indulged man, even though he had his own sense of loneliness as an orphan. And that this man could go to Gethsemani and do what he did, and then get to be who he was in terms of the world and the relationship that Gethsemani was to have in the world and the inspiration it was to give to the world. Not all particularly Thomas Merton, but at the same time that faith that we have to keep emphasizing, the grace of God working through him. No one has been able to explain it, for me at least.

Kilcourse: That's probably why he was as transparent about it or at least as open about it because he realized that was the story that was being told.

Ford: Yes, yes.

Kilcourse: Not his own story, but the story of God.

Ford: Yes.

Kilcourse: How would you describe Merton's place in Catholic intellectual life as a Catholic philosopher and theologian?

Ford: I think that he was growing more and more all the time from *The Seven Storey Mountain*. *The Seven Storey Mountain* was for people like Frank Sheed and Fulton Sheen another *Confessions* of Augustine—that was one of the blurbs that was on the book. And I think that one of the big things here was that people could find out that somebody could leave the world, and the kind of world that he had, and go into that place. Gabriel Marcel has a line (I think Marcel), "It was not so much that I believed in faith, but that I believed in the faith of somebody else first." I think that, here again, Merton was a great instrument in terms of being a step toward a faith of one's own, because you were reading this man who was doing this thing, and then got to go beyond this. In that respect it was a kind of awakening about the implications of the faith, and then of course as it went on, the implications of this as it was going out to politics and to society and to the contemplative life and so on. He was beginning to go beyond the laity and influence a lot of the clergy, and I think it's not unfair to say that Merton had some effect on the Second Vatican Council—I don't think there's any denial of that. That being said, if you talk about him being a theologian and philosopher, then I would have to say—and I'm not in a position to judge theology—but I'd have to say philosophically he was certainly not structured. I suspect he was not theologically, but what he had was this great poetic insight into the core of philosophy and the core of theology, and this was something you didn't get through a discursive process. I'm convinced that he had this insight into truth that a theologian and a philosopher could look at their own and say, "I should have thought of that, I should have seen this." Then, I think also he had a gift of prophecy. He was a prophet of our time. And I don't think those of us who were around him then understood this well enough. I know I've told you before that when I was sitting at my desk in Baltimore and I got the phone call about his death, I wondered if ten or fifteen years from now anybody would ever hear of Thomas Merton. And I think we now know that his influence has gone far beyond even what those of us who loved him suspected. About twenty-four languages, now, I think he's been translated into. Touching people, especially young people, nobody had ever touched. So I would never classify him as a theologian or a philosopher as such, but as a poet who could really get to the core of what a lot of theologians were missing and what a lot of philosophers did miss.

Kilcourse: What spiritual writers most influenced Merton? You mentioned Meister Eckhart.

Ford: Yes, but I wouldn't be capable. . . . I think again the fantastic accomplishments of this man. He read and read and read, so I wouldn't be able to say who . . . I know that he went through stages. He went to the Desert Fathers. He didn't start off at this end, he went back to the Desert Fathers and came through. The reason I mention Meister Eckhart is because I think that he, in the later years, had great effect on him. This getting to God beyond God, for example. It was not recognized at first. All the people who read books about him added that all up. People talk about so many other people influencing Merton, and I think that Meister Eckhart is overlooked. I think Dan [Walsh] told me this one time, too.

Kilcourse: That will be a good assist for the readers of *The Merton Annual* and the interview, Meister Eckhart. What of Merton's own writings attracts you the most in your reading?

Ford: That would be difficult. I'd go back to (even though he considered it to be corny later on) I think *The Seven Storey Mountain* for all of us, a beginning. *Conjectures of a Guilty Bystander* was another one. *The Sign of Jonas.* One of the best pieces I think he ever did, a short piece, was the introduction to the Japanese edition of *The Seven Storey Mountain.* That was a good hunk of work. And of course *New Seeds of Contemplation* you can always pick up and get good insight. It's hard for me to single out stuff, because everything he did I thought was good. He gave me a lot of things that had not been published. Among other things he had was an article on Camus, which may have been published since then, because Brother Patrick [Hart] gets all of this stuff published somewhere. But he maintained that Camus was moving up toward Christianity. Again, he was just pouring out material.

Kilcourse: You were also a close friend of Dom Flavian Burns, who was abbot at Gethsemani at the time of Merton's death. What can you tell us about their influence upon each other?

Ford: Well, not very much. I was away when Father Flavian got to be abbot. I do remember one thing. I think Father Flavian told me this himself. The tension between Abbot Fox and Merton—too many people looked at it in a very negative way. This is not the question you asked me, but I think it has a bearing on this question. I've always tried to figure out why the stress was there. I was having dinner one night with Bob Giroux. And I was talking about this thing, and this tension, and "there's one thing," he said, "that you must never forget. Merton was an orphan." And even though he had other people taking care of him, the trust that took care of him and so on and got him out of jams and the like, he was an orphan. And I think that there was this paternal relationship between Father Abbot and Merton, if you see that relationship in this light. But the interesting thing, and the thing I eventually want to get to in terms of this is that Merton needed the abbot's strength. So it was also kind of restrained, but at the same time, I think Merton, even though there was tension and irritation at times, had the affection of a son. Maybe I'm completely wrong about this, but this is the way I guess I've read it. Consequently, when Father Flavian came in, who had been junior to Merton, why this was a different ballgame altogether. The story that I get, that I find so amusing, is when he was talking about going to Bangkok, that he went to Father Flavian and said, "I want to get permission to do this,"

I think maybe he was suspecting that he was going to get a "no." But then Father Flavian turned to him and said, "Make up your own mind." And Merton couldn't quite handle this for awhile. So maybe this is a complete distortion, but you were asking for personal opinion, and I'm giving it. I think that Merton had an affection for Abbot Fox. Hostile, maybe at times, but that's going to be true of any family, of father-son relationships.

Kilcourse: That's part of the relationship.

Ford: Sure.

Kilcourse: Sudden affection.

Ford: Yes.

Kilcourse: Wasn't Dom James Merton's confessor?

Ford: Yes, this is interesting. I don't think, again, from the outside, that we people who look at the abbey know what community means in a Trappist monastery. The closest we get to it is a family. But there's a twist here to it that I don't pretend to understand. But it's there, a kind of affection there, and inevitable tensions that you're going to get in any family. But at the same time, it's a source of fantastic growth, or destruction. I think the spirituality has to come out of that tension.

Kilcourse: In *The Seven Mountains of Thomas Merton,* Michael Mott mentions you and your wife Gladys once being on an abbey picnic, including Merton and the nurse with whom he fell in love. Do you have any insights or reflections about this crisis late in his life?

Ford: Crisis can depend on viewpoint. It can be anything from loss of a loved one to the dissolution of an adolescent crush. I do not really know what Merton felt about this matter. But you asked for a viewpoint. So I'll give one with the caution that my wife does not agree with me completely in this matter.

First, I think that this event takes up too much space in Michael Mott's book. Second, I would make, from my viewpoint, a distinction between love and infatuation. If one stands back and looks at this in some detached way, the fact that a fifty-some-odd year-old monk was during a hospital stay smitten by a beautiful young nurse, young enough to be his daughter, one could certainly have varied reactions.

One could be just plain amusement. At some other extreme there could be talk of love crisis.

We use the word "love" today so very casually that we can easily forget its implications—commitment, dedication, loyalty, to some extent abandonment of self. Infatuation can be many things, from glandular reaction to very real human feeling, if perhaps fleeting, the later can lead to the former but. . . . Even though there are some love poems which were published, I can only wonder if they are born in the deep feeling of Abelard (Heloise) or Kierkegaard (Regina) or Dante (Beatrice)—where the unattainable leads to more romantic thoughts than would the sustained actual encounter. Here I but guess.

Gladys, Fr. John Loftus, and I took the young nurse to Gethsemani for a visit and a picnic. She and Merton had some private conversation, and subsequently there were other brief meetings. It at least got to be such a matter that like some adolescent Merton was making night telephone calls from the gatehouse. Some would certainly justly question Merton's judgment in the matter. And while I am happy for any beautiful human relationship—and I hope I am not a hardened unromantic—I believe that in this Merton made a fool of himself. I believe that the reported response of Abbot Fox was quite appropriate. He laughed at him. And haven't we all been in positions we felt to be very very serious when even a smile could shake us. If one talks about Merton and love, then I would have to talk about the abbey where Merton loved for decades with men in community, keeping promises, sustaining irritation to do something productive with it, growing in dedication to an unfolding mystery.

But I do not think this episode should be overlooked or dismissed. It may have had a beautiful effect on even more than two lives. So all of this for me is speculation. One thing I am certain of is that I definitely agree with his taste in young nurses.

Kilcourse: Twenty-five years after Merton's death, we're still making efforts to follow his vision of spirituality. What do you see as the most urgent but unfulfilled parts of his vision which we still need to undertake?

Ford: It was easy for some people like myself to isolate aspects of life—religion here, work there, family life and vocation, other compartments of life—to fail to work at integrating these into a wholeness of life that is Christian. This was not so much a deliberate stand as an unawareness. I believe that Merton awakened us to see that the search for the Kingdom must be attained through efforts in the political, economic, and social climates in which we live and that a Christian response is demanded in these issues. Silence is a loud denial of required response.

Merton was a counterculturalist, sensitive to the weaknesses in a society and church which he loved so much he was giving his life for it. There was a time for honest critical response. Too often we have hidden cowardice with the conviction that certain issues are just none of our business.

We have to realize that faithfulness to the Church is more than assent to Creed; it is responding to the often harsh message of the Gospels where Christ placed some social burdens on our consciences. Merton can in this matter ever be a gadfly reminding us through his work and life that new issues must be faced with some old tried and true values—those of Jesus!

Kilcourse: We'll put an end to this. Jack, from your point of view as a friend of Merton's, how would you evaluate Thomas Merton's interests as they're expressed in many of the Merton circles and activities that claim his name and spirit?

Ford: I think that there would be so many ways to look at this. And I guess I would have to look at it in terms of the needs of the people involved. To imagine that Merton was going to be out there as a vehicle of one kind for all people to use to get to the truth would be a distortion. Because I think we have different needs. And so I think some people need to be continually immersed in Merton himself, going back and looking at his works and seeing the implications of these. I think others of us would want to see Merton as a direction, who through his works urges us to look beyond him, in other words, not to have him be an end in himself but to have us breaking more the ground he plowed to begin with. So I think those would be at least two paths. And, of course, Merton the artist will be viewed not only by what he said but by what persons bring to his work.

Kilcourse: How do you think the Church and the world will remember Thomas Merton one hundred years after his death, and how should we remember Thomas Merton one hundred years after his death?

Ford: I have difficulty grasping a question like that. I think that Merton has not been simply a popular writer sustained by a particular age. The roots of his writing go too deep for that. I believe he will be read as something of a prophet of our time, but that he will also become part of a tradition of spiritual writing that has nourished the Church.

As for how we should remember him? That he was a man loved enough by God to use him effectively in a confused world. That he loved God in himself and God in us. If we remember that, the rest is a matter of footnotes.

Kilcourse: Jack, thank you for a delightful conversation.

Critical Turn Ahead!: 1992 in Merton Scholarship and Publication

Michael Downey

Where to begin? And where to end? It makes no difference where I begin, for I shall be there again in time. In my own "raids on the inarticulate," T. S. Eliot's words from the *Four Quartets* have often provided just the right kind of nudge:

> "In my beginning is my end."
> "In my end is my beginning" ("East Coker")

> "We shall not cease from exploration
> And the end of all our exploring
> Will be to arrive where we started
> And know the place for the first time" ("Little Gidding")

The same lines come to mind when faced with the Mertoniana that continues to appear year by year. Where do I begin in a bibliographic essay of works appearing in 1992, which both anticipates the twenty-fifth anniversary of the death of Gethsemani's most celebrated son, and marks a new era in the Merton legacy?

Is there any end to it? Is it just one thing after another? With Qoheleth I find myself plagued with the haunting suspicion that there is really nothing new under the sun. And I must admit that, at times, I share Dominican Richard Weber's sentiment expressed on the concluding page of the final issue of *Spirituality Today*. Weber wonders: ". . . when does the publishing of Mertoniana end? Where is the point when publishing anything he wrote begins to cheapen his true reputation? Will we have, next year perhaps, the new Merton book: *Whiter and Brighter: The Laundry Lists of Thomas Merton?*" (44/2 [Summer 1992] 200).

I do not judge it to be my task to provide an inventory list of each and every item of 1992 Mertoniana. Nor is it my task to separate wheat from chaff. It is more a matter of recognizing some of the gems in the 1992 Merton collection. No one of them can be appreciated if all are lumped and tangled together.

It is my purpose to single out those strands that I consider to be the more valuable of the lot, not only in terms of their distinctive contribution to the collective Merton fund, but also in terms of how well they will wear in the long run. By way of conclusion I shall suggest what is the most serious challenge that yet awaits us in our common work as students and scholars in the field of Merton studies.

Books

William H. Shannon's *Silent Lamp: The Thomas Merton Story* (N.Y.: Crossroad, 1992) has received warm reception and appreciative reviews. What Shannon does is tell the now familiar story of Thomas Merton, but with a sharp eye for the contours of Merton's spirituality. Shannon zooms the lens so that Merton the monk is brought into sharp focus, and the author's own contemplative poise yields a picture that many have been anticipating for some time. What we have here is a reflective biography by one who is altogether familiar with Merton the man and monk. The most striking feature of Shannon's work is that he is able to familiarize the reader with the life and times of his subject, inviting to a thoroughing appreciation of Merton—as if for the first time. But he does this without ever slipping into the irksome "my chum Tom" idiom, or worse, into the mixed message of some Merton mystagogues: "no-one-outside-the-monastic-life-can-possibly-understand-our-Father-Louis."

One of the more distinctive features of Shannon's work is also the most problematic. The chronologies that are provided at the end of chapters or groups of chapters are not well integrated in view of Shannon's overall aim. The chronologies list significant events and dates in the world at large, together with key events and dates in Merton's own development. These chronological listings are like appendeges at the close of chapters. There is no explicit connection made between the chronological data, especially the events taking place in the world at large, and the Thomas Merton story as Shannon tells it.

It might be argued that it is the task of the reader to make such connections. But the reader is left wondering why Shannon deemed certain world events and dates worthy of inclusion in his chronicle, while
others were excluded. What is unclear is Shannon's principle of inclusion and exclusion, especially since there seems to be no explicit
effort to demonstrate whether and to what degree the events chroni-
cled influenced Thomas Merton and the community at Gethsemani
of which he was a part.

Shannon's reflective biography is a book which I would put in
the hands of any student or scholar of Thomas Merton. We are, once
again, in debt to one who stands at the forefront of Merton scholarship.

Authors often have little to do with the way publishers and book-
sellers market their work. In much of the publicity that heralded the
appearance of *Silent Lamp*, it was set against Mott's work and lauded
for not tangling the reader in details. I am still somewhat staggered
by the odious comparisons between this book and Michael Mott's *Seven
Mountains of Thomas Merton*. Jejune judgments claiming that Mott's
work is bogged down with facts and details belie a jaundiced view of
a work that is an inestimably valuable source in understanding the
Merton story, as well a paradigm of literary grace. They tarnish Mott's
exhaustive biography, and slight its singular significance, even if not
quite enough of the monastic Merton is mirrored in Mott's pages.

Thomas Merton: Spiritual Master. The Essential Writings, edited with
an introduction by Lawrence Cunningham; foreword by Patrick Hart;
preface by Anne E. Carr (N.Y./Mahwah: Paulist, 1992) is the ''keeper''
of the year. It seems that, as with Shannon, publishing and publicity
personnel have had their own way with this book. Cunningham is
expert enough to know better than to call this judiciously selected and
edited collection *the essential writings*. Yet that is what is claimed. Who
decides these things in Mahwah? Or New York?

Without doubt, we have here the most solid, foundational selection of the broad range of Merton's writings to date. We do not really
get a taste for Merton's poems here, and that is to be lamented. But
what is provided is rich fare, artfully arranged and presented. Cunningham's entrée is in itself worth the price ($14.95 paperback). Anne
E. Carr's preface is exquisite, just as we have come to expect of her.
Patrick Hart's foreword provides helpful remarks about the period of
Merton's life when he was either master of students or master of
novices at Gethsemani (1951–1965). But the real merit of the work lies

in Cunningham's understanding of Merton the master. His understanding of Merton as sapiential theologian and his definition of Merton as a "spiritual master" is perhaps the best hermeneutical stance auditioned thus far in Merton studies. What is also a most delightful surprise is that Cunningham perhaps unwittingly demonstrates that he is himself a master at his craft: a discerning guide; a careful and insightful teacher; a graceful sage of measured word and deep respect for the words and wisdom of another.

The Springs of Contemplation: A Retreat at the Abbey of Gethsemani, ed. Jane Marie Richardson (N.Y.: Farrar, Straus, Giroux, 1992) is a transcription of two series of talks given during retreats at Gethsemani: the first in December 1967; the second in May 1968. These two retreats at Gethsemani were occasions for contemplative nuns to gather together to discuss with Merton the pressing issues facing religious and contemplative life. It is useful to note that Merton did not seek official permission to meet with the nuns or to give them conferences. Nor did the nuns require or request permission to participate. What we have here, then, is vintage, off-the-cuff-Merton; anything but the domesticated variety. And it is fresh. What Jane Marie Richardson has accomplished in these pages is quite impressive. From audio tapes that are at times barely decipherable, she has provided a clean and sharp rendering of the retreat conferences. Oddly, more of the flesh-and-blood Merton comes through in these pages than in the tapes. Particularly admirable is the way in which Richardson has been able to keep the dialogical character of the retreat conferences. Here we have Merton talking about whatever issue is raised, doing theology on his feet, passing breezy asides about the state of affairs in the Church and religious life, calling for a more prophetic critique on the part of religious and contemplatives vis-à-vis the world of which they are a part. And, of course, he is speaking with women. One would be hard pressed to detect even a hint of nascent Mertonian feminist consciousness in these pages. And to the editor's credit, she does not pretend that there was one. But for any thorough understanding of Merton on the contemporary renewal of religious and contemplative life, this book is a real treasure, handsomely produced.

Thomas M. King's *Thomas Merton: Mystic at the Center of America* (Collegeville: The Liturgical Press/Michael Glazier Books, 1992 [vol. 14, The Way of the Christian Mystics]) promises more than it delivers. In this work, King provides a helpful study of Merton on "the self," "contemplation," "freedom," and "others." In many respects he covers much the same ground as Anne E. Carr's splendid study, *A Search for Wisdom and Spirit: Thomas Merton's Theology of the Self.* Some of King's investigations of Merton's understanding of different types of prayer and contemplation are instructive. But the book seems to work against itself partly because the terms "prayer," "contemplation," and "mysticism" are used without a great deal of precision. What is nowhere to be found in these pages is a clear explanation of what the author means by the term "mysticism" and, more importantly, just how Merton may be understood as a mystic. King's work takes up themes already raised in Raymond Bailey's ponderous study of Merton *on* mysticism, in John J. Higgin's early investigation of Thomas Merton's theology *of* prayer, and in William H. Shannon's *Thomas Merton's Dark Path.*

Much more needs to be said about Merton the mystic. Before the conversation can proceed to anyone's advantage, however, more terminological clarification is in order. Merton did not use the term mystic or its cognates with any great regularity, particularly in reference to himself. Further, Merton did not tell us much about his own experience of prayer. In this he differs from Teresa of Jesus, John of the Cross, or Elizabeth of the Trinity and others who provide descriptions of their mystical experience. A Fourth and Walnut epiphany does not a mystic make, at least not in the classical sense of the term. But such an experience does provide as good a starting point as any for a discussion of Merton the mystic. Or Polonnaruwa. Neither one is treated in King's work. Not even given a nod. It is also quite striking that King pays little attention to Merton's poetry. If there are veins of mysticism to be mined in the Merton corpus they lie in the poems, especially the antipoetry of the later years. George Kilcourse has consistently and effectively examined the poetry as a source for understanding Merton's spirituality. His *Ace of Freedoms: Thomas Merton's Christ* (Notre Dame: University of Notre Dame Press, 1993), a carefully crafted study of Merton's Christology, is the first critical systematic theological investigation of Merton's poetry.

Because of the questions King's book raises, it is my hunch that it will provide stimulus for further serious critical investigation, not of Merton on prayer or contemplation or mysticism, but of Merton the mystic. This is fruitful terrain, especially in view of David Cooper's carefully argued, though by no means universally accepted thesis that

Merton failed as a mystic (see David D. Cooper, *Thomas Merton's Art of Denial: The Evolution of a Radical Humanist* [Athens, Ga.: University of Georgia Press, 1989], ch. 6, "Failed Mysticism," 166–91). Future forays into the landscape of Merton's mysticism will be greatly enriched by the ongoing work of Bernard McGinn, *The Presence of God: A History of Western Christian Mysticism* (vol. 1, *The Foundations of Mysticism: Origins to the Fifth Century* [N.Y.: Crossroad, 1991]), who maintains that the central category governing discourse about mystical experience in the Christian tradition is not "union" but "presence."

Book Chapters

In *Spiritual Guides for Today* (N.Y.: Crossroad, 1992) Annice Callahan devotes a chapter to "Thomas Merton: A Living Mystery of Solitude," 97–116. This is a helpful little introduction to the life and spirituality of Thomas Merton. Useful for undergraduate courses, Callahan situates Merton alongside five other twentieth-century spiritual guides, three Roman Catholics, one Jew, one Anglican. Callahan's strong suit is also something of a handicap. Her writing is straightforward, direct. This is very helpful in working with undergraduate students who tend to value clarity and precision in expression. But when taken either in part or as a whole, Callahan's writing is a bit clipped. The style is staccato. The reader is provided with basic, reliable information. But the net effect is that we have just skimmed the surface. But in teaching Merton to college or university students, Callahan's work will serve as a fine primer.

Conrad C. Hoover's, "Going Deep into the Truth: Thomas Merton and Spiritual Direction in a Cross-Cultural Context," in *Common Journey, Different Paths: Spiritual Direction in Cross-Cultural Perspectives* (ed. Susan Rakoczy [Maryknoll, N.Y.: Orbis, 1992] 67–77) is worthy of note. His exposé is built on Merton's conviction that the contemplative experience is already embedded in the traditions of all peoples. He contends that we can do nothing more helpful than to help others uncover their own proper identity and destiny as they come to know the Christ dwelling within. While Hoover does not say much about Merton the spiritual guide that has not been said before, the fact that he brings his insights on spiritual direction to bear upon a much wider cross-cultural conversation advances the discourse about Merton a significant step in the right direction.

Varia

There are a few other items worthy of note. Thomas Merton, *The Monastic Journey* (revised edition with foreword by Patrick Hart; Kalamazoo: Cistercian Publications, 1992 [Originally published in Britain and U.S., 1977]). This collection of essays takes up issues pertinent to monastic, solitary, and contemplative living. Written during his later years, these articles are expressive of Merton's more mature reflections on the monastic vocation.

Merton: A Film Biography, produced by Paul Wilkes/Audrey L. Glynn is now more accesible and available in a more affordable video cassette (First Run Features. 153 Waverly Place. New York, N.Y. 10014).

It should also be noted that the French-born New Yorker Thomas Merton was judged worthy to be included in the encyclopedia published to mark Kentucky's bicentennial. See the entry by Robert E. Daggy, "Thomas Merton," in *The Kentucky Encyclopedia*, ed. John E. Kleber (Lexington, Ky.: The University of Kentucky Press, 1992).

Perhaps one of the more noteworthy developments is that Thomas Merton's *The Seven Storey Mountain* is now available on audio cassette (read by Sidney Lanier; abridged by Jacob Needleman and John Hunt/Spiritual Classics on Cassette [Berkeley: Audio Literature, 1992]; two cassettes). Such a recording will be of inestimable value to the visually impaired, the elderly, the infirm. It should also receive a warm reception by those who have welcomed the renaissance of "listening in" which has been occasioned by the advent of "A Prairie Home Companion," "Radio Reader," and other such audio programs.

The Need for a Critical Turn

At the close of the first twenty-five years of Merton studies, it may be appropriate to suggest some of the tasks that yet await us in our common work. Above all else it seems that the most pressing task is to connect the discourse within the circle of Merton studies with the discourse in other fields. We need to make room for a greater variety of voices in our ongoing conversations, even and especially those voices which might seem to interrupt and unsettle commonly held perceptions about Merton the man and the monk. Merton *aficionados* need an *aggiornamento*. The windows need to be opened, new light thrown on the subject, fresh air breathed into our lungs, new blood let flow

through our veins. Much of the Merton conversation is claustropho-
bic, a bit like *"deja vu* all over again.''

A new generation of Merton scholars will have different perspectives and a different task. Their work will not primarily be that of making the literary legacy of Thomas Merton available to an ever widening
circle of readers. It is rather more a task of bringing a heightened critical hermeneutic to bear on the life and legacy of one who no doubt
will stand up well under the most rigorous constructive critique. What
is being suggested here is not that a cadre of insensitive smart allecks
try to air Merton's dirty laundry. Rather it is to suggest that if the conversation around Merton is to be brought to a new plateau, a far greater
measure of constructive critique is called for.

It is now more commonly recognized that the Merton circle is
really quite small. Its canons tend to be narrow. They are implied rather
than explicit. Studies of Merton that veer away from the hagiographi-
cal tend to be shunned. Consider the cool reception given David
Cooper's astonishing study of Merton. Even if Cooper may not have
a feel for Merton's monastic matrix, he volunteers a brave and refreshing critical interpretation of Merton, based on Merton's own writings,
rather than on the lore. We need more critical studies like his. And
Anne Carr's. Or George Kilcourse's. These critical investigations signal the direction where the studies will be moving in the next generation of Merton scholarship if Merton is to continue to speak from age
to age.

In conclusion, I should like to provide an example of a critical
question that has yet to be brought to bear on the Merton corpus in
any rigorous or systematic fashion. If all Christian spirituality is *ipso
facto* Trinitarian, why is it that there is so little explicitly Trinitarian language in Merton's writings? Since the affirmation of God as triune is
central and essential to Christian faith, why do Merton's writings seem
to rely so little on explicit Trinitarian symbolism? (*Pace*, William Koch's
research on pneumatology in Merton's canon, a study pertinent to the
Trinitarian theme). It is conceivable that there is a particular way that
Merton perceived the basic truth that the doctrine seeks to articulate,
but that he expresses it in a way that requires skillful and careful translation. Or it may be that the prevailing Christian doctrine of God had
in Merton's time so marginalized the Trinitarian dimension (because
of its esoteric and speculative character) that he gravitated toward a
more generic Christocentric monotheism. But because it is to be ex-

pected that authentic Christian faith and spirituality in some way reflect the particularities of symbols and events of Christian faith, the seeming absence of reliance on Trinitarian, as well as pneumatological, language and symbolism in Merton's writings on Christian life is an area awaiting rigorous, critical investigation.

Reviews

Lawrence S. Cunningham, editor. *Thomas Merton: Spiritual Master. The Essential Writings*. New York: Paulist Press, 1992. 437 pages. $14.95 paperback.

Reviewed by Walter E. Conn

This may be the book bargain of the year: two books in one modestly priced volume. For, in addition to over 350 pages of selected writings by Merton, the buyer also gets about eighty choice pages of editorial commentary and apparatus: a brief foreword by Patrick Hart, O.C.S.O.; a short preface by Anne E. Carr; a long introduction (and brief introductory notes to each selection) by Lawrence Cunningham; a five-page chronology of Merton's life; and a six-page select bibliography of books by and about Merton.

Perhaps we should consider the Merton writings first. I will focus on the list of items selected, knowing that their substance needs no recommendation to readers of the *The Merton Annual*. The editor's precise intention was to bring together the essential writings of Merton specifically as "spiritual master," not to produce another general *Thomas Merton Reader*. Cunningham explains the systematic process of consultation he employed to avoid an idiosyncratic selection. The method worked: given the limitations of space, most readers will find little to quibble about. The selections are divided into two groups: Autobiographical Writings (arranged chronologically) and Spiritual Writings (ranging from 1958 to 1968, but arranged in only a rough chronological order).

Not surprisingly, the autobiographical group begins with about forty pages from *The Seven Storey Mountain* (part two, ch. 1, sec. ii–v) where Merton recounts the friendships and other influences at Columbia leading up to his declaration to Father Ford at Corpus Christi: "Father, I want to become a Catholic." Next we find "Fire Watch, July 4, 1952," the epilogue to *The Sign of Jonas*. Next comes about forty pages from the first half of part three of *Conjectures of a Guilty Bystander*, which include the "Fourth and Walnut" conversion. This selection is followed by some fifty pages from the posthumously published *A Vow of Conversation: Journals 1964–1965*, covering New Year's Day to Easter, 1965. Then we have the complete text of the short essay *Day of a Stranger*, a 1965 piece detailing life in his new hermitage. This autobiographical group ends with selections from *The Asian Journal*, including the Polonnaruwa experience.

The group of Spiritual Writings begins with several sections from the second part of *Thoughts in Solitude* (1958): "The Love of Solitude." It also includes "The General Dance" from *New Seeds of Contemplation*, the prose-poem "Hagia Sophia," the introductory essay from *The Wisdom of the Desert*, and "Herakleitos: A Study" from *The Behavior of Titans*. A particularly valuable inclusion (more than sixty pages) in this group is "The Inner Experience," the first four parts of a 1959 manuscript on contemplation in which Merton tried to augment Neo-Scholastic formulations with insights from Eastern mystics. This important transitional work was previously available only in back issues of *Cistercian Studies* (complete) and in *Thomas Merton's Dark Path* by William H. Shannon (selected passages). The work of Merton's later years is represented by "Learning to Live" from *Love and Living*, "Contemplation in a World of Action" and "Is the World a Problem" from *Contemplation in a World of Action*, "Rain and the Rhinoceros" from *Raids on the Unspeakable*, and "A Christian Looks at Zen" from *Zen and the Birds of Appetite*. Finally, in "A Letter on the Contemplative Life" and the co-authored "Contemplatives and the Crisis of Faith," we have, from the year before his death, Merton's long-held consistent view on the search for God: one who risks entering and sharing the solitude of the heart begins to understand what is beyond words—"the intimate union in the depths of your own heart, of God's spirit and your own secret inmost self, so that you and he are in all truth One Spirit" (427). Obviously, both groups of generous selections are packed with vintage stuff.

Now for a few words about the other book in this volume—the editorial material. Brother Patrick Hart's helpful foreword focuses on Merton's duties in the 1950s and 1960s as master of scholastics and master of novices at Gethsemani, vitally important experience for the transformation of his life and writing. Anne Carr's extraordinarily rich preface zeroes in on Merton's key distinction between the false self and the true self: "Genuine autonomy is found only in self-forgetfulness . . ." (10).

Finally, Lawrence Cunningham has written what is not only a superb introduction to this collection of writings, but a penetrating literary and theological introduction to Merton's life and work. An opening section sketches the broad lines of Merton's life, explicating both its American and cosmopolitan dimensions. There follows a section on Merton "The Monk" in which Cunningham argues that monasticism, a fundamental way of being a Christian, is the interpretative key to understanding the many Mertons. "Thomas Merton as Theologian" explains Merton's dual theological education: the official Neo-Scholastic manuals of his studies for the priesthood and his voracious reading in monastic and mystical literature. Cunningham argues for Merton as a monastic theologian, attempting to know the self in order to know God, focusing on the *experience* of God's loving presence, struggling to bridge the gap between "theology" and "spirituality," between head and heart. A section on "Merton the Social Critic" explains Merton's social involvement as intrinsic to his evolved understanding of monastic life: "His life was to be a 'No!' to everything that hid the beauty of [the] world as it came from the hands of God and had been redeemed in Christ" (44). In "Merton and the East," Cunningham presents Merton as a new kind of monk, extending the boundaries of the contemplative life, reaching for levels of spiritual development which are "universally recognizable" though culturally and doctrinally diverse (46). A final section considers Merton as a "Spiritual Master," a great teacher who has mastered a doctrine and a way of life. I cannot think of any interested reader—from novice to master—who will not learn much from this introduction.

Thomas M. King, S.J. *Merton Mystic at the Center of America.* Collegeville: The Liturgical Press/Michael Glazier Books, 1992 [vol. 14, The Way of the Christian Mystics]. 160 pages. $12.95 paperback.

Reviewed by Annice Callahan, R.S.C.J.

This book on Thomas Merton as a mystic at the center of North America reveals the unity of his spirituality. It discusses four basic themes in his writings: the self, contemplation, freedom, and other people.

In the section exploring Merton's notion of the self, King notes some of the developmental changes that Merton underwent as a Trappist monk: an initial attraction to the monastic goal of immersion in the anonymity of the group; his inner conflict as writer and monk; his growing acceptance of his identity as writer and monk; his defence of autonomy; the death of his secular ego and of his religious identity through a Zen immersion in the anonymity of nature and immediate experience; a movement from a philosophy of the individual to a contemplative sense of the person; a recognition of the need for the human development of an ego-identity before an emphasis on its loss; the contrast between the empirical ego or false self and the true inner self nourished by transcendent experience (1–36).

In the chapter on contemplation, King distinguishes three forms of contemplation about which Merton wrote: metaphysical, natural, and infused. I particularly appreciated King's discussion of Merton's belief that metaphysical intuition of the ground of being is a form of natural contemplation, and that it is foundational for the Christian life. At the same time King is careful to observe the differences that Merton perceived between a metaphysical intuition and infused contemplation (37–52). I also appreciated King's reflections on *The Ascent to Truth* and the revised *New Seeds of Contemplation* in which Merton affirmed the primacy of intellectual knowledge in the act of contemplation over and against an anti-rational notion of mysticism (52–64). I found King's review of Merton's notions of Paradise and the Fall uncritical in view of our postmodern understanding of the new story of creation and of the emergent universe (64–68). I valued King's emphasis on Merton's unitive approach to contemplation in art and life (64–75).

King portrays well Merton's prophetic insight into several potential sources of our contemporary North American unfreedom: attachment to our social identity and to social conformity; mass movements; technological culture; propaganda; slavery to our appetites (86–96). He also delineates how religion and art can be sources of deliverance according to Merton (93–96). I agree that Merton remained resolutely theistic throughout his writings and even in his dialogue with Zen (103–04).

I wondered why the third chapter on freedom was not put first since it contains so much biographical material. In face of the data presented in recent reliable Merton biographies by such authors as Monica Furlong, Michael Mott, Anthony Padovano, and William Shannon, I was surprised by the tentativeness of the author's conceding the possibility that Merton had fathered a child (77).

In the final section, "Others," King explores three paradoxes in Merton's life: the lack of opposition between solitude and society; between contemplation and action; and between monasticism and the concerns of society. Merton came to realize that solitude can heal the fictional self constructed by the anonymous crowd so that our true self can find community in Christ. He considered the hidden ground of love based on a personal experience of God to be the point of communion for ecumenical and interfaith dialogue (107–20). Merton came to see the unity between contemplation and action not only as a charism but also as the movement of finding our creative freedom in God to act on our own and to do the work of God in the world (121–29). His first fervor at having become a monk separate from the world gave way to his final conviction that a monk is intimately in the world. He also concluded that the monastic ideal of peace of heart had become a national need (129–40).

The epilogue captures the challenge that Merton offered North America. He raised a prophetic voice that affirmed the value of mysticism as a way to, and form of, social justice.

As a Jesuit and a theologian, Thomas King is sensitive in chapter 3 to Merton's integration of faith and North American culture. In chapter 4, he indicates ways that Merton promoted justice in the service of faith. In the epilogue, this theologian names the paschal mystery of Merton's surrender, his *suscipe*, letting go of his speech, identity, freedom, and community of friends to find these gifts transformed.

This clear and concise book is a significant contribution to the burgeoning corpus of secondary literature on Merton. It covers a great deal of ground in limited space. It combines frequent citation of Merton and reflective appraisal on King's part. The focus on four themes offers a frame for understanding Merton's exeriences and images of himself, God, monasticism, the Catholic Church in ecumenical and interfaith dialogue, and North American culture. At the same time, it serves as a helpful introduction to Merton's life, writings, and themes of his spirituality. It will be a valuable resource for undergraduate and graduate students, teachers, scholars, and others wanting to learn more about Merton, monasticism, the Roman Catholic Church in North

America, and North American culture. The bibliographical apparatus at the back is simple and straightforward. It invites us to be mystics in and of North America.

William H. Shannon *Silent Lamp: The Thomas Merton Story*. New York: Crossroad, 1992. 304 pages. $22.95.

Reviewed by Francis Kline, O.C.S.O.

Jamais Vu: A Thomas Merton We Have Not Seen

William H. Shannon calls Thomas Merton ''easily the most important and influential writer on the life of the spirit in the twentieth century'' (13). If this is so, one must welcome this new book into the virtual library on Merton and discover on what shelf in that variegated room it might go.

The book turns out to be a unique study. The author calls it a ''reflective biography'' (7), because he chooses carefully significant events and experiences of Merton's life to organize his thoughts and to guide his considerations toward some definite statements about his subject. Shannon's work does not replace and, indeed, does not approach in literary elegance Michael Mott's exhaustive biography *The Seven Mountains of Thomas Merton* (Boston: Houghton Mifflin, 1984), but it does assume the advantage of consulting all that has already been written in order to forge some new convictions about Merton. Shannon's book has the perspective of time. His purpose is nothing less than to trace the development of Merton's spiritual journey. For Merton's was not just a boat with wild sails on an open sea, but a sturdy bark with a powerful engine determined to reach the appointed shore. Certain of his circumstances, he designed his ship and furnished it and occasionally offered it some serious frustration. But on the whole, Merton was a fortunate man—even a chosen vessel, whose course was marked out for him long before he realized it. One has to look deeper into the mystery of Merton's relationship with God in order to discern the course his voyage took. We are just now at a place to begin to appreciate this and we can be grateful to Shannon for starting us off.

William H. Shannon was for a long time a professor at Nazareth College, Rochester, New York. His Merton studies have put him in the forefront of the field. For example, he is the general editor of the Merton correspondence, a formidable task, since the Merton output continues to astonish the computer dependent. More than all this, Shannon speaks from the vantage point of American Catholic culture, where he is almost a contemporary of his subject, and certainly a sympathetic one (8).

In order to pursue his objectives, Shannon considers the Merton story against the background of the Catholic Church and the changes that it underwent before and through the Second Vatican Council. This includes the Cistercian Order of the Strict Observance and its reappropriation of its twelfth-century heritage and, further back, the primary ascetic tradition of the Greek and Egyptian East. Finally, he has a keen eye for western culture itself, as it moves through profound upheavals, which cannot fail to bring their influence to bear on any evaluation of Merton.

The tale can be told only by one who has shared the experience and gotten the meaning. Shannon's book does not pretend to compete with the well-known biographies and studies of Merton, but, on the contrary, will probably introduce a new spate of Merton studies which take as their premises these convincing themes:

> (1) that Merton's life was a success because his spirituality came to view an ever-widening horizon and even glimpsed the peaks of universal truth.

> (2) that Merton remained essentially faithful to his monastic vocation. This is the thesis that best accounts for all the known facts of Merton's life and thought from his entrance into Gethsemani to his death in far-off Bangkok (no mean feat for any thesis!)

> (3) that Merton picked up the torch of human existence as he found it and with the insatiable thirst for transcendent truth and silence that could have come to him from God alone, he made his very life into a lamp for those with him and after him. Merton, as a spiritual guide, can be

trusted because his life was authentic. We come to him to hear the unspeakable and to learn about the unknown.

A refreshing feature of Shannon's work is the chronology which gets interspersed with chapters or blocks of chapters. It provides salient facts and happenings of the time contemporary with the Merton story as well as the cardinal points in Merton's own biography. The chronology frequently reads like a separate work layered through the context of the author's intended presentation of Merton. But the counterpoint between the Merton themes and the world beyond, while attractive and impressionistic, leaves many loose ends untied. Feeling disjointed, we are left to make our own connections between Merton in the monastery and the world outside it. But the chasm is too wide. To be sure, the chronology can serve as a gauge measuring the contemporaneity of Merton's moves and feelings, but it leads us on to other questions. How much was Merton affected by what was going on outside (that is, before the late 1950s and early 1960s)? Even more to the point, how many of Merton's later preoccupations were distilled in the mix of the Gethsemani community life and its particular culture? We need to be better informed about the way all those events of the yearbook affected the monastery in general and Merton in particular. Merton certainly learned of events and was influenced by his generation living beyond the monastery walls by his numerous contacts and reading. But he was also shaped by the men with whom he lived and by the peculiar subculture they created on the margins of society. In a future study, Shannon's chronology might be more selective and more related to Merton and his life at Gethsemani. In this work, the chronology acts like a wayward crutch with a mind of its own when it comes to literary unity.

Merton, Contemplation, and Scholasticism

Father Shannon writes a remarkable paragraph in his introduction (8–9), made sterling by quoting Merton's own poetic images, on the archetypal symbol of "home." Merton had been constantly uprooted during his formative years and remained a wanderer until his stability of twenty-seven years at Gethsemani. But what he had experienced during his first twenty-six years profoundly affected how he would be stationary in Kentucky. Merton interiorized his lessons in rootlessness. He learned to avoid calling any place "home." The word, spoken in deprivation and longing, became sacred and equivalent to God. The wound, once so great, now was the sign of redemption. For it carried him past the clutches of human habitation and gravitational points dear to our kind, onto the transcendent nature of God. This contemplative theme gets well-earned attention in the pages to follow.

Our author writes of an "ascetic atmosphere of the pre-Vatican II Church" (130). If the Church was ascetic, monasticism certainly had a lot to do with it. Quite simply, asceticism is an essential ingredient to monasticism. If Merton suffered a certain ambivalence toward his writing because he was trying to become a monk, he was probably being faithful to his monastic calling, just as others in the Church were offering sacrifices in the spirit of the general spirituality of the time. However, that Merton came to see the difficulty of squaring monastic life with a writing career as a *pseudoproblem* is a *non-sequitur* (135). The problem does not go away in any monk's life. One refines the ambivalence. One trusts one's experience to go on writing (if we are a Merton), but the ascetic effort remains and needs to become transformed as one's art develops. Integration of one's gifts into one's personality does not mean the demise of asceticism or that one should have never allowed the specter of the sacrifice of one's art to come and haunt. One must first determine how essential the gift is to one's personality, or, in other words, whether Christ's call includes the gift with its own new ascetical demands.

The contemplation-art dichotomy, clearly set forth by our author (136) represents another and separate issue. The blurring of the scholastic focus in Merton's development and his growing awareness and trust in a more integrated, if less predictable experience, is valid for all of us in the latter decades of the twentieth century. So is the liberation from repressive and over-generalized ascetic practices, practiced for their own sake, which apparently plagued the Catholic Church at large as it hastened to find shelter from a secularly rampant culture in a safe if windless port before the Second Vatican Council (161–63).

But Scholasticism is not thereby dismissed from the podium of truth. It must still have something to say, if it was ever valid, though perhaps in a different way. Art, considered in our time as the apogee of self-expression, is going to appear oversized and delinquent in any Scholastic or Neo-Scholastic scheme, while, in an early medieval mind set (that is, in the eleventh and twelfth centuries, before the Scholastic period) it is going to appear in scale and tame. That Merton's perspectives on art and contemplation shifted during his lifetime, states only that our philosophic framework has also shifted. But to what it has shifted, if it indeed has moved to a definite place, no one can as yet say. And if monasticism is no longer the predominant charisma in the Church, its preternatural emphasis on asceticism need no longer be broadly or rigidly applied by people outside a monastery cloister.

Artists join together contemplation and art in one way. Surely, monastics join them in another. What Merton achieved in his own life, in his period and in the given ecclesial situation, may be directive for those in his own milieu in and out of monasticism. Yet monastics of a later time must continue to pose the question of how they should be ascetics and artists, and how asceticism and art prepare them for the gift of contemplation. The distinction between monastic and other contemplatives was perhaps rightly not Shannon's concern. Yet it needs to be the concern in any future study of Merton by a monastic.

Merton and Monastic Renewal

Merton's critique of community as he knew it in a crowded and fast-changing Gethsemani is not to be taken lightly (147–60, 248–62). Apparently, the routine of observances in the Gethsemani of the time was still largely considered to be the end in itself and not yet enough the means to contemplation. The priority which contemplative prayer enjoys in our Order today is in no small way due to Merton, his teaching, writing, and influence. But the issue is not black and white. Merton's contemporaries in the monastery undoubtedly enjoyed contemplation. Yet who will deny that the life was heavily structured? The debate here is on emphasis, focus, and a changing cultural climate both sacred and profane. Some in our Order today look back longingly to the days when there existed structures, schedule, and symbolic rituals aplenty. After the demise of many usages, some of them assuredly formalistic, monastics tend to read back into them meanings and significance which they scarcely enjoyed when they were actually lived. Despite the nostalgia, very few in our monasteries today consider a mere return to a former observance a desirable thing. To a great extent, the new approach to the monastic life which Merton hoped for (Is it exactly what he hoped for?) has come about in the legis-

lation of the General Chapters of the Cistercians of the Strict Observance in the years following 1967. Still, Merton's strident criticisms
of community life as it was then seem a bit curious to a later generation of monastics.

Merton the Solitary

Father Shannon lumps together in one chapter (13) Merton's
efforts on behalf of monastic renewal and his move to the solitude of
the woods in 1965. One gets the impression that the eremitical life holds
the key to a successful redrawing of cenobitic life, and very well it may.
Several ideas set forth here in this chapter, however, need to be examined.

Merton says that in the woods, he is a ''nobody'' (251) and the
seclusion of the hermitage no doubt gave him the anonymity he sought.
But many monks find the routine of the community, the good zeal of
monks which honors the other brother's opinion, and the humility of
silence, including the voluntary avoidance even of sign language, a
sure way to anonymity in the community and total dependence on
God. What stands revealed is the intense inner life with God that leaves
no room for ambition, no desire for any office or charge in the monastery, no need for publication. The far greater challenge is to remain
in the cloister and confront the demons of power and sway, taste and
the will to influence. Let the one who can accept this grace do so. For
those who posses great gifts from God, the way is usually to shoulder
responsibility for using these gifts effectively. The time may come, even
for these, to leave off the exercise of responsibility, as Merton did, when
he exited community life. But for the majority of monks, there remains
the great anonymity of the cenobitic life, with its poverty of will, schedule, and autonomy. The life of continual solitude away in a hermitage
represents a different dimension.

In fact, the eremitical life follows on the successful struggle in
community against one's own demons and the *powers of the air*. This
traditional transition from one to the other, as embodied in *Rule of St
Benedict* (=*RSB*) seems lost in Shannon's chapter 13. The discussion
of the Antonian form of monastic life underwent a much further development in Evagrius and Cassian before it was ever taken up by the
RSB or by any later monastic reform. As an inspiration, it has progeny
like Abraham, but as a direct model, it is a distant ancestor. Merton's

move to solitude may have been just the shot in the arm that institutional monasticism of the time would respond to. In this, he was a prophet, as in almost everything else he did. But his *transitus* to the woods is hardly an object for broad imitation. Merton himself did not do all that well in solitude. The last pages of the Mott biography do not make for edifying reading. This fact does not neuter the salutary effect of Merton's eremitical life for himself or for the Cistercian Strict Observance or for his readers. The hermit life is now officially recognized in the Constitutions of our Order [See CST 13, St 13.3.A], and a large part of the credit for it is due to Merton and his disciples. Still, the hermit life has not replaced the cenobitic life, to any significant degree. It continues to be rare because so few do well in extreme solitude. In sum, applying the eremitical life as a balm to an ailing cenobitism is a far too simplistic operation.

Merton the Visionary

By moving to the woods, Merton only heightened the already existing tension in his life between the anonymity needed for contemplative prayer and his call and "mission" to the world. Given the evidence of his ultimate monastic fidelity, and his extraordinary honesty and self-knowledge, one is convinced that he would have kept thriving spiritually on this paradox and would have eventually overcome it in his own person. In the meantime, he remains a riddle, an incarnated koan that will continue to fascinate and impart wisdom.

After the initial hurdles in monastic life had been cleared, as Father Shannon demonstrates, toward 1957–1958, Merton's broader vocation *ordini et orbi* (to the Order and to the world) accelerated with savage and exhilarating speed. In ten short years until his death in 1968, he catapulted a large portion of the monastic tradition into the contemporary world. The intense, briefer final chapters of Shannon's book (chapters 11–14 and the conclusion) trace the trajectory that Merton's life ultimately became. They are a vindication of the author's purpose in presenting his work and make for fascinating and thought-provoking reading.

Jane Marie Richardson, S.L., editor. *The Springs of Contemplation: A Retreat at the Abbey of Gethsemani.* Thomas Merton. New York: Farrar, Strauss, Giroux, 1992. 285 pages. $22.00 hardcover.

Reviewed by Mary Damian Zynda, C.S.S.F.

In the years immediately following the Second Vatican Council, Thomas Merton felt it necessary to speak to contemplative religious women (prioresses and abbesses), leaders of religious houses, whose responsibility it was to guide their sisters through the rough transition upon which the Church was embarking. Merton ". . . realized that their vocation demanded a new maturity within a patriarchal system" (ix). So he invited twelve women (without permission from his abbot, of course!) to visit Gethsemani in order to facilitate learning and dialogue. This effort was Merton's "pastoral outreach" to these contemplative women and his contribution to assisting them in the formation of a vision which could carry them into the future; it is a vision which was responsive to contemporary society, culture, economics and to the challenges and proposals of Vatican II.

Merton gave two retreats to these sisters, one in December 1967 and the other in May 1968, the last year of his life. *The Springs of Contemplation* distills the wide variety of topics on which he spoke and leaves us with a concentrated sample of the experienced, mature Merton. Loretto Sr. Jane Marie Richardson's efforts in transcribing and editing these talks constitute a significant contribution, edifying for both contemplative and active religious, those involved in professional Merton studies, for women, and for serious Christians in general. The text is a valuable edition filled with the sharp insight, thoughtful wisdom and practical spirit of Thomas Merton.

Merton began the December 1967 retreat by addressing the topics of "Presence, Silence, and Communication," all of which are elements integral to the monastic life. "Genuine silence is the fruit of maturity, a blending of many positive and negative aspects" (10). Understanding the psychological dynamics of the cloistered community, Merton pointed out that silence provides "some distance and time in order for people to collect themselves" (11). Discovering and nurturing an individual identity within a community, while requiring distance and space, is not an individual effort. Merton called on religious institutions to assist in forming human beings who are whole. This said, however, he also asserted that it was the proper role of the community to foster the growth of saints: people who are more than just fully developed human beings.

A realist with a keen awareness of American society, culture, and politics in the 1960s, Merton turned his conference entitled "Changing Forms of Contemplative Commitment" to the task of challenging the sisters to reexamine their religious traditions and lifestyles in light of their contemporary social reality. He reminded the leaders that renewal did not mean just being *more* Carmelite, *more* Cistercian, or *more* Franciscan. Rather, what was needed would be a reexamination of their respective traditions with an eye toward bringing their own contemplative spiritualities into more dynamic dialogue with the world around them. Contemplative commitment, Merton emphasized, is a commitment to all humanity: "Where there is human presence we have to be present to it. And wherever there is a person, there is to be a personal communication. There God can work. Where there is presence, there is God" (31).

In the conference entitled "Responsibility in the Community of Love," Merton addresses the prophetic nature of the contemplative. For Merton this nature rested fundamentally on prayer and is supported by the community. He reinforced the primary fact that contemplative communities must respond to the Word of God, and this response is intimately related to the prophetic call of the contemplative. It is precisely within this contemplative call that he encouraged the sisters to live fully their vocation as religious women and not rely upon clerics to define their vision. He urged them to stand on their own two feet, take risks, and make necessary changes to develop personally and communally. Speaking specifically to personal growth, Merton challenged these leaders to respond seriously to the need for healthy psychological development among their sisters, as encouraged by the Council which recognized the need for religious to grow into mature adulthood.

The contemplative community should be charismatic, Merton claimed in this conference, and all community members should be women available to God's call at any time. He expounded upon Cassian's understanding of prayer as the attainment of purity of heart, the necessary posture which for Merton provided the basis for hearing the call of God.

Merton's activist tone intensified in the conference "Contemporary Prophetic Choices," where he stated that as contemplatives ". . . we have to rock the boat" (80). A prophet himself to a Church involved in worldly power, Merton asserted that "the great problem of contemplative life, of religious life, of the priesthood and of everyone else, is that we have been corrupted by that power" (81). Prophets are not acceptable to authority, warned Merton, they must question everything. This is the contemplative's charism to freedom.

The freedom of true psychological maturity concerned Merton in his last conference "Respect for Each Person's Diversity in Community." One cannot be spiritually mature without first achieving psychological maturity. A male religious, no less than a great contemplative authority, Merton was convinced of the real need for more communication between men and women contemplatives. He stated, "Men contemplatives should be in the position to appreciate the values of women more. You have to remember that men are jealous of women, as you probably know if you had brothers. I think one of the problems of the American male today is that he is terrified of women. He constantly has to hit women over the head to prove he's the boss. Advertising also ties into this image business, the macho male. But it seems to me that men in contemplative life should not necessarily have that drawback" (108). The dialogue between male and female contemplatives, therefore, constituted for Merton an opportunity to depart from the psychological immaturity of the culture which, left unchallenged, would compromise the development of an authentic spiritual maturity in both the individual contemplative and the community.

The contemplative life as prophetic in nature and function was Merton's point of departure as he opened the May 1968 retreat. In the first two conferences, "Contemplative Life as Prophetic Vocation" and "Prophecy, Alienation and Language," Merton reinforced the need for contemplatives to become self-actualized so as to maintain their presence in American culture and society. Merton reaffirmed ". . . before we can become prophetic, we have to be authentic human beings, people who can exist outside a structure, who can create their own existence, who have within themselves the resources for affirming their identity and their freedom in any situation in which they find themselves" (136). Asserting his own prophetic voice he stressed, "If we are to live up to our prophetic vocation, we have to realize that whether we're revolutionary or not, we have to be radical enough to dissent from what is basically a totalitarian society. And we're in it'' (133).

Continuing his analysis of American culture, Merton told the sisters that the prophetic vocation demanded they be deeply aware of the many contradictions in life. He pointed out, ''. . . our prophetic vocation consists in hurting from the contradictions in society . . . the contradictions in the Church . . . and the contradictions in our own backgrounds and our own Christian lives . . .'' (157). Recognizing these contradictions, he suggested a contemplative response to the situation: silence (the monastic practice that would communicate the protest of contemplatives). ''People should be able to sense that our silence comes from a deep reflection and honest suffering about the contradictions in the world and in ourselves'' (158). For Merton, this prophetic function was the fundamental root of the contemplative life, a life which demands the kind of self-knowledge and risk-taking that challenges not only American society, but the global village as well.

Throughout history, asserted Merton, women—especially contemplative women—have been oppressed and suppressed by the ''feminine mystique.'' Merton's third conference, ''The Feminine Mystique'' naturally flowed from the two previous. Here Merton acknowledged the evil of this mystique which has prevented women from being strong prophetic voices in the Church and in the world. Real women, women who are whole, women like Teresa of Avila, did not compromise their prophetic vocation and effected change in the Church and the world as well. Merton insisted that ''it is time to end this mystique, which does no one any good'' (163).

Religious women have been harmed from the beginning in the Church, Merton pointed out, by both the feminine mystique and the Church's severe gender bias. ''Being a person, is what has to be emphasized'' (172). ''We need a whole new theological anthropology, a whole new understanding of what a human being is, what a woman is, what a man is'' (172–73).

Merton would be remiss if he did not explore the benefits of Zen with the sisters. In ''Zen: A Way of Living Directly,'' he pointed out that ''Zen was nothing but John of the Cross without the Christian theology'' (177). Presenting Zen as a way of life, and not merely as another form of contemplative prayer, he offered the sisters a spiritual tool which could sharpen their inner awareness as well as their awareness of the world around them.

Contemplative life is a life of obedience. However, in "Acting in Freedom and Obedience," Merton clarified the fact that religious obedience is not a question of submission to authority nor is it an instrument for keeping an institution going properly, ". . . [O]bedience is meant to free us so that we can follow the Holy Spirit. We respect the authority of others and obey it, but we also have to follow our own conscience" (229). Religious obedience, Merton believed, "makes a person supple, free from attachments to self-will . . ." (227) which allows a person to live the prophetic vocation of total availability to God.

Merton included other conferences which addressed the topics of asceticism, penance, and celibacy, all of which, for him, conspire to create the contemplative heart: a heart desiring to love God alone, and seeking therein to love all of God's creation.

Thomas Merton's many and varied messages to these contemplative leaders twenty-five years ago prophetically challenge us today. For persons engaged in their own inner process and aware of how that process impacts all of creation, *Springs of Contemplation* will be an asset, an inspiration and a challenge to the journey toward wholeness and prophetic Christian witness in the world.

Denise Levertov. *Evening Train*. New York: New Directions, 1992. 128 pages. $17.95. *New and Selected Essays.* New York: New Directions, 1992. 266 pages. $21.95 hardcover.

Reviewed by Emily Archer

If there is any poet in these times whose work elucidates "contemplation in a world of action," it is Denise Levertov. "The poet stands open-mouthed in the temple of life," wrote Levertov in 1965, exploring the etymology of *contemplation*. Nearly thirty years later, this poet continues to gift us with the in-springs of her own attention to the world, with poems that emerge awake and breathing. Denise Levertov has two new volumes from New Directions that witness the world and her service to art. *Evening Train,* Levertov's seventeenth book of poems, attends to the perceived coming and going of Being in mountains, mists, moons, birds, as well as to the anguishing absence of being in the "barbaric fairgrounds" of our own making ("On a Theme by Thomas Merton"). *New and Selected Essays* assembles a mosaic of Levertov's thinking about her vocation and poetics from the 1960s to the 1990s, placing her newest colorations alongside older ones. In these new volumes one can see ever more clearly a "poet in the world" but not of it, and her calling as poet an honor and task she now sees as "work that enfaiths."

True to her publisher's name, Denise Levertov is always exploring "new directions," within and without. *Evening Train* provides passage to a new landscape, the Pacific Northwest. Appropriately, "Settling" is the title of the first poem. However, those familiar with Levertov's themes of pilgrimage, journey, process, and flux will note that the verb is present participle—"settling" not "settled." For while Levertov feels "welcomed here" (Seattle), she says she's come "to live, not to visit." Living means exploring, watching, waiting for being. One subtitle for this book could have been a combination of the first poem title and last—"Settling . . . Suspended"—for the poems that follow the landscape of this new terrain take us with Levertov ever more deeply into the inscape of between. Poised between the quotidian and the numinous, between knowing and unknowing, between faith and doubt, Levertov celebrates the mystery of their minglings with visionary poems that are the fruit of true contemplation.

One special object of contemplation in this new book is a mountain, whose power "lies in the open secret of its remote/apparition" ("Open Secret" 14). Clouds and mists variously illumine the mountain, conceal it, transform it, and float it above the tree line, shaping her faith in the "vast presence, seen or unseen" ("Settling" 3). Thus we find Levertov also settling into a new inscape rich in attention to a presence often experienced as absence, learning from a landscape that still resists humanizing intrusions and scrutiny. Mists in turn rest, rise, veil, efface, and in one poem, transform the mountain, such that

> majestic presence become
> one cloud among others,
> humble vapor, barely discernible,
>
> like the archangel walking
> with Tobias on dusty roads ("Effacement" 7).

This mountain rings its changes upon one who has taken a post like the heron to wait for Being, "whatever hunger/sustains his watchfulness" ("Myopic Birdwatcher," 92). The poetry in *Evening Train* is an invitation to ride with an Advent traveller, a watchman who tells us of the night, a psalmist who affirms the possibility of day.

For Denise Levertov, being a poet in the world has always meant being a witness to night and the shadows of our own making. Her "political poetry," despite critical controversy, remains powerful into the 1990s. Part VI, "Witnessing from Afar," delivers up close the continuing horrors of war in all its forms—the Gulf War, AIDS, miseducation, media hypocrisy, technological violence, abuse of earth and human beings—through the transforming power of images that awaken the reader as no documentary realism can. Levertov has "seen a lot" of war over the years as an active protester who travelled to Vietnam. Yet "no knowledge/nor dark imagination/had prepared her" for "the world's raw gash/reopened" in the Gulf War ("Witnessing from Afar the New Escalation of Savage Power," 82). There can be neither peace in the world nor in the cells of our body, her poems convince us, as long as we continue to construct monoliths and systems of our inappetite desires. "In the Land of Shinar," a vivid reworking of Genesis 11, makes the Tower of Babel our own, imagines our lives darkened by the hour in an enlarging eclipse of wisdom. One day, she prophesies, the

> weight of dream and weight of will
> will collapse, crumble, thunder and fall,
> fall upon us, the dwellers in shadow (85).

Poems in part VIII, "The Tide," speak to a different kind of power, being, dwelling. The antithesis to a self-clutching, power-driven existence is modeled by "Christ the Poet,/who spoke in images" ("What the Figtree Said," 111). With extraordinary empathy, Levertov imagines the arduous yielding this poet endured in "Ascension," relinquishing the comfortable limits of cells and senses for another kind of birth:

> Fathering Himself.
>   Seed-case
>   splitting,
>
> He again
>   Mothering His birth:
>   torture and bliss (116).

It has been Levertov's recent habit to let poems of spiritual longing and Christian themes occupy the last section of her books. These poems testify to one of her "new affinities of content" (in an essay by that name) and to a faith shaped by its ecstasies, doubts, and incompletions. There is the growing sense, as well, that in serving her art, Levertov also serves "Christ the Poet," for here is one as willing to speak *Thou* to the lowly, disgusting multipede ("Embracing the Multipede," 107) as to grasp "the rich silk" of God's garment and suffer "no embrace" ("Suspended," 119). Here is a poet as empathic with a fruitless figtree as with Christ stumbling under "Incarnation's heaviest weight . . . this sickened desire to renege" ("Salvator Mundi: Via Crucis" 114). Levertov even imagines God's own suffering in one of the most remarkable poems of the book, "On a Theme by Thomas Merton" (based, she notes, on "one of the tapes of informal lectures Merton gave at Gethsemani in the 1960s" [120]). God asks Adam, "Where are you?" and Levertov explores the exile:

> God's hands
> palpate darkness, the void
> that is Adam's inattention,
> his confused attention to everything,
> impassioned by multiplicity, his despair.

God gropes for a "Fragmented Adam" who dizzies himself at "a barbaric fairgrounds," absent amidst the world's chaos, a black hole in the fabric of creation:

> . . . Fragmented,
> he is not present to himself. God
> suffers the void that is his absence (113).

No false lights or "whirling rides" carry the reader through the objects of attention in this book; rather, the *tenebrae* of faith and memory. The fifth section and metaphoric center of the book, "Evening Train," remembers travellers "gone into the dark" who have shared and shaped Denise Levertov's journey: a dancer, a washer-woman, an uncle, her Welsh mother, her Jewish father. And at their core is "Dream Instruction," a poem dwelling, surely by no accident, at the physical center of the book. There the poet finds herself "in the language-root place," learning not from any human mentor (as she acknowledges H. D., Duncan, Rilke, and Williams to be) but from the

Old Mother, who "has come to live in what happens, not in the telling" (60). Suspended between the rush of past and future, between memory and desire, the poet learns the new direction her vocation must take:

> and I have now, as the task before me, to *be*,
> to arrive at being,
> as she the Old Mother has done
> in the root place, the hewn
> wooden cave, home
> of shadow and flame, of
> language, gradual stillness,
> blessing (61).

In *New and Selected Essays*, Levertov has collected prose from over thirty years of writing about a servant poetics, a *melos* clearly heard within the constellated themes of this book, within its progression to new tonalities and affinities. Thus, rather than arranging the essays in chronological sequence, Levertov's prose score registers subtle new directions within essays grouped by abiding concerns.

Four essays, for example, show a continued affinity for the work of William Carlos Williams and its implications for her own art. A relatively recent (1989) essay compares Williams's and Eliot's temperaments and approaches to aesthetics. Yet it is also an essay which, while addressing those artists' response to indigenous culture, expresses Levertov's own sense of being always on the circumference of community and place. The English-born Levertov still feels "substantially 'out of sync' with American culture" after four decades and is astonished by what she perceives as America's "constant need for self-definition" (59). That self-conscious sense of place so prevalent and grounding in much American literature may be a deficiency in her own art, she admits, but "it's something which I've had to manage without" (60). The last essay in the book, "An Autobiographical Sketch," explains the early formation of this identity of margins, "unsupported by a community" (258). Yet it may be this very "deficiency" that enables Levertov "to witness from afar" with such clarity, and to greet with empathy those marginal beings who reveal Being in the mysteries of experience.

Denise Levertov has always been at the center, however, of a modern poetics of non-traditional forms and lineation, and her contribution there is widely recognized. Readers familiar with Levertov's instruction in form and line will be glad to have under one cover "Some Notes on Organic Form," "On the Function of the Line," and "Technique and Tune-up." "Organic form" is a term Levertov used effectively in the late 1960s to image the process of "letting the experience lead [the poet] through the world of the poem, its unique inscape revealing itself as he goes" (69). In the 1980s, however, Levertov declares the "need for new terms" ("I have almost given up using the word 'organic' since it has been taken up by the shampoo manufacturers" [76]). "Exploratory" now seems to her the best term for a poetics of the inner voice and for a poetry that emerges "vertebrate and cohesive" (77).

Another group of essays deals with such questions as: Who is the poet? What is the poet's responsibility to the world? For over three decades Levertov has stressed the importance of the artist as servant, an attitude she believes keeps the aim of her aesthetics in perspective and the "inessentials" from distracting her attention. Everywhere in her poetry and prose this calling is apparent, but does not go unchallenged. When asked to offer a statement on the relationship of genre to gender at an MLA symposium of women's issues, Levertov stated that the notion that "genre may be determined by gender" is foreign to her aesthetic, that various expressions of gender are made under various sorts of cultural pressures and historical trends. Genre is entirely "a matter of the relation of form to content" (102). And true service to art will transcend "any inessential factor—including gender" so that the work retains "its numinous, mysterious energy and autonomy, its music, its magic" (103). Levertov's own work is testimony to this aesthetic, for one is always aware of a womanly eye in the vision she imparts, but it is finally the vision one remembers.

An early 1980s essay, "Poetry, Prophecy, Survival," revisits certain questions from "The Poet in the World," the title essay of her most notable prose collection heretofore (New Directions, 1973). With two decades of reflection in the interim, Levertov has strengthened her conviction that the poet must be psalmist as well as prophet (another strong melodic line)—praising as well as raging—in order to serve "the trembling web of being" in our age. A poetry of affirmation has as much to do with politics as a poetry of anguish; otherwise, we lose "the vision of the potential for good" and a redemption worth struggling for (144). She poses a related issue in two essays concerned with biography, using the tragic responses to Anne Sexton's life and work as an example of what must not happen. "Biography and the Poet," the newest essay and previously unpublished, challenges the disturbing trend of misplaced curiosity in literary biography, stimulated in large part by "confessional poetry." A prurient interest in the poet's sexual, medical, or psychological life is bound to obscure the work itself. What, she asks of any poet's biography, will add "valuably to what we receive from the subject's creative opus"? (173). Levertov is looking for biographies like Walter Jackson Bates' *Life of Keats*, for which the poems themselves remain the focus throughout.

Levertov might have had in mind the controversial biography of Anne Sexton by Diane Wood Middlebrook (1991), which contains many transcripts of Sexton's psychiatric sessions. Levertov wrote "Anne Sexton: Light Up the Cave" in 1974 shortly after Sexton's suicide-death, deeply concerned over the epidemic tendency she observed to identify the artist's life with self-destruction rather than creation. Anne Sexton's example has been so romanticized and sensationalized that suicide and creativity, depression and poetry are stubbornly linked in the minds of many admirers. Many want to equate Sexton's destructive proverb " 'thrust all that life under your tongue!' " (192) with artistic activity. But they rarely remember, quotes Levertov from *The Death Notebooks*, that Sexton also wrote

> Depression is boring, I think
> and I would do better to make
> some soup and light up the cave (193).

Thus we have in Denise Levertov an artist who has a clear, yet humble sense of what the world needs from its poets. No less so, Levertov also knows what she as a poet needs from her own kind. By 1992, Levertov's explorations have carried her from a preoccupation with form, terms, and techniques, toward an affinity for content. Her new affinity *for* content is an important development, as it coincides with the particular "affinities *of* content" she announces in the book's first essay by that name. "Form is never more than a *revelation* of content," she asserted in 1965 (revising Robert Creeley's projectivist maxim: "Form is never more than an extension of content"). Levertov seems to be journeying further and further toward the often elusive source of that revelation, toward the essence of what *is*—the "I am that I am."

"Some Affinities of Content" is the expressed evidence that Levertov is learning her lesson well from the Old Mother of "Dream

Instruction": she is coming "to live in what happens, not in the telling" (*ET* 60). Yet this doesn't mean Levertov has abandoned form.
Recalling the process of composing *Mass for the Day of St. Thomas Didy-
mus* (*Candles in Babylon*, 1982), Levertov explains coming to the piece
at first as an "agnostic" and preoccupied mostly with form, the traditional elements of a Mass. But what happened in the telling was that
by the time she arrived at the *Agnus Dei*,

> I discovered myself to be in a different relationship to the
> material and to the liturgical form from that in which I had
> begun. The experience of writing the poem—that long swim
> through waters of unknown depth—had been also a conver-
> sion process, if you will (250).

This is "work that enfaiths," she explains, a bold reversal of the usual
"faith that works." Her abiding faith in Keats's "truth of the imagination" has led her to discover analogies "between the journey of art
and the journey of faith" (249). Many of Levertov's new directions have
come from walking the gift-strewn path of that discovery.

"The poems to which I look for nourishment and stimulus are
more and more those with which I feel an affinity that is not necessarily stylistic at all," admits Levertov in the fall 1990 (2). She realized
those affinities as being of two sorts, essentially similar in direction:
various nature poems of the Pacific Northwest and poems of religious
concern. The voices of nature poets Hayden Carruth and Sam Hamill,
or the spiritual poems of Czeslaw Milosz and Lucille Clifton provide
"testimonies of lived life, which is what writers have a vocation to give,
and readers (including those who write) have a need to receive" (21).
Levertov's movement toward Christian belief has been consistent and,
she states in "A Poet's View," is "not incompatible with my aesthetic
nor with my political stance, since as an artist I was already in the
service of the transcendent . . ." (243). She has come to live in the
happening of her own faith, a process of breathing and becoming,
much like the process of writing a poem.

New and Selected Essays is unquestionably a testimony of lived life,
still living. But it is to her poetry that one must finally return to explore Denise Levertov's greatest contribution to art. *Evening Train* invites us into a country of diaphanous beauty, where mists shape the
sure light of presence. Whirling rides and evening train, the darkness
of chaos and the darkness of the divine—Levertov attends it all with

keen night vision. In the re-readings and contemplation her poetry invites, we may get a glimpse also of the language-root place, to a word that enfaiths. It is difficult not to speculate, having read this luminous book, that when God asks Denise Levertov "Where are you?" the answer is "Present."

Jay Tolson. *Pilgrim in the Ruins: A Life of Walker Percy.*
New York: Simon & Schuster, 1992. 544 pages. $27.50.

Reviewed by Patrick F. O'Connell

The name of Walker Percy was connected in my mind with that of Thomas Merton almost from the time of my first acquaintance with each. Sometime in the mid-1960s, I came across one of those magazine surveys in which famous people recommend books they've recently enjoyed. Among the group was Thomas Merton, enthusiastically touting Percy's first novel *The Moviegoer*, a choice which, as I recall, the compiler thought rather racy for a cloistered monk. At the time I had read little or nothing by Merton, though one or two of his books were around the house, and knew of Percy only because the last page of my paperback copy of *To Kill a Mockingbird* contained an advertisement for *The Moviegoer*, which did indeed sound rather racy ("a *Catcher in the Rye* for adults only"). It was only years later, after becoming much more familiar with the work of both men, that I realized why Merton was so favorably impressed by Percy, though I continued to wonder how Merton had come across the novel in the first place. That question (along with others of considerably more significance for Percy's life and art) has now been answered by Jay Tolson in his fine life of Walker Percy, *Pilgrim in the Ruins.*

Tolson's biography has a thesis, but is by no means thesis-ridden. In his preface the author says a major focus of this book will be to examine "how, and to what extent, Percy's life constituted a heroic, or at least an exemplary, life" (12). He sees Percy's decision in his early thirties to abandon his medical career (already interrupted by a bout of tuberculosis, contracted in the Bellvue Hospital morgue) and become a writer as a sort of Pascalian gamble: writing provided a way to confront both the challenges of his own family heritage (which included not only a distinguished record of public service but the suicides of his father and grandfather), and the broader crises of meaning for humanity, America and the South in the mid-twentieth century, with the resources of an art profoundly influenced by his conversion to Catholicism and his reading of Kierkegaard and other existentialist philosophers. While pointing out that the "interest of an exemplary person depends largely on the complexity, and sometimes the enormity, of his or her flaws" (12), Tolson sets his enterprise in opposition to the sort of "debunking" biography which "seems to have no higher goal than, as Elizabeth Hardwick once said, to 'diminish the celebrated object and aggrandize the biographer' " (13). Tolson's respect for his subject and his perceptive yet unobtrusive interpretation of Percy's "life-project" insure that neither of these results will occur.

Tolson finds Percy's life story to be "something of a mystery" (12), not only in the conventional sense but in the deeper, Marcelian understanding as a participation in transcendence, which can be examined and analyzed but not definitively "solved." His actual presentation of the events of his subject's life is quite straightforward, with no attempt to preempt the reader's own judgment as to the "exemplary" or "heroic" character of Percy's life and work; he is thereby more convincing than would be a more blatant attempt to persuade or any artificial manipulation of his data to reinforce his thesis. Percy emerges from Tolson's presentation as a complex, frequently testy, sometimes uncertain human being, with definite limitations in ideas and idiosyncrasies in behavior, but finally as a genuinely admirable person and a novelist and essayist of rare power and insight.

The main outline of Percy's life has been well known to interested readers for some time through numerous interviews and biographical chapters in critical studies: his birth into an illustrious Southern family which included a Civil War hero, a U.S. Senator, and influential lawyers and businessmen; the suicide of his father when Walker was thirteen, and the drowning death of his mother three years later; his adoption by his cousin William Alexander Percy, "Uncle Will," minor poet and author of an important memoir on the changing South, and the most significant influence on Walker's personal and intellectual development; his education at North Carolina and Columbia Medical School, followed by a stay at the famous Saranac Lake clinic after contracting TB; his marriage to Mary Bernice (Bunt) Townsend, and subsequent entrance of both into the Roman Catholic Church; his long literary apprenticeship, which culminated in the publication in 1961, when Percy was forty-four, of *The Moviegoer*, which went on to win the National Book Award; his interest in the theory of language, which not only informed his fiction but resulted in numerous essays on the central importance of symbols and symbolmaking for human identity; his writing of five more novels, which earned him a reputation as one of the most significant American novelists of the second half of the twentieth century.

Tolson enriches this basic biographical framework with a wealth of new and fascinating detail. He traces the background of the Percys and the Phinizys (Walker's mother's family) as it extends through five Deep South states. He carefully examines the circumstances of Percy's mother's death and convincingly refutes the rumors that it too was suicide. He considers in depth the profound influence of Will Percy's Southern romantic-stoicism on his young cousin, who eventually rejected Will's philosophy of life but never diminished in respect for his integrity. Tolson also reveals the surprising fact that Will Percy was himself a fallen-away Catholic, courtesy of his Louisiana Creole mother.

One of the central threads running through the book is Percy's lifelong friendship with Shelby Foote, who became a novelist long before Walker thought of writing fiction, and whose advice and support were crucial for Percy both professionally and personally. While Percy's reputation later outstripped his friend's, Shelby's recent celebrity as principal commentator for the Public Television *Civil War* series, which has made him probably better known and certainly more recognizable than his fellow novelist, would surely have both pleased and amused Walker. Tolson also explores the influence of novelist and fellow-convert Caroline Gordon on Percy's initial experiments in writing fiction; her instruction and encouragement were Percy's most important training in the novelist's craft. Tolson also reveals that Percy's investigation of language theory actually predated by some months the discovery that his daughter Ann was suffering from a severe hearing loss: Bunt and Walker's successful struggle to assist their child to surmount her handicap is itself an inspiring story of determination, perseverance and love.

The author also details the bizarre, or perhaps providential, circumstances which led to Percy's winning the National Book Award, even though his publisher hadn't even submitted *The Moviegoer* for consideration: the fact that A. J. Liebling's interest in Louisiana politics, specifically Huey Long, led him to pick up a new novel with a Louisiana setting, which impressed him so much that he passed it on to his wife, novelist and NBA judge Jean Stafford. The lack of enthusiasm of Alfred Knopf (and even more so of Mrs. Knopf, who airily dismissed the award winner's offer to sign a copy of his novel) is wryly described, as is the sharp observation of rival publisher Robert Giroux, which led Percy to switch firms and resulted in a mutually satisfactory association for the rest of Percy's career.

Tolson also relates that Walker's brother Phin had been in the same PT-boat squadron as the young John Kennedy (and had actually witnessed the ramming of Kennedy's boat and pleaded, in vain, that the boat he was on check for survivors), and that while Walker was an enthusiastic Kennedy supporter, Phin turned down an offer to coordinate this old friend's Louisiana campaign, and voted, as he usually did, Republican! The Kennedy election encouraged Percy's own commitment to social change, as did his association with a number of progressive church people, and while he remained in a number of ways a cultural conservative, he became a strong supporter of civil rights, both publicly in his writing and privately as a member of the Community Relations Council in his home town, Covington, Louisiana. (In his later years, he would be an equally committed and articulate supporter of the pro-life position on abortion.) These are just a sampling of the many strands of Percy's life which Tolson weaves together skillfully and compellingly, concluding with a sensitive discussion of Percy's struggle with cancer and his death on May 10, 1990.

Tolson is particularly good at relating Percy's own background and experiences to characters and events in the novels, while remaining free of any simplistic attempt to reduce the art to a commentary on the life, or vice versa. But he does point out, for example, the extent to which the character of Aunt Emily in *The Moviegoer* draws on that of Uncle Will; how Will Barrett's father in *The Last Gentleman* and *The Second Coming* is an amalgam of a number of the Percy men; how the genesis of *The Second Coming* is to be found in the sudden arrival at Percy's door of an old fraternity brother, a retired business executive from North Carolina who told his wife he was going out for cigarettes and impulsively hopped a bus for New Orleans; and the way in which Percy's own unsettling experiences during his 1934 visit to Germany found their way into his final novel *The Thanatos Syndrome*.

Tolson wisely eschews providing capsule plot summaries of the novels or any developed critical commentary of his own, but he does give a thorough sampling of the initial reviewers' responses to each of Percy's books, as well as an account of longer studies which appeared during Percy's lifetime, so that the reader is able to get a good sense of the reception which the various books received (particularly as Tolson freely expresses his own agreement or disagreement with many of the evaluations he cites, both positive and negative).

Somewhat more problematic, perhaps, is Tolson's tendency to focus on the distinction between the aesthetic and the moral dimensions of art to the point that they sometimes seem at odds. He writes, "Artist though he was, Percy became and remained a moralist who saw the end of art not in formal perfection but in the adequacy of its gesturing toward the truth that would make him free" (11). He sets up a kind of running contrast between Percy's approach and that of Shelby Foote, who is presented as a representative of the modernist creed of self-contained "objectification of sensibility, of an affective exquisiteness," an "elevation of sensibility above all else" (493).

While Tolson pays tribute to Percy's "artistry and resources as a novelist," in particular his keen observation of social manners, his "high comedic ends," his control of language, and his examination of "the human heart in conflict with itself" (492), he seems at once distrustful of an emphasis on formal concerns and somewhat doubtful that the excellence of Percy's fiction can be sustained on purely formal grounds. He justly stresses that Percy saw his fiction as a vehicle for raising fundamental questions about the human search for meaning, and as a means of suggesting, often in the most indirect ways, answers to some of these questions. He rightly points out, "Faith as a means of knowledge, as perhaps the highest form of knowledge, was the enabling condition of Percy's art. It was the substance of his artistic vision, and the final justification of his labor" (493). But he seems unaware that the goal of "formal perfection of the work" is also at the heart of the Thomistic aesthetic of Jacques Maritain's *Art and Scholasticism*, for example, which according to Tolson was one of the "staples of Percy's reading" (237) at the time of his initial experiments in writing fiction.

In calling him "the most important American moralist since Ralph Waldo Emerson" (13), Tolson not only reveals his deep appreciation of Percy's thought, but places him in a context where the specifically aesthetic, formal, fictive aspects of his writing are implicitly accorded a subordinate role. It is perhaps instructive to see the progression Tolson uses in his opening reference to the "life story of Walker Percy—physician, novelist, philosopher, moralist" (11). It remains to be seen whether this strategy of shifting the ground for a defense of Percy's lasting significance is ultimately to be a successful one, or if it will simply reinforce the suspicion in some quarters that the novels are basically cleverly disguised didactic treatises. At any rate, this issue does not detract from the admirable job Tolson does of presenting the story of Percy's life with clarity, order, and insight.

In the context of that story, Percy's relationship with Thomas Merton had a relatively minor but not insignificant impact on both men. The two were contemporaries (Merton a year older) who had a number of things in common: each lost both parents at an early age (Percy being more fortunate in his guardian than Merton in his); each had actually been at Columbia during the same period (Percy of course in the medical school); each settled, finally, in the South. Most importantly, each was a convert to Roman Catholicism, a writer, and a person who resonated strongly to the insights of existentialist philosophy.

Tolson provides a succinct account of the two men's contact with one another, which began when Merton wrote an appreciative letter to Percy in January 1964 about *The Moviegoer*, which a monk visiting from another monastery had requested and received from Percy and later passed on to Merton (thus the solution to the mystery of how Merton had come across it in the first place). Merton recognized and applauded the quest for existential integrity at the heart of the novel, and he admired what Tolson calls the "art of indirection and reticence" (315) with which the theme is conveyed. This initiated a correspondence which continued until shortly before Merton's death. Merton was equally enthusiastic about Percy's second novel, *The Last Gentleman*, which he called, in a pre-publication letter to Robert Giroux, "one of the sanest books I have read in a long time" (330), though one wonders what Merton made of the novel's satiric portrait of the "pseudo-Negro" Forney Aiken, whose experiment in dying his skin is clearly modeled on that of Merton's friend John Howard Griffin. Merton actually contributed ideas and suggestions on Bantu metaphysics and other topics for the work in progress which was to become *Love in the Ruins*, but he did not live to see it published.

Tolson also describes the one, curiously unsatisfactory visit of Percy to Gethsemani (for an editorial board meeting of the journal *Katallagete,* held at Merton's hermitage), when "both turned awkward and shy" (341), Percy persisted in addressing Merton as "Father Louis," and their conversation remained somewhat inconsequential and forced. But he points out that their mutual respect was not lessened by the encounter, and their epistolary contact continued to flourish. One of their common interests was the race question, though Tolson does not include my favorite Percy-Merton story, mentioned by Michael Mott, in which Percy mailed to Merton a racist card he had been given which included the instruction, "Pass this Card on to another White man"; Percy's sardonic comment was, "Well, you're a white man, aren't you?" (*The Seven Mountains of Thomas Merton* [Boston: Houghton Mifflin, 1984] 492).

Tolson does point out that Merton's linkage of the racial issue with the Vietnam War, "might eventually have opened into a wider political rift between the two men" (342) had Merton not died soon after, since Percy was much less sure of the immorality of the war than was Merton; though one wonders what the author of the scathing "Letters to a White Liberal" in *Seeds of Destruction* (New York: Farrar, Straus and Cudahy, 1964) would have made of being called "a more doctrinaire liberal" (316) than Percy. Though the contact lasted less than five years, because of Merton's untimely death, it was clearly an important one for both men, and Tolson gives it its due, even saying that for Percy the beginning of the correspondence "served as a partial antidote to the shock of the Kennedy assassination two months before. It might not have put Percy back on the right track immediately, but it reminded him what his best track was" (316).

Tolson's discussion also suggests further areas of exploration, not only in the areas of literature and race relations, but in the two men's shared antipathy to Cartesian dualism: some of Percy's statements about the shortcomings of Descartes' anthropology sound remarkably like the Merton of *Zen and the Birds of Appetite* (New York: New Directions, 1968) and other late works. It would be interesting to examine how Percy's solution to the problem, a Peircean "triadic" theory of language as symbol and link between persons, compares to Merton's endorsement of the primordial, preverbal unity of subject and object found in Zen. Some of the information provided by Tolson could serve as a starting point for such a project.

Unfortunately, extrapolating from Percy's own mistaken comment that Merton had gone to Burma, Tolson states that he died there rather than in Thailand (342; see the 1984 interview with Victor A. and Dewey W. Kramer, "A Conversation with Walker Percy about Thomas Merton," in Lewis A. Lawson and Victor A. Kramer, eds., *Conversations with Walker Percy* [Jackson: University Press of Mississippi, 1985] 310, 317). This is one of a handful of errors which an alert, and religiously literate, editor should have caught. He also refers to Romano Guardini as "Guardino" in one place (386), and confuses the Elizabethan poet and musician Thomas Campion with the Jesuit martyr Edmund Campion (466). He contrasts Sartre's atheism with Percy's "convinced fideism" (238), though elsewhere he makes clear that Percy considered faith "wholly compatible with reason" (200), a position antithetical to fideism. He misquotes Stephen Dedalus' declaration "Non serviam" (James Joyce, *Ulysses* [New York: Random House, 1934] 582; see also James Joyce, *A Portrait of the Artist as a Young Man* [New York: Viking, 1964] 117 as "non servo" [491], which is not only the wrong tense [present for future] but the wrong verb ["servo" (I keep) for "servio" (I serve)]). Actually, Latin does not seem to be Tolson's strong subject, as he also uses the impossible form "annum mirabilis" (223) for "annus mirabilis" (or "annum mirabilem"). There is also a possible source of confusion when Tolson states that the Forney Aiken section of *The Last Gentleman* is "blatantly lifted" from John Howard Griffin's account of passing as a Negro in *Black Like Me*, and then goes on to note that the "entire episode . . . is a pretty rough sendup of what southerners often derisively refer to as 'northern liberals' " (308); Griffin, of course, was a Texan. There are also a couple of evident misprints: "journal" for "journey" (306) and a missing word in the sentence: "An artist needs *not* to see or his work too clearly" (371).

These, however, are minor blemishes on a major achievement. Taken together with Patrick Samway's recent edition of Percy's previously uncollected non-fiction pieces (*Signposts in a Strange Land* [New York: Farrar, Straus and Giroux, 1991]), *Pilgrim in the Ruins* is a splendid summing up of Walker Percy's life and career, and an essential starting point for further exploration of his contributions to contemporary literature and thought.

Thomas Merton. *The Merton Tapes*. Fourth Release of
Lectures. Kansas City: Credence Cassettes, 1988
(Released 1991). 7 cassettes (60 min. each). $8.95 each.

Reviewed by Dewey Weiss Kramer

Father Louis (Thomas Merton) begins one of his weekly talks to
the Gethsemani community with the remark that the Thomas Aquinas
text under discussion contains nothing really new; his brothers already
know the facts of which Aquinas writes: "But it's the *attitude* we get
from it" that is crucial, Merton says. Potential auditors can take note.
They might also wish to consult the reviews of the first three releases
(*The Merton Annual* II, 314–19: review of 19 tapes; III, 311–20: 30 tapes;
and V, forthcoming: 18 tapes) since similar strengths, weaknesses, and
methodology apply.

Auditors of those first groups, just like Merton's novices, will
not find much new; they will, however, find much that is crucial. As
with the earlier lectures, although the conferences were intended as
instruction in the monastic life, Merton's teaching usually applies easily
to non-monastics as well. In fact, the strongpoint of this most recent
grouping, and its organizing principle, is first: the emphasis on *practical* applications of spiritual topics discussed; and second: the fact that
the majority of the topics themselves tend to involve the world beyond
the monastery. In no other group thus far is there as much concrete
advice for pursuing a right attitude—for prayer, for a keener awareness of the present lived moment, for finding an effective grounding
for one's own life, whatever its circumstances.

Credence Cassettes does not provide dates for the individual conferences, but these selections clearly reflect the later Merton who has
left behind him all *contemptus mundi* and has turned toward a loving
embrace of the world, not, however, without criticizing it at the same
time. Victor A. Kramer's review of the first nineteen tapes noted their
value as "documentation" (in addition to the spiritual instruction) of
Merton and Gethsemani. In the choice of tapes presented here, Credence Cassettes has documented aspects of the final stages of Merton's personal journey. Thus, the final tape of the series, "Monasticism
and Marxism" (AA2461), consists of the audio portion of his lecture

at the Bangkok conference, the last public appearance before his death (available also as video and printed in *The Asian Journal*). That lecture's topic, "Monasticism and Marxism," is a striking example of Merton's conviction of the necessary interrelationships between the monastic and the secular realms. Side B of tape AA2459, "Sanctity," is further demonstration of this attitude. Identified by the announcer as a lecture given "during" the Bangkok trip, Merton delivers a "chapter talk" of the sort often given to his novices or the assembled community, but now addressed to a group of Indian monastics. Typically for this series, his "spiritual" teaching is firmly ensconced in a secular context: his remarks on prayer are set against a well-articulated description of the tensions in Church and world engendered by the renewal of Vatican II and the Cold War respectively.

The political element is not the main aspect of the "world" presented in this series, however, but rather the right use of and appreciation of the universe and its beauty. This thrust is heard especially in tapes AA2457, "Justice for all of Creation," and AA2458, "Developing a Conscience"; but it is perceptible also in his approach to the cross and death, and spiritual direction (in "The Cross: Victory over Death," AA2455) and prayer (in "Sanctity," AA2459). This is also the rationale for including the rather slight conferences on literature ("Lyric Poetry," AA2460).

Highpoints of this series of seven tapes are the four conferences in which Merton uses Aquinas's *On the Ways of God* as his point of departure ("Justice . . ." and "Developing . . ."). It is here that the master teacher and spiritual guide is at his finest. Nor is the poet absent: celebration of gamboling calves, beautiful in their awkwardness, can constitute genuine "seeds of contemplation" for the listener.

Contributors

Emily Archer is a doctoral student at Georgia State University and has published in *Studies in the Literary Imagination.*

Annice Callahan, R.S.C.J., is associate professor of spiritual theology at Regis College in Toronto. Her publications include *Spiritual Guides for Today* and *Spiritualities of the Heart* (ed.).

Walter E. Conn is professor of religious studies at Villanova University and editor of *Horizons, The Journal of The College Theology Society.* He has written extensively on Christian conversion.

Roger J. Corless is professor of religion at Duke University. He is involved in the East/West dialogue and in ecumenism.

Michael Downey, associate professor of theology at Bellarmine College in Louisville, is the editor of *The New Dictionary of Catholic Spirituality.* His publications include books and essays on Christian spirituality and worship.

John Ford, a retired educator, lives in Louisville.

Roberto S. Goizueta is a member of the faculty of theology at Loyola University, Chicago. Associate editor of the *Journal of Hispanic/Latino Theology,* he has written about liberation and Hispanic/Latin American theologies.

Rosemary Haughton, an internationally renowned writer and lecturer, lives at Wellspring House in Gloucester, Massachusetts.

E. Glenn Hinson is professor of historical theology at the Baptist Theological Seminary at Richmond in Virginia. He has written widely in ecumenism and spirituality.

George Kilcourse is professor of theology at Bellarmine College in Louisville. His most recent publication is *Ace of Freedoms: Thomas Merton's Christ.*

David King teaches at Kennesaw State College in Georgia and has published poems in the *Georgia State Review.*

Francis Kline, O.C.S.O., is abbot of Mepkin Abbey, Moncks Corner, South Carolina.

Dewey Weiss Kramer teaches at DeKalb College in Clarkston, Georgia, and is a founding editor of *The Merton Annual.*

Victor A. Kramer, a founding editor of *The Merton Annual*, serves as general editor of the Georgia State Literary Series and has books in process about James Agee, Walker Percy, and Thomas Merton.

Patrick F. O'Connell teaches theology at Gannon University in Erie, Pennsylvania. He is a regular contributor to *Living Prayer.*

Steven Payne, O.C.D., is a member of the Institute of Carmelite Studies. He was editor of the Carmelite journal *Spiritual Life.*

Tina Pippin teaches in the department of Religion and Bible at Agnes Scott College in Decatur, Georgia. She is a vocational deacon in the Episcopal Church.

Katherine M. TePas is assistant professor in the religion department at LaSalle University in Philadelphia. She recently completed her doctoral dissertation on Aelred of Rievaulx at The Catholic University of America.

Rembert Weakland, O.S.B., is archbishop of Milwaukee.

Mary Damien Zynda, C.S.S.F., is on the staff of Bethlehem House at the Abbey of the Genesee in Piffard, New York, and has written on Merton and Evelyn Underhill for *The Merton Annual* 4 (1991).

Index

MAKE IT AN ANNUAL EVENT FOR YOU

The Merton
ANNUAL

$\mathcal{J}\!\mathit{erusalem}$ $TM.\ '60$

As the years pass, Thomas Merton's reputation as a spiritual writer and advisor only increases. *The Merton Annual* publishes articles about Thomas Merton and about matters of major concern in his life and work. Its purpose is to continue to develop his message for our times and to provide a regular outlet for substantial Merton-related scholarship. *The Merton Annual* includes as regular features reviews, review-essays, a bibliographic survey, interviews, and first appearances of unpublished, or obscurely published, Merton materials, photographs, and art.

Place a standing order, and have volumes billed and shipped to you automatically each year.

PLACE A STANDING ORDER

Phone: 1-800-858-5450 • Fax: 1-800-445-5899

The Liturgical Press
P.O. Box 7500, St. John's Abbey
Collegeville, MN 56321-7500

Back Issues (Volumes 1-5) of

The Merton
ANNUAL

are available from

AMS Press, Inc.
56 East 13th Street
New York, NY 10003
Fax (212) 995-5413